Labour Policy—
False And True

A Study In Economic History
And Industrial Economics

by

Lynden Livingston Macassey

Labour Policy—False And True
A Study In Economic History And Industrial Economics
by Lynden Livingston Macassey

ISBN: 978-93-62764-30-0

Published by

DOUBLE 9 BOOKS

2/13-B, Ansari Road
Daryaganj, New Delhi – 110002
info@double9books.com
www.double9books.com
Tel. 011-40042856

ABOUT THE AUTHOR

Lynden Livingston Macassey was a barrister and labor lawyer. Lynden Macassey was born on June 14, 1876, in Carrickfergus, Larne, County Antrim, as the son of engineer and attorney Luke Livingston Macassey. He was educated at Bedford School and Trinity College in Dublin. The Middle Temple called him to the Bar in 1899. Between 1901 to 1909, he taught economics and law at the London School of Economics. During World War I, he became embroiled in industrial unrest among munitions workers on the River Clyde and co-authored a report with Lord Balfour of Burleigh in 1915. His proposals were incorporated into the Munitions of War (Amendment) Act of 1916. In 1916, he negotiated agreements establishing joint committees of employers and shop stewards on the River Clyde. He did, however, back the controversial deportation from Glasgow of militant labour leader David Kirkwood. In 1922, Macassey was appointed as a labour assessor for the British government on the Permanent Court of International Justice in The Hague. His seminal work, Labour Policy: False and True, was also released in 1922. Macassey died in London on February 23, 1963.

CONTENTS

PREFACE

Portions of some of the chapters in this book have already appeared in *The Times*, the *Quarterly Review*, the *Edinburgh Review*, the *Nineteenth Century*, the *Sunday Times* and the *Evening Standard*, and are now incorporated in their proper place in the larger scheme on which they were originally written. I am indebted to the proprietors of those publications for their kindness in permitting me so to reproduce them.

An old friend and valued colleague of mine in the Department of Shipyard Labour—Mr. C. F. Farrar—did me the great service of assisting to get the book through the press.

To my Secretary, Miss K. I. Toogood, I owe the preparation of the Index.

L. M.

August 12th, 1922.

INTRODUCTION

Our great industrial difficulty, under modern conditions, is to combine human development with human work, and persuade people to be industrious. Formerly, men worked to benefit themselves; now, they are apt to refrain from working for fear they may benefit other persons. The injury to employers from such a course is evident; but the detriment to the workers themselves is less obvious, and the calamitous effect on the community is seldom realized. That difficulty is what we call "the Labour problem"; a knowledge of the principles on which it can best be solved is our chief national necessity.

This book strives to criticize the wrong, and indicate the right, solution. The test which it applies is whether a solution places the community before section or party, or is one designed primarily to advance sectarian interests, political or industrial, either avowedly, or speciously, under professions of solicitude for the public good. Nowadays, one has to look well below the surface of words, however distinguished may be their origin. There is little to choose between the revolutionary Socialist, whose solution consists in thrusting industrial democracy into supreme economic or political power through ruthless direct action and then socializing industry, and the constitutional anti-Socialist, who would solve the problem by pledges to inaugurate a new industrial Heaven and Earth, and other "ninepenny-for-fourpence" promises, which he has no honest conviction can be redeemed, and which, if he seriously considered, he would know can never be fulfilled. On the whole, during the last few years, the latter has proved the greater menace to the nation.

Policies for the solution of the Labour problem fall, broadly speaking, into two main categories. Those which insist upon, or imply, the reconstruction of industry by eliminating private enterprise and the capitalist. Of this type is the policy for which the Labour Party stands—the vague abstraction of "nationalization and democratic control." All other policies are of the type which postulates, as essential to industrial progress, continuance of the so-called capitalistic organization of industry with, however, amendments and reforms of varying character. There is not always that clear-cut distinction. Many opponents of the Labour Party's policy are advocates of the particular method of socializing industries known as municipalization, and even of the State running certain quasi-industrial ventures like the Post Office. Such overlapping and border-line cases must always occur. Human affairs can never wholly be regulated by precise formulae; were that possible, the world would be a dull place wherein to live.

If the Labour problem is to be solved, there must be more clear thinking, critical analysis, and decisive action on the part of the general public, who forget how vitally they are interested. With the object of placing before them its various elements in logical sequence and balanced perspective, I have, after much consideration, adopted the following scheme for this book: I set out in Part I the policy of the Labour Party for solution of the problem, and examine its fundamentals; next, I describe in Part II the Government's Labour policy, so far as it has been declared, or evidenced in departmental practice, and consider it; then, lastly, I outline in Part III what, in amplification of the Government policy and in opposition to that of Labour, I conceive to be the true solution, and the one most calculated to promote the interests of the nation.

The Labour Party heralds itself as "the true national democratic party," and as such claims to have formulated a national Labour policy, which, on the most superficial examination, exhibits many indications of purely sectarian objectives. My effort has been to appraise that policy critically but fairly, and see how far it is likely to advance the common welfare. This cannot be done unless one clearly appreciates the industrial root on to which the so-called national democratic party has recently been grafted, and from which it draws all its nurture and virility. Part I, therefore, explains in some detail the history and constitution of the Labour Party, and also the nature of the root, which, called by the most euphemistic name, is merely a particular species of Socialism. At the moment, the Labour Party does not seem unduly proud of its lineage, nor inordinately anxious to force upon the attention of the country its real socialistic aims. But it is essential that they should be laid bare, and this I endeavour to do in Part I, not by quotations from Labour leaders' speeches, which express considerable difference in views, according to the forum, are not conspicuous by consistency, and are regarded as of no binding force by the Party. I give actual extracts from official documents published by the Labour Party, not generally known or accessible to the ordinary reader, and which state, if not with clarity, at any rate in its own language, the principles to which the Party declares that it has pledged the allegiance of all its followers.

The Labour Party arraigns before the bar of public opinion the present Government, and, indeed, all past "Capitalistic Governments," and charges them with having neglected the interests of the workers, and of being devoid of any consistent Labour policy. Such an accusation, if sufficiently repeated, obtains a certain validity of currency, because the public know little of what has been really achieved under Government direction. I hold no brief for the present Coalition Government—I have often criticized its unfortunate opportunist action in regard to industrial matters, and do so freely in this book—but it is vital that the public should understand, if only as the foundation on which to build a new and amplified Labour policy, what it and former Governments have done, at the expense of the nation, for the workers of the country. This is the theme of Part II, and, as any future solution of our Labour difficulties must be materially influenced by the effect upon industry, upon employers and employed, of the emergency measures taken by Government for the regulation of Labour during the war, a chapter in Part II is devoted to this important matter.

In Part III I then proceed to the true purpose of the book—to indicate in broad outline what seems to me to be the only possible Labour policy for the future. It must satisfy, and be attuned to, the human qualities of the workers; Part III, therefore, starts with a description of the aspirations and sentiments of the workers as I found them in real life, and then proceeds to set out the principles that I think should govern the three greatest relationships in industry—that of the Government to industry—that between employers and employed—that between industry and the community.

In my treatment of the subject I have tried to avoid academic disquisition, and to produce a discussion fitting as closely as possible to the actual realities of workshop life, as they came within my practical experience, first, as an engineer, and, later, in discharging for Government the duties of many war-time offices involving the control of labour. My own ascertainment of facts is opposed in many respects to what has been stated by other writers, but some three thousand close and intimate conferences during the war with employers' organizations, Trade Union executives, district and branch committees, together with many mass meetings—at all of which careful notes were taken—to say nothing of having one's finger daily on the pulse of over one million men, supply me with a groundwork of facts sufficiently convincing at any rate to my own judgment.

That the Labour problem can eventually be solved with success by resolute perseverance along the line of principles suggested in Part III I feel certain. In the robust common sense of the British employer and the British workmen I have the utmost confidence. Of its ultimate triumph I am convinced. Time after time, during the war, when an industrial catastrophe seemed inevitable, I have seen common sense, acting on the national genius for compromise, serve to prevent both sides from going over the brink of the abyss that suddenly yawned. Along these principles a solution can be secured that will be stable and satisfactory alike to employers, the workers and the community. The first essential step to a solution is knowledge of the ingredients that make up the Labour problem, and there is no book, as far as I am aware, available to the general reader that states the matter plainly from a wide and practical experience quite as I have striven to do. That is my apology for publication of this book.

My criticisms, I trust, will leave no rancour; I have stated my views with directness, but in words I have weighed, and there is nothing behind them, for I am neither an employer nor a politician. I am but anxious to see a brotherly, just and nation-saving solution of the problem. Labour and I have had many a fierce tussle in the past, but I think we have learned to respect each other. No section of the community so revels in and honours straightforward and downright criticism as does Labour, provided it is really honest and the critic is sincere. It is something to be able to say, after so much official controversy as I have had, that on no occasion did we ever descend from discussing principles to personalities. I hope this book may not contain a single involuntary lapse from that standard, as I count myself fortunate, in spite of acute differences in economic views, to enjoy the friendship of many persons, both great and humble, in the Labour movement, a valued possession I would not lightly jeopardize. It is with principles, and principles only, that this book is concerned, and not with persons.

PART I
THE LABOUR PARTY'S FALSE POLICY

CHAPTER I
THE LABOUR PARTY'S CONSTITUTION AND ITS DEFECTS

There are two great Labour organizations: the Trades Union Congress, with its Executive, the General Council, which represents the industrial wing; and the Labour Party, with its National Executive or Executive Committee, representing the political wing. The distinction between industry and politics—at no time kept clear—is fast disappearing.

Origin of the Labour Party

The Labour Party dates from 1900—when the Labour Representation Committee was formed on the initiative of the Trades Union Congress, the Independent Labour Party, the Social Democratic Federation, and the Fabian Society. Of 15 Committee candidates who ran at the subsequent General Election of 1900, 2 were returned—the late Mr. Keir Hardie and Mr. Richard Bell—9 Trade Unionist members being also returned, but not under the auspices of the Committee. Before 1900 prominent Trade Unionists had stood individually for Parliament, and had, from time to time, been elected. The first effective steps had been taken in that direction by the Labour Representation League established in 1869, after the Reform Act of 1868. In 1874, 13 candidates went to election, and the first two "Labour members" were elected, one being the late Right Hon. Thomas Burt. In 1880, 3 were returned; in 1885,11; in 1892,14; in 1895,12. The successful Labour candidates stood on an industrial and not a "Socialist ticket"; where Socialists did stand they received scanty support. At the election of 1885, the Social Democratic Federation ran a candidate in Kennington and one in Hampstead: the former polled only 32 votes, the latter 29.

In 1886, the Labour Representation League having been dissolved, the Electoral Labour Committee was constituted by the Trades Union Congress. It soon fell under the influence of the Liberal Party, and this led to Mr. Keir Hardie's campaign, opened at the Swansea Trades Union Congress in 1887, for an independent Parliamentary Party representing Labour. Mr. Keir Hardie himself fought Mid-Lanark as an Independent Labour candidate in 1888 unsuccessfully, but was returned for South-West Ham in 1892. At his instance the Independent Labour Party was founded in 1893; it sent 28 candidates to the poll in 1895, with no success. But the political activity of the Independent Labour Party soon roused the Trades Union Congress. In 1899, at the Plymouth Conference, the Congress passed a resolution directing its Parliamentary Committee to arrange a conference of Trade Unions, Co-operative and Socialist Societies, to secure the return of an increased number of Labour members to Parliament. As part of the machinery the Labour Representation Committee was formed in 1900.

The constitution of the Labour Representation Committee in 1900 was as follows: 41 Trade Unions, with a membership of 353,070 members; 7 Trades Councils; 3 Socialist Societies, adding a further membership of 22,861, making a total of 375,931. At bye-elections between the General Elections of 1900 and 1906, three prominent candidates of the Labour Representation Committee were elected: Mr. (now Sir) David Shackleton for Clitheroe, the late Mr. Will Crooks for Woolwich, and Mr. (now the Right Hon.) Arthur Henderson for Barnard Castle. The Newcastle Trades Union Congress of 1903 passed a strong resolution enjoining political independence, and instituted a parliamentary fund. At the General Election in 1906, out of 50 candidates sponsored by the Labour Representation Committee, which in that year re-christened itself "the Labour Party," 29 were elected. Under the chairmanship of Mr. Keir Hardie, the Parliamentary Labour Party was immediately established with all the paraphernalia of a separate political party in the House of Commons. At the General Election of January 1910, out of 78 candidates, 40 were elected; at that of December 1910, out of 56 candidates, 42 were elected; at that of December 1918, out of 392 candidates, 59 were elected. At the last election in 1918, with a total vote in Great Britain of 9,690,109, 2,375,202 were polled by Labour.

Reconstitution in 1918

At the Labour Party Conference at Nottingham in January 1918, a revised constitution was proposed, which was ultimately adopted in London at the Party Conference on February 26 of the same year. The case for the new constitution was put before the Nottingham Conference by the Secretary to the Executive Committee, the Right Hon. Arthur Henderson, in these words: "It was no use the Executive using anything in the nature of a social programme or talking about building up a new social order and reconstructing society until they had taken into very careful consideration their present position as an organized political force. They had done so, and came to the unanimous conclusion that Labour, as politically organized in the existing circumstances, was altogether inadequate to the great task that lay immediately before it. They had never in the proper sense claimed to be a national political party. This limitation was inherited from the resolution carried at the Trades Union Congress in Plymouth in 1899. They were a political federation consisting of Trade Unions, Socialist bodies and Co-operative Societies, but in recent years they had developed what were called Local Labour Parties." Mr. Henderson said the real question to be decided was whether, for the purposes of best attaining political power and of so advancing its party programme, the Labour Party should scrap the whole of its existing political machinery and build up a political organization from a new foundation depending only upon individual membership. "Speaking as an old electioneerer," he continued, "he did not mind saying that if they had to begin afresh that would be the ideal at which he would aim, but in view of the close proximity of a general election he could imagine no greater mistake than to attempt to create a new organization based solely upon individual membership." The Party ultimately decided to adhere to the existing scheme of a central industrial federation, but to graft on to it such a form of electoral constituency organization, linked up with the Local Labour Parties or Trades Councils, as would bring the federation and the constituencies into close contact with the Annual Conference and the National Executive of the Labour Party.

In the new constitution the Party thus expressed its intention:

> "(a) To organize and maintain in Parliament and the country a Political Labour Party, and to ensure the establishment of a Local Labour Party in every county constituency and every parliamentary borough, with suitable divisional organization in the separate constituencies of divided boroughs.

> "(b) To secure for the producers, by hand or by brain, the full fruits of their industry, and the most equitable distribution thereof that may be possible upon the basis of the common ownership of the means of production and the best obtainable system of popular administration and control of each industry or service.

> "(c) Generally to promote the political, social and economic emancipation of the people, and more particularly of those

who depend directly upon their own exertions by hand or by brain for the means of life.

"(*d*) To co-operate with the Labour and Socialist organizations in the Dominions and Dependencies with a view to promoting the purposes of the Party, and to take common action for the promotion of a higher standard of social and economic life for the working population of the respective countries.

"(*e*) To co-operate with the Labour and Socialist organizations in other countries, and to assist in organizing a Federation of Nations for the maintenance of freedom and peace, for the establishment of suitable machinery for the adjustment and settlement of international disputes by conciliation or judicial arbitration, and for such international legislation as may be practicable."

The new constitution maintains the Party as an industrial federation of Trade Unions, Socialist Societies, Trades Councils, and Local Labour Parties; but it establishes the principle of individual membership of the Party through membership of the local organization. Every man and woman, therefore, may now join a Local Labour Party. It is intended to form a Labour Party in every parliamentary constituency, as a unit of organization to which Trade Union local branches and Local Trade Councils, Co-operative, Socialist, and other such societies will be affiliated, and to which each individual local supporter of the Labour Party will adhere. Every candidate for Parliament must be chosen or approved by the local organization and accepted by the National Executive. He must stand as a Labour candidate, and, if elected, must agree to act in harmony with the constitution and standing orders of the Party, and accept the decisions of Party meetings. He must include in his electoral address those issues defined by the National Executive as the Labour Party's programme for the election.

The official adherence of the Co-operative movement to the political Labour Party is rather interesting. For many years when motions were brought forward in the Annual Co-operative Congress in favour of the Co-operative movement taking up political activity, these resolutions were invariably rejected by overwhelming majorities. However, in 1918, at an emergency conference of the Co-operative movement in London on October 16 and 17, it was decided to take political action. The reasons which led the Co-operative movement to this decision were taxation of Co-operative dividends, the alleged neglect of the Government to make greater use of the Co-operative movement in dealing with the national food supply, and alleged unfair treatment of the staffs of the distributive societies under the Military Service Acts.

For the year 1917, prior to its reconstitution, the Labour Party's membership was as follows:

123   Trade Unions, with a total membership of   2,415,383;

239   Trades Councils and Local Labour Parties;

3   Socialist Societies with a total membership of   47,140,

making a total affiliated membership of 2,465,131, which also included the membership of the Co-operative and Women's Labour League affiliations. For the year 1920, the membership of the Labour Party was 122 Trade Unions, with a total membership of 4,317,537, 492[1] affiliated Trades Councils and Local Labour Parties, 5 Socialist Societies, representing a membership of 42,270, making a total membership of 4,359,807, which also included the membership of the Co-operative and Women's Labour League affiliations.

The Socialist Societies are the Fabian Society, which, in 1921, returned a membership of 1,770; the Herald League with a membership of 500; the Independent Labour Party with a membership of 35,000; the Jewish Socialist Party (Poale Zion) with a membership of 3,000; the Social Democratic Federation with a membership of 2,000.

By the accounts of the Party the total receipts for the year ending December 31, 1920, were £62,000 odd, of which £49,000 represented affiliation fees.

The Trades Union Congress

Turning from the Labour Party to the Trades Union Congress, "Labour's Annual Parliament," this, when founded in 1868, consisted of 34 delegates, representing about 20 societies with an affiliated membership of 118,367. In 1919, although all Trade Unions were not included, it had grown to 851 delegates, representing 266 Unions and an affiliated membership of 5,283,676. In 1921 it consisted of 810 delegates representing a membership of 6,417,910. It may now be taken to represent industrially the organized labour of Great Britain, and has the largest Trade Union affiliated membership in the world.

The Trades Union Congress must be distinguished from the General Federation of Trade Unions which was created under its auspices in 1899—now representing an affiliated membership of about 1½ millions— and the chief object of which is to maintain Trade Union rights, and to assist financially or otherwise affiliated Unions involved in disputes with employers or employers' organizations.

The National Joint Council

A scheme for co-ordination of Labour forces was recently worked out by a Joint Co-ordination Committee representing the Parliamentary Committee of the Trades Union Congress and the Executive Committee of the Labour Party. A National Joint Council has been constituted representing the General Council of the Trades Union Congress, the Executive Committee of the Labour Party and the Parliamentary Labour Party. Its duties are to consider all questions affecting the Labour movement as a whole, and to make provision for immediate action on questions of national emergency, and to endeavour to secure a common policy and joint action, whether by legislation or otherwise, on all questions affecting the workers as producers, consumers or citizens. The expenditure of the Council is met in equal proportions by the General Council of the Trades Union Congress and the Executive Committee of the Labour Party. The scheme also provides for the establishment, under joint control of the General Council and of the National Executive, of four departments organized to deal with research and information, international affairs, publicity and legal matters. In the memorandum which recommended the scheme for the National Joint Committee, it was pointed out that in view of the enormous growth of the Labour movement and the importance of presenting a united front upon the great problems which lie before it, the need for co-ordination was becoming daily more important. "If Labour is to realize its ideals it must formulate a common policy and secure the maximum of common action. The effectiveness of the Labour movement has in the past been dissipated by overlapping functions, by duplication of effort, and by confusion arising from conflicting policies." The scheme is described as one which enables Labour to speak with one voice on all questions of national importance, and to pursue one uniform policy in support of its common ends.

The Parliamentary Labour Party

What the Parliamentary Labour Party is, must also be explained. In 1906, 29 Labour members were, we have seen, returned to Parliament; they were then constituted into a distinct Parliamentary party, Mr. J. Keir Hardie, M.P., being elected Chairman, and a Vice-Chairman, Secretary and Whips being also appointed. It is the practice of the Parliamentary Party at the beginning of each session to review the resolutions passed at the various conferences of the Labour Party and to take them as indicating the principles on which the Parliamentary Party should proceed. About the commencement of the session there is a joint meeting between the Parliamentary Party and the National Executive of the Labour Party for the purposes of deciding the various objects in respect of which Bills should be introduced into Parliament or motions made. A general review of the Parliamentary Labour Party's activity since 1906 will be found in the *Labour Year Books* for 1916 and 1919.

The Labour Party, a Class Party

The Labour Party claims to be "the true national democratic party" in challenge of the old party system. It recommends itself to the electorate as "the party of the producers, whose labour of hand and brain provides the necessities of life for all and dignifies and elevates human existence," "Producers have been robbed," it says, "of the major parts of the fruits of their industry under the individualist system of capitalist production; and that is justification for the Party's claims."

The constitution of the Labour Party when examined definitely disproves the contention that the Party either is or ever can be, while that constitution lasts, a national democratic political party. By a political party one understands, according to our British traditions, a party whose members are united in support of common political principles, and not a party whose object is to advance its own material interests. Whatever the Labour Party may call itself, it is in fact a class party—that appears clearly from its history. Up to 1900, when the Labour Representation Committee was constituted, it was definitely Trade Unionist in its organization. In 1900, as has been shown, seven local Trades Councils were, for the first time, brought in along with three Socialist Societies, but they only accounted for 22,861 out of 375,931 affiliated membership. Between 1900 and the revision of the constitution in 1918, the Party was obviously still comprised, in the main, of industrial Trade Unionists. Individual members were, as has been explained, nominally introduced into the Party in 1918, by throwing membership open to members of Local Labour Parties and Trade Councils. It is impossible, because the Labour Party has not the figures itself, to give any comparison between the number of individual members of Local Labour Parties and Trades Councils who are not Trade Unionists and the 4,317,537 members of the affiliated Trade Unions in 1920. But one thing is quite clear—the individual member is wholly swamped by the Trade Unions' membership and power. If the accounts of the Labour Party are examined for 1920, it will be found that of the total affiliation fees of £49,000, only about £1,382 is contributed by Trades Councils and Local Labour Parties, which include a certain number of individual members, and £524 from five Socialist bodies; so that practically the whole of the income of the Labour

Party comes from the Trade Unions; they naturally exercise the right to dictate policy and run the Party machine. When it comes to the selection of the local Parliamentary candidate, if a Local Labour Party or Trades Council runs a candidate they must themselves provide for the whole expenses of the election, and that puts a serious difficulty in their way; on the other hand, if a Trade Union selects a candidate it is enabled, by means of its parliamentary levy, to pay the whole costs of his election. As a result, in the great number of cases, Trade Unionist candidates, with the financial backing of their Unions, are accepted as Local Labour candidates—true carpet-baggers in the real sense of the term, and probably wholly unknown to the district. One may learn from experience the basis on which the Trade Unions select candidates. It is considered a matter of prime importance by every Union to have members of its own in Parliament, and its first consideration is whether he is a sound and trusty member of his particular organization. As it is considered essential that only men should be selected by a Union who have an intimate knowledge of the working of the Union, the branch secretary or the district delegate or district secretary or a member of the executive or the general secretary of the Union is generally chosen, and he, it should be noted, is picked out, not for his political experience or enthusiasm, but as a trusty protagonist of his own trade body; he, therefore, goes into Parliament primarily to advance the industrial interests of his own particular Union and, so far as is compatible with that, of Labour in general. This needs clearly to be understood by the general public of this country. The Labour Party has no right to protest against those who would institute a campaign against it on the ground that the Labour movement, as at present constituted, is definitely class and sectarian in its objects. There is ample justification for that attack in the Labour Party's own pamphlet *Trade Unionism and Political Action*. The Labour Party will not for a very long time, if ever, be a Party solely of individual membership; that would mean that the Party would have to cut itself off from the enforced contributions of affiliated Trade Unions, and rely upon the voluntary contributions of its individual members.

The Labour Party prides itself on being the party of brotherhood—an admirable sentiment, one too seldom encountered in the industrial world to-day. We are entitled to test such a profession by examining to what extent the spirit of fraternity operates amongst the 122 different Trade Unions which are members of the Party. If any one part of the community is torn by internecine strife it most certainly is the Trade Union section. Consider for example the question of demarcation of work. If we take trades like those of the shipwrights and the joiners, they are separated by thin divisions; so much so that in one port shipwrights do work which in another port is done by joiners. If anywhere there is the least invasion by one trade into the work of the other the most unbrotherly struggles ensue, resulting almost invariably in one Union or the other calling their respective members out and so stopping work in the port. Time after time during the war I had the fitting out or refitting of urgently needed vessels held up by these kinds of fratricidal disputes. Again, take trades like engineers, members of the Amalgamated Engineering Union, and plumbers, members of the Plumbers' Union—between them there is the most bitter animosity. Certain pipes on board ship are, according to the custom of the port, bent and fitted by the members of one Union, and certain other pipes, possibly of the same material but a little larger or smaller, or of the same size but of a different material, are bent and fitted by members of the other Union. After the Jutland fight, I had most vital naval repairs held up owing to the whole of the engineers in one large district going on strike because plumbers had been put on to bore a few holes in the outer casings of searchlights, as there were no available engineers to do the work. Instances might be multiplied indefinitely of this industrial enmity which is to form the basis of the new political brotherhood. We have again the perennial dispute between the Amalgamated Engineering Union and the National Union of Railwaymen in respect of the men in the railway engineering shops, or the acrimonious controversy, growing in intensity, between the General Workers' Union, representing the unskilled or semi-skilled men, and the Amalgamated Engineering Union. The former Union asserts the right of an engineering employer to promote its members from the job of general labourer "on the floor" to work semi-automatic or other similar machines "in the shop," which without question the man is usually quite competent to do; on the other hand the Amalgamated Engineering Union, or its district committee, claims that no person, however competent, can be put on to work any of those machines unless he is a member of the Amalgamated Engineering Union and receives in respect of the work the prescribed rates of pay. So then we have this curious paradox that the Labour Party, which knows that there exists, and is quite incapable of extinguishing, this spirit of industrial hostility amongst the various sections of its Trade Union membership, still professes its ability to instil and enforce the spirit of social brotherhood throughout the whole electorate. "By their works ye shall know them," The truth of the matter is that the sole cohesive political force which the Labour Party can exert, apart from the Trade Unions' industrial compulsion on their members, are the promises of better times, less work, more time for leisure, more money to spend, by the abolition of what it calls the "capitalistic" or private employer, and the suggestion that thereby there will be some fund of money made available for distribution amongst the members of the Party.

The Party's Want of Leadership

What about the Labour Party's leaders? Labour undoubtedly possesses outstanding men of tried experience, ability and judgment, and others, untried as yet, but of equal capacity and ability. I had the good fortune during the war of serving at different times directly under the Right Hon. A. Henderson, the Right Hon. G. N. Barnes, the Right Hon. John Hodge, and the Right Hon. G. H. Roberts. I had also the opportunity of comparing their ministerial gifts with those of other Cabinet Ministers and Ministers of State. The Labour Ministers did not suffer from the comparison; their respective records are unsurpassed for foresight, decision, balance of judgment, statesmanship, organizing and administrative ability, power of evoking the loyalty of their departments and commanding the confidence of the public. The weakness of a Labour Government will assuredly not lie in the personnel of its Ministers *if* they lead—but will they be allowed to lead? So far the signs are not encouraging.

Nobody who has not seen the working of the Trade Union machine from inside has the remotest conception of the difficulties of the Trade Union leader, or of the tyranny to which he is subject. He is in the first instance usually a paid official of his Union, and if he takes or advocates any political or parliamentary action which is considered in any way to invade or infringe the trade rights and privileges of his Union, he will assuredly fall from office at the next Union election. Every leader must, therefore, keep one eye upon his own position and the other upon the political principle which he is disposed to advocate. This makes it exceedingly difficult for any Labour leader to take a strong independent line which may excite even the suspicions of ill-informed sections of his followers, still less their hostile opposition. I saw over and over again during the war how frequently large committees of Trade Unionist leaders would agree with the Government in London on the adoption of some measure—it may have been for the suspension of a trade custom in order to expedite production—and how it became quite impossible to obtain their active assistance afterwards to put the agreement into operation among their members, with the notable exception of some few whose sturdy independence I never ceased to admire. But these, unfortunately, perhaps as the result of their qualities, have little influence in political Labour.

There is another aspect: the great unwritten law of the Labour movement is solidarity at any price, and it frequently happens that the leaders, in order to avoid splitting the Party, will adopt, against their own better judgment, the proposals of extremists rather than face disruption. The action of constitutionalists in the Labour movement, in ultimately taking part in the recent formation of the Council of Action, notwithstanding their own earlier protests, is a case in point.

No political party is immune from intrigue or from cabals and conspiracies against its accepted leaders, but it is not an exaggeration to say that the Labour movement is more impregnated than any other movement in this country with those unlovely tendencies. You have only to follow the course of a branch committee or a district committee election, or the election of an executive committee-man or general secretary of a Trade Union, to realize the prevalence and power of personal jealousies. This is notoriously so in the political Labour world. Nothing cuts so deeply at the roots of independent leadership as incessant conspiracy and intrigue.

CHAPTER II
AN OUTLINE OF THE LABOUR
PARTY'S GENERAL POLICY

To appreciate the Labour Party's industrial policy, it is necessary to know, at least in outline, the general policy of which the former is a part. As the basis of all social reform it is contended that "the individualistic system of capitalist production based on the private ownership and competitive administration of land and capital, with its reckless profiteering and wage slavery, its glorification of the unhampered struggle for the means of life, and its hypocritical pretence of the survival of the fittest, must go." With it must be eradicated the "monstrous inequality of circumstances which it produces, and the degradation and brutalization, both moral and spiritual, resulting from it"—"along with it must disappear the present political system, enshrining the ideas in which the capitalistic system naturally finds expression." The Labour Party advances a new basis of social reorganization; it proposes to reconstruct society on four pillars resting upon the common foundation of "the democratic control of society in all its activities." These four pillars are: "(1) Universal enforcement of the national minimum; (2) the democratic control of industry; (3) a revolution in national finance; and (4) the surplus wealth for the common good."

A National Minimum Standard of Living

The principle of the national minimum, it is claimed, contrasts sharply with the principle of the capitalistic system, expressed either by Liberal or Conservative policy. By the national minimum is meant the assurance for every member of the community of a standard of life conferring a reasonable minimum of health, education, leisure and subsistence. One chief element is a legal minimum wage, to be revised according to the level of current prices. As part of this national minimum, the ambiguous principle of "equal pay for equal work" is postulated in all occupations in which both sexes are engaged. The Party also demands that the Government shall prevent unemployment, and should it fail to secure for every willing worker a suitable situation at the standard rate of wages, it shall provide such a worker with maintenance in the form of out-of-work benefit paid through his Trade Union. The National

Unemployment Insurance Scheme should, it is insisted, be extended, on a non-contributory basis, to every occupation. What is affirmed as a fundamental is that "in one way or another remunerative employment or honourable maintenance must be found for every willing worker by hand or by brain in bad times as well as in good." Complete provision against involuntary destitution in sickness and in health, in good times and in bad, must be assured for every member of the community.

Effective Personal Freedom

Democracy, the Labour Party asserts, implies effective personal freedom, and involves the complete removal of all war-time restrictions on liberty of speech, publication, press, travel, choice of residence, kind of employment, and especially of any obligation for military service. These sentiments, strange to say, come from the Party which denies the right of the non-Union operative to work; and which claims for Trade Unions the right to picket and the other privileges afforded by the Trade Disputes Act, 1906. On the same principle, complete political rights are demanded for every adult irrespective of sex, and for every minority, the right to full proportionate representation in Parliament. The abolition of the House of Lords is demanded, with the elimination from any new second Chamber of any qualification based on heredity. Separate statutory legislative assemblies are claimed for Scotland, Wales and England, with autonomous administration in local matters; Parliament at Westminster to be merely a Federal Assembly for Great Britain, controlling the Ministers responsible for departments of central government; these Ministers, with others representing the Dominions and India, to form a Cabinet for federal affairs of the British Commonwealth.

Socialization of Land and Industry

The Labour Party stands for the removal from industry of the private employer and the capitalist, the introduction of a new "scientific re-organization of the national industries," purged from the degradation of individual profiteering, and regenerated on the basis of the common ownership of the means of production; the equitable sharing of the output among all who assist in any capacity in production; and the adoption of "democratic control of industry."

Accordingly the Labour Party would immediately establish the common ownership of land, the common ownership and administration of railways and canals, and their consolidation with harbours, roads, posts, telegraphs, and the ocean-going steamer lines into a national service of Communication and Transport, to be worked "unhampered by capitalist, private or purely local interests, and with a steadily increasing participation of the organized workers in the management, both central and local, exclusively for the common good." So also it would erect a score of national central electrical generating stations, with which all municipal electrical plants would be connected for distribution purposes. For similar reasons, the Party demands the immediate nationalization of coal-mines, with steadily increasing participation in the management, both central and local, of the various grades of persons employed; and insists that the retail distribution of household coal should be undertaken by the municipal authorities or county councils, the purpose to be achieved being the distribution in every local district of household coal of standard quality at a fixed and uniform price "as unalterable as the penny postage stamp." The State expropriation of profit-making industrial insurance companies is urged, also the assumption by Government of the whole business of life insurance. Much stress is laid upon the alleged necessity that Government should take the manufacture and retailing of intoxicants out of the hands of persons who find profit in promoting the utmost possible consumption of them, and that each local authority should deal with "the trade" within its district on the basis of local veto or limitation of licences or other system of regulation.

Admittedly alive to the evils of centralization and the restrictions of bureaucracy, the Party claims a free hand for local authorities, assisted by grants-in-aid from Government sources, to extend widely the scope of municipal enterprise. Local authorities should, it is asserted, not only retail coal, but supply milk, and engage in other similar spheres of trade. All members of local bodies ought, it is said, to receive their necessary travelling expenses, and also be paid for time spent by them on the public service.

The Labour Party would re-organize the whole educational system from the nursery school to the university "on the basis of social equality"; "each educational institution, irrespective of social class or wealth, to be open to every member of the community on terms within his reach"—everything in the nature of military training to be absolutely prohibited. In regard to public health, the Labour Party holds that Government should build at the national expense the requisite number of dwelling houses, spacious and healthy, each having four or five rooms, larder, scullery, cupboards, and fitted bath, spaced not more than ten or twelve to the acre, and provided with a garden. National provision for the prevention and treatment of disease, and the care of orphans, infirm, incapacitated, and aged persons is also included as an indispensable part of Labour's policy.

In regard to agriculture and rural life, the Party has formulated a number of proposals based on the Government's immediately assuming control of the nation's agricultural land, and—

"ensuring its utilization, not for rent, not for game, not for the social amenity of a small social class, not even for obtaining the largest percentage on the capital employed, but solely with a view to the production of the largest proportion of the food-stuffs required by the population of these islands under conditions allowing of a good life to the rural population with complete security for the farmers' enterprise, yet not requiring the consumer to pay a price exceeding that for which food-stuffs can be brought from other lands."

The means proposed to attain this end are large national farms, small holdings made accessible to practical agriculturists, municipal agricultural enterprises, and farms let to Co-operative Societies and other approved tenants, under a national guarantee against losses due to bad seasons. All distribution of agricultural food-stuffs—from milk and vegetables up to bread and meat—is to be taken out of the hands of dealers and shopkeepers, and is to be effected by Co-operative Societies and local authorities "with equitable compensation for all interests expropriated or displaced."

The Labour Party also advocates Government importation of raw materials and food-commodities, and Government control of the shipping, woollen, clothing, milling, and other similar industries; the rationing both of raw material and of food commodities, and the fixing of all prices on the basis of accurate costing, so as to eliminate profiteering. It is, the Labour Party says—

"just as much the function of Government, and just as necessary a part of the democratic regulation of industry to safeguard the interests of the community as a whole and those of grades and classes of private consumers in the matter of prices, as it is by the Factory and Trade Board Acts to protect the rights of the wage-earning producers in the matter of wages, hours of labour and sanitation, or by the organized police force to protect the householder from the burglar."

A Revolution in Public Finance

A complete revolution in national finance is overdue, in the opinion of the Labour Party. Too long, it says, has our national finance been regulated on a basis opposed to the teaching of political economy, according to the views of the possessing classes and the desire for profits of the financiers. There ought to be such a system of taxation "as will secure all the necessary revenue to the Government without encroaching on the prescribed national minimum standard of life of any family, without hampering production or discouraging any useful personal effort, and with the closest possible approximation to equality of sacrifice." The Labour Party accordingly would institute direct taxation of all incomes exceeding the necessary cost of family maintenance, and the direct taxation of private fortunes both during life and at death for the redemption of the National Debt. It opposes taxation calculated to increase the price of food or necessaries of life, and holds that indirect taxation of commodities, whether by customs or excise, should be limited to "luxuries." It would retain and increase the excess-profits tax and, until nationalization of minerals, the mineral-rights duty. The unearned increment of urban land and mineral values it would divert by taxation wholly into the public exchequer. Death duties would be regraduated and heavily increased, so as to turn into the national coffers all the wealth of every person deceased in excess of a quite moderate amount to be left for family provision. In addition, the Labour Party stands for "conscription of wealth," described as "a capital levy, chargeable, like death duties, on all property, with exemption of the smallest savings up to £1,000, but rising rapidly in percentage with the value of the property, for the purpose of freeing the nation of as large an amount as possible of its present load of interest-bearing debt." Co-operative Societies would be left entirely free from this levy.

The Surplus Wealth for the Common Good

The fourth principle of the Labour Party's policy of social reconstruction is "the diversion to the common good of the surplus over the expenditure required for the maintenance of the national minimum of life." This surplus is said to be embodied in the riches of the mines, the rental value of lands superior to the margin of cultivation, the extra profits of fortunate capitalists, now alleged to be absorbed by individual proprietors, and devoted to the senseless luxury of the idle rich. It is to be secured by nationalization and municipalization, and by steeply graduated taxation of private income and riches. From it is to be drawn the new capital which the community day by day will require for the perpetual improvement and increase of its various enterprises, and for which it is said to be dependent now on the usury-exacting financier.

> "It is in this proposal for the appropriation of every surplus for the common good—in the vision of its resolute use for the building up of the community as a whole instead of for the magnification of individual fortunes—that the Labour Party, as the Party of the producers by hand or by brain, most distinctively marks itself off from the older

political parties, standing as these do essentially for the maintenance unimpaired of the perpetual private mortgage upon the annual product of the nation that is involved in the individual ownership of land and capital."

International Co-operation

From Labour's home policy we turn to foreign affairs. Its international aims are "peace and co-operation between nations; the avoidance of anything making for international hostility; the development of international co-operation in the League of Nations," and "an ever-increasing intercourse, a constantly developing exchange of commodities, a steadily growing mutual understanding, a continually expanding friendly co-operation among all the peoples of the world." "Imperialism," defined to mean extension of empire over countries without reference to the wishes of the inhabitants of those countries, is repudiated as rooted in capitalism, and springing only from a desire for profits and for selfish exploitation of the natural resources belonging solely to those inhabitants. "Protectionism" in any form, whether by prohibitions on imports, embargoes, tariffs, differential shipping or railway rates, for the purpose of limiting the amount or restricting the free flow of foreign commodities into this country, is unreservedly condemned. Protection for the benefit of a particular trade, or all trades, while it may conduce to the immediate advantage of Labour, is presumed to operate to the greater ultimate advantage of the capitalist, and to strengthen his position. Anything tending to such a result is "contrary to the true interests of Labour." Protection is said to lead to capitalistic rings, combinations and trusts, higher prices, diminished consumption, reduced employment. This being so, Labour favours the free importation of all foreign goods, and their sale at rates as low as are consistent with their manufacture under unsweated labour conditions in their land of origin.

No Protective Tariffs

All tariffs, especially if differential, must, so Labour contends, inevitably create international friction, retaliation, enmity, and ultimately active hostilities, and are to be more especially discarded, inasmuch as they are the favourite instrument of capitalistic groups eager to make profits out of international ruptures. Labour accordingly objects to the protection of key industries for purposes of national safety. "It is impossible to make either the British Empire or the British Isles self-contained or self-supporting. Even if practicable, the policy of self-sufficiency would indicate a provocative intention to maintain a national condition of perpetual preparation for war." Therefore, except so far as is necessary to avoid the spread of disease or prevention of accidents, there must be no restriction on the transit or importation of any commodity. Imperial preference is likewise rejected as a selfish attempt to reserve for the inhabitants of the British Empire the raw materials and markets of the Empire, a course incompatible with any kind of lasting peace, having regard to the resentment it would provoke amongst the nations excluded from participating in these raw materials or from supplying our imperial markets. Labour calls for "the open door" in all our Colonies and Dependencies, and in "non-adult countries," meaning by this term "exploitable countries" like China and Africa. The position of the capitalist has been so undermined by Labour's attack at home that capital, in Labour's opinion, is now making its real profits and consolidating its power by expropriating natives, and compelling them to work for low wages.

Freedom of International Trade

In order to free Europe from "the rivalries of Capitalism—Imperialism—Protectionism, which poisoned international relations between 1880-1914," Labour desires to see an economic side of the League of Nations developed so as to secure the removal of all economic barriers and maintain equality of trade conditions. But surely it was Labour itself that called loudest for self-determination, which has so grievously impaired the economic restoration of Europe. A World Economic Council of the League ought to apportion the supplies of food-commodities and raw materials and maintain credit in the various countries so as to ensure fair allocation of raw materials, the furtherance of production, the development of international lines of communication, and the prevention of exploitation by trusts. As an alternative to "the present profit-making capitalistic economic system," Labour proposes to use for purposes of international trade, an organization on a world-wide basis of the different national Co-operative movements. So long as foreign trade remains under the control of the competitive and capitalistic system, Labour asserts that its general international aims can never be attained.

CHAPTER III
THE LABOUR PARTY'S
ADOPTION OF SOCIALISM

I. MEANING OF SOCIALISM

Socialism is too amorphous to admit of any workable definition. Each age exhibits schools of thought, industrial and philosophic, which define Socialism in different ways according to contemporary political circumstances, economic conditions and industrial tendencies or their interpretation of them. There is no more interesting study than to trace out the variant meanings of "Socialist" from its first appearance in the *Co-operative Magazine* of November 1827 up to the present time, and to note its successive contractions and extensions in political, ethical, economic and social implications as decade succeeded to decade.

The Common Characteristics of all Socialistic Creeds

But certain brands of Socialism can be described if not defined. The one common characteristic is abolition of the "capitalistic organization" of industry. If we call this A, then we can say that all schemes of Socialism can be reduced to the general formula $A + x$, where x is a symbol standing for a very large number of variables which comprise the methods by which the capitalist is to be extinguished; the terms on which the present capitalists will be compensated or otherwise expropriated; the persons or authority in whom the means of production—and probably there should be added distribution and exchange—will be vested; the persons or body to be responsible for the organization of industry and for its control; the means by which capital will be found and prices regulated; the relation in which the new industrial system will stand to the community, and the various socialized industries to one another. These are the practical points to which attention should be directed rather than academic definitions.

Of the term "capitalism" and what is implied by it all kinds of definitions are current. Socialists of different schools have their own definitions embellished with epithets which vary in virulence according to their particular trend of thought. Employers too have their definitions, but it will be sufficient for our purposes if we take capitalism to mean the existing scheme of industrial organization. The basic vices of capitalism, according to all Socialists, are that it is a system under which the owner of the capital employed in industry possesses and controls the whole business of production and sale of the output, buying, just as he buys raw materials for his business, the labour power of the workman, paying him as little for it as possible, and that in the form of a wage merely in respect of the time he is at work; a system under which the employer maintains a reserve of unemployed labour in order to provide for the variations in trade, while recognizing no responsibility in respect of the workman at times when the employer cannot or is not prepared to provide him with work. Under such conditions the workman is said to occupy a quasi-servile status, to be a wage-slave and entitled to no voice at all in the control of the industry. That, without the usual garnish of abuse, is probably a fair description of the present organization of industry as it is envisaged by the Socialist. The two great incidents of capitalism which the Socialist therefore seeks to eradicate are: the private ownership of land and capital; and the employment on a wage-basis of hired labour. If only capitalism could be abolished the workman would no longer see his employer and other capitalists appropriating, in the shape of rent and interest and profits, all the value of the product which the labourer is said to create over and above the amount of his wages.

To capitalism, it is customary, and, indeed, necessary for his argument, for the Socialist to attribute all the ills from which industry suffers and most evils to which the community is heir. With the exit of capitalism the Socialist says that unemployment would disappear and adequate maintenance be secured for sickness, old age and other incapacity, equality of opportunity afforded to all, full scope provided for individual expression and development, and a universal millennium inaugurated. In the minds of some Socialists there seems no limit whatsoever to the mephitic influence of capitalism. Dr. Shadwell, in his discerning articles in *The Times* [2] on "The Revolutionary Movement in Great Britain," mentions that the *Daily Herald* of February 2, 1921, found the cause of influenza in capitalism, and argued that unless the latter is destroyed it will destroy mankind; conversely Dr. Shadwell logically suggested we may assume that if capitalism is abolished influenza will disappear!

We are now in a position to distinguish the principal schools of Socialism that exist to-day. One will not find them formulating their principles as crisply as I set them out. My object is merely to indicate the main outlines.

State Socialism

First we have the State Socialist who advocates that the State should acquire, as he generally says, the means of production, distribution and exchange, or, to reduce it to practical terms, land and the national industries. Taking, for example, a concrete case—the railway industry—the State would take over all the railway undertakings in the country from the various companies of shareholders who now own them and, under most schemes of State Socialism, would compensate the shareholders by paying them, in State securities, something approaching the capital value of the net maintainable revenue of the undertakings. Under this system the State steps into the shoes of the original owners of the railways and acts as the employer controlling the industry and employing the workmen just as the private owners previously did. The industry would be run by a Government Department in Whitehall and, the State Socialist says, will be run in the interests of the community and not for private profit, inasmuch as the Government Department is, through its ministerial head, responsible to Parliament, which represents the community.

Syndicalism

The next school is that of Syndicalism, which, curiously enough, was really in its origin a British conception evolved in the revolutionary phase of the Chartist movement, but afterwards touched up and elaborated by Continental Socialists, especially in France, as by G. Sorel. Under this system, the private owner would be evicted by the workers, who would form some consolidated body, usually in the shape of an industrial Union, including all persons concerned in the operation of the industry, and that body would carry on the industry solely in the interests of the workers. Possession of the industry would be secured by the workers seizing the political power in the State, or, as is more generally advocated, by direct pressure of such a kind, in the form of a general strike or otherwise, as would enable the workers in all industries by concerted action to seize the means of production. Regarding, as the Syndicalist does, the capitalist as an idle and useless parasite who battens on the labour of the workers, no compensation would be paid to owners. The Syndicalist has not quite made up his mind whether he will include the technical and administrative staff in the industrial Union which will own and operate each industry, nor has he worked out the relation to the State of individual industries or industry as a whole.[3] Most Syndicalists assume that the State and its legislative, administrative and executive organizations, as we know it, will cease to function and come to an end under a syndicalistic regime, and that the country will be governed by some organization representing the workers as a whole. Except amongst certain revolutionary elements, Syndicalism has not a strong hold on British labour.

National Guildism

Next we come to the school of Guildsmen, of which that section known as the National Guilds have worked out their theory in the greatest detail. This school says that State Socialism would mean a rigid bureaucracy, and, so far as the workers are concerned, little advance on the capitalistic regime, because the workers would really be in the employment of the State and enjoy little or no voice in the control of industry. On the other hand, they say that the syndicalistic conception is doomed to failure because it makes no provision for including the supervisory, technical, managerial and administrative staff in the industrial organization that controls each industry, nor allows any safeguards for the consuming community against the selfish exercise of monopolies upon which the people are dependent for their necessary commodities and services. Accordingly the National Guildist proposes that the system of craft Trade Unionism that exists in this country should be replaced by industrial Unionism under which all manual workers employed in each industry would be enrolled in a comprehensive Trade Union embracing the whole of the industry, which in course of time would be expanded into an industrial Guild that would also include all the supervisory, technical, managerial and administrative staff, and that this Guild should be entirely responsible for the control and organization of the work of the particular industry. Exactly how the Guilds are to acquire the means of production in each industry is not yet developed; some advocate acquisition by the State for a small payment to the owners and then transference by the State to the Guilds; others the forcible acquisition by the Guilds after such gradually intensive action on the part of the workers as will bring the capitalistic system of organization of the industry to an impasse. A Guild Congress for each industry will regulate the affairs of that industry, and a National Guild Congress of all industries the affairs of all the industries in the country. Prices and other matters in each industry which affect the consumer will be regulated by arrangement between the

Guild and local and central organizations representing the consumers, and general matters in all industries affecting the community will be adjusted by negotiations between the National Guild Congress and National Consumers' Organizations. Those who desire to follow out Guild Socialism both as an industrial and a political conception should read that most interesting and brilliantly written book by Mr. G. D. H. Cole, *Guild Socialism Re-stated*; and investigate the Building Guilds.

Nationalization and Democratic Control

In Great Britain, political, industrial and social schemes of reconstruction have never followed strictly logical lines; they have invariably assumed a character of compromise, thereby giving effect to national idiosyncrasies of temperament. Accordingly we find a large body of Socialist opinion in this country advocating what it calls "nationalization and democratic control." Perhaps the best illustration of what is meant by that baffling phrase is afforded by the scheme of the Miners' Federation of Great Britain for the reorganization of the coal industry. In that scheme, which is explained in the Bill presented to Parliament by the Miners' Federation in 1920, the basic proposal is that the State should buy out the coal owners and that there should be established a National Mining Council. Since the Miners' Federation as at present constituted could not appoint the technical workers, this Council would be composed, as to one-half, of representatives of the manual workers in the coal industry, and as to the other half by representatives of the Government. If, however, the Miners' Federation could appoint the technical workers, I rather gather that they would not have been prepared to acquiesce in such duality of control. Under their proposal, the one-half of the National Mining Council representing the workers would be appointed by the Miners' Federation and the other half would be persons appointed by the Government to represent the technical, administrative and commercial sides of the industry together with other persons to represent the consuming community. This Council would determine the annual output, fix prices and control finances. In addition, there would be District Councils for each coal-mining district, one-half elected by men working in the district, and the other half being technical and administrative persons and representatives of the National Council. Further, there would be Pit or Colliery Committees at every colliery comprised exclusively of the managerial, technical and manual workers. The manager as the person responsible for the governance of the mine, would be responsible to the Pit Committee, and the Pit Committee and the manager would be responsible for conducting the colliery.

It will be observed that this scheme of organization, which is probably what the most thoughtful sections of Labour have at the back of their minds as the kind to be applied to a well-organized industry, differs from State Socialism in that the State is not the direct employer, and differs from Syndicalism in that the workers have not autocratic control, and differs from Guild Socialism in that the conduct of the industry is not entirely by a Guild representative of all persons concerned in the industry, but by a Council consisting as to one-half of representatives of the miners and as to the other half of Government representatives.

CHAPTER IV
THE LABOUR PARTY'S
ADOPTION OF SOCIALISM

2. HISTORY OF THE ALLIANCE

It is impossible to understand the present connection between the Labour Party and Socialism without some small acquaintance with the history of Labour's attitude to Socialism in the past. That involves a retrospect of Trade Unionism. Up to 1825, anything in the nature of a Trade Union was rigorously suppressed by the Combination Laws, which, after considerable agitation, were repealed by the Acts 5 Geo. IV, 95 and 6 Geo. IV, 129. Although full freedom was not thereby secured for Trade Unions, yet for the first time the right of collective bargaining was recognized—a process of negotiation in course of which organizations of workmen could withhold their labour in order to secure the rates of wages or conditions of employment that they desired. As was naturally to be expected, this led to an increase in the number of Trade Unions and of their power. But fortune proved unkind. At the outset of their development there occurred the financial crash of 1825, which caused wholesale commercial ruin and widespread closing of works, reductions of wages and unemployment for the four or five years following, with continual strikes by way of resistance to wage reductions. The poverty and destitution of the working-classes as compared with the wealthier section of the community led to dissemination among the workers of revolutionary ideas, political and socialistic. One can read in the newspapers of the time, even as far back as 1829, familiar doctrines—that Labour is the only source of wealth—that the working-men are the support of the middle and upper classes, the nerves and soul of production, the foundation of the nation. From 1829, and particularly through the Chartist days of 1835-1842, the Trade Union movement which had previously concerned itself mainly in endeavouring to increase wages and improve conditions of employment, was actively associated with the middle classes in prosecuting revolutionary aims.

Labour's Struggle for Political Power, 1825-1832

From 1829-32, the struggle swayed around the Reform Bill. Both Labour and the middle classes combined to regard the enactment of that measure as the opening of the door to social progress. Its failure to provide for universal manhood suffrage shattered the hopes of Labour. Revolution had for some time been whispered; a school of advanced Labour thought, when working out to its logical conclusion the theory that labour was the sole source of value, had evolved the doctrine of class-war.

Labour's Alliance with Revolutionary Socialism, 1832-1842

Stung by disappointment through exclusion from the suffrage, organized Labour embraced these revolutionary doctrines, arrayed itself definitely against Parliamentary government, and insisted that the workers' only hope of salvation lay in direct application against the community of their economic power. Robert Owen about that time was the leader of socialistic thought in this country, and Labour adopted and adapted certain parts of his policy as its official programme. Owen's notion substantially was that the machinery of production should be owned not by the community, but by the particular section of workers who used it, and that the Trade Unions concerned in each industry should be transformed into national companies to carry on the trade. Profit-making and competition were to be eliminated. The labour of the miner, for example, would exchange on some time-basis with the labour of the agricultural labourer. One enthusiastic Owenite, William Benbow, elaborated the theory of the general strike as the means of enforcing the transfer of industries from the capitalists to the workers. This was the first official adoption by organized Labour in this country of socialistic conceptions. The movement, however, collapsed in 1834, and was succeeded by what is now known as Chartism. That term was at the time merely understood to mean democratic parliamentary reform, its immediate object being the conquest of political power, and its ulterior purposes, so far as organized Labour were concerned, were the establishment of communist colonies, the common ownership of land and of the means of production, social reform, democratic political organization, greater freedom for Trade Unions and improvement in wages and working conditions. There was thus a combination of mixed forces working indiscriminately for social reform, Trade Unionism and democratic parliamentary government. The dominant notion was to obtain parliamentary power which was thought a sufficient means to reform society, reorganize industry and purge the nation of every kind of social and industrial disorder. As is well known, there were two distinct parties in the Chartist movement, those who advocated physical force and those who confined their argument to moral suasion.

The year 1842 marks the culmination of Chartism and will be remembered as the year of the general strike in the North of England, and of the apparent imminence of a social revolt; but the collapse of the general strike and the repressive action of the government took, for the time being, all driving force out of the agitation. When times improved, and trade started to prosper, Chartism lost ground; the Trade Unions began to detach themselves from schemes of social revolution, and to make their immediate objective the improvement of the conditions of the workers in regard to wages and employment. Chartism continued as a political movement, with varying fortunes, up to the year 1849. What it achieved up to 1855 is thus summarized by Mr. Beer in Vol. II of his *History of British Socialism*, p. 190:

> "After a desperate contest of thirty years' duration, Chartism had come to an end. It had not been a struggle of a plebs for equal rights with the patriciate to spoliate and enslave other classes and nations, but a class-war aiming at the overthrow of the capitalist society and putting production, distribution, and exchange on a co-operative basis. The working-class was apparently defeated.

> "Baffled and exhausted through erratic leadership, untold sacrifices, and want of proper mental munitions, they retired from the field of battle, bleeding and decimated, but little aware of the great results they had achieved. They only saw the shattered ideals and broken hopes that lay strewn on the long path they had been marching and counter-marching from 1825 to 1855, not knowing that it was from the wreckage and debris of those shattered ideals that the material was gathered for building and paving the road of social progress.

> "The advance which Great Britain had made in those thirty years in social reform and democracy was enormous. The Chartist period witnessed the first real Factory Act (1833), the first mining law for the protection of child and female labour (1842), the Ten Hours' Day (1847), the reduction of the newspaper stamp (1836), the Abolition of the Corn Laws (1846), the repeal of the Corresponding Acts (1846). It bequeathed to the working-classes the co-operative store and co-operative production, more successful trade unions, and international sentiments. It forced the thinking men of the nation to regard the Labour problem as a serious subject for investigation and discussion. Finally, it imbued the

thinking portion of the working-class with the conviction that Liberalism must first do its work, before Labour could come into its own, both in the legislature and in the factory. In short, from the catastrophes of 1832, 1834, 1839, 1842 and 1848, the lesson emerged that the revolutionary policy of 'all or nothing,' of a sweeping triumph by one gigantic effort, of contempt for reform and of the supreme value of a total and radical subversion of the old order, were foredoomed to failure. The generation that succeeded Chartism went into Gladstone's camp and refused to leave it either for the social Toryism of Benjamin Disraeli or for the social revolution of Karl Marx."

Labour's Renunciation of Socialism, 1842-1885

Onwards from the year 1842, although individual Trade Unionists and certain societies, which included no doubt members of the working-classes, continued to promote Socialism, the British Trade Unions advocated no scheme of Socialism as part of their official objects. They contented themselves with improving their organizations, increasing their members, making provision for friendly society benefits and of introducing methods of collective bargaining instead of class-war and of strikes. Mr. Beer again states the position at p. 195 of Vol. II, *History of British Socialism*:

"The twenty years following upon the collapse of Chartism formed the golden age of middle-class Liberalism. The glamour of its doctrines as set forth by Mill in his essay 'On Liberty,' the phenomenal growth of British trade and commerce, the unrivalled position of Great Britain as the workshop of the world, made British Liberalism the lodestar of all nations striving for freedom and wealth. Competition as the regulator of economic relations, free trade as the international bond of peace and goodwill, individual liberty as the sacred ideal of national politics, reigned supreme, and under their weight the entire formation of social revolutionary ideas of the past disappeared from view. The working-classes formed a part of triumphant Liberalism.

"Gladstone, surveying his hosts in 1866, appeared quite justified in telling his Conservative opponents that there was no use fighting against his social forces, 'which move onwards in their might and majesty and which ... are marshalled on our side.' He might have addressed the same eloquent words to the leaders of the International Working Men's Association, who with Karl Marx at their head, were precisely at that time making a serious attempt to resuscitate Chartism and detach the masses from the Liberal Party. Socialism and independent Labour politics came to be regarded as exotic plants which could never flourish on British soil.

"The trade unions renounced all class-warfare and merely tried to use their new citizenship (1867) and their growing economic organization—the first trade union congress took place in 1869—with a view to influencing the distribution of the national wealth in their favour. Their aim and end was that of a plebs striving for equality with the possessing and ruling-classes. It was, despite some struggle for the legalization of trade unionism, a period of social peace, and it lasted till about 1880."

This state of things continued in fact up to about 1885, and until that date Socialism formed really no part of official Trade Union principles.

The Era of Constitutional State Socialism, 1885-1905

Mr. and Mrs. Sidney Webb in their *History of Trade Unionism*, revised edition, 1920, p. 374, describe the principles of the Labour Party about 1885 as follows:

"*Laissez faire* then was the political and social creed of the Trade Union leaders of this time; up to 1885 they undoubtedly represented the views current among the rank and file; at that date all observers were agreed that the Trade Unions of Great Britain would furnish an impenetrable barrier against Socialist projects. Within a decade we find the whole trade union world permeated with collectivist ideas, and, as *The Times* recorded as early as 1893, the Socialist Party supreme in the Trades Union Congress. This revolution in opinion is the chief event of Trade Union history at the close of the nineteenth century."

These two talented authors analyse the causes. They attribute it in great measure to the "new unionism" of 1889 which was itself largely the result of the wide circulation in Great Britain of Henry George's *Progress and Poverty* during the years 1880-1882; the lecturing of the late Mr. H. M. Hyndman and Mr. William Morris and other disciples of Karl Marx; revelations of certain "well-intentioned if somewhat sentimental philanthropists" of their experiences in the sweated industries and slums of our great cities, as, for example, Mr. Charles Booth's great work, *Life and Labour in London*; depression in trade; the great Dock Strike in 1889.

The attitude observed by the Trades Union Congress in regard to socialistic proposals is instructive. Up to 1887, at five successive conferences, amendments in favour of the nationalization of land had been continuously rejected; at the Swansea Conference in 1887, a resolution in no very definite terms was accepted in its favour. The extreme socialistic conception of the advanced Trade Unionist of the nineties was State Socialism to be secured by constitutional political action. The power of action was to be derived from every working-class Socialist becoming a member of his Trade Union, of his local Co-operative Society, of his borough council, urban or rural district or county council. This represented substantially the full socialistic creed of official Labour up to about the year 1905. Mr. and Mrs. Sidney Webb thus epitomize it:

> "In short, there was from the collapse of Owenism and Chartism in the eighteen-thirties and -forties right down to 1900 practically no sign that the British Trade Unions ever thought of themselves otherwise than as organizations to secure an ever-improving standard of life by means of an ever-increasing control of the conditions under which they worked. They neither desired nor sought any participation in the management of the technical processes of industry (except in so far as these might affect the conditions of their employment or the selection of persons to be employed), whilst it never occurred to a Trade Union to claim any power over, or responsibility for, buying the raw materials or marketing the product." — (*History of Trade Unionism* (1920), p. 653.)

The New Syndicalist Revolutionary Ferment of 1905

Between 1905 and 1910 new socialistic beliefs of a Syndicalist character began to be absorbed by sections of Trade Unionists, especially the miners and the engineers, who soon exhibited a spirit of revolt not only against the capitalistic system, but more especially against the limited aims of contemporary Trade Unionism. There commenced, and up to the beginning of the war, continued a definite struggle in the Labour movement between the constitutional Trade Unionists who held tight to their ideals of State Socialism, and the revolutionary industrial Unionists, led by James

Connolly, and Tom Mann, who preached their doctrine of Syndicalism, advocating first the abolition of craft Unionism—the system under which all workmen of a particular craft, for example, engineers, are enrolled in their own craft Unions irrespective of the industries in which they work— and its replacement by industrial Unionism, that is to say, the enrolment in one Trade Union representing each industry of all men engaged in that industry irrespective of their particular craft or occupations, such as to a limited extent prevails in the railway, mining and transport industries; secondly, the appropriation of the means of production in each industry by the manual workers who would produce the output, charge the price and conduct the industry. Connolly, who was afterwards executed for complicity in the Irish Rebellion of 1916, came from the United States of America in 1905, and persuaded the Socialist Labour Party of Glasgow to link up forces with the American Industrial Workers of the World. Mann, who was recently the Secretary of the Amalgamated Engineering Union, brought the seeds of revolutionary Syndicalism from Paris and sowed them personally by means of a widespread campaign.

Without any doubt, the Socialist Labour Party, an organization not, however, affiliated to the Labour Party, has contributed more than any other agency to the spread of Syndicalism in England. It describes itself as "a revolutionary political organization seeking to build up a communist movement in this country." It works "to sweep away the mass of debris which was once known as the parliament institutions," Those who want to appreciate its activities in these directions ought to follow them in Dr. Miliukov's *Bolshevism—An International Danger*, and I can personally vouch for and add to his testimony. The Socialist Labour Party was indubitably the power behind the revolutionary propaganda before the war among the miners and the railwaymen, and to some extent among the dockers, and it was responsible for many of the numerous "irritation strikes" in 1911-14 and for the Clyde strikes in 1916. Its disloyal action during the war, through the medium of the workers' committees and shop steward organizations, is later described. The S.L.P. and the I.W.W. were the original founders of the "Hands Off Russia Committee." Such has been the revolutionary ferment leavening English and Scottish Labour since 1905—to it we largely owe our present recurrent outbursts of industrial insurrectionism.

The Socialist Societies

There are, as previously explained, certain Socialist Societies definitely affiliated to the Labour Party; others are unofficially recognized, and there are yet others not recognized, either officially or unofficially, which comprise numerous persons who through their Trade Union or local organizations, or individually, are members of the Labour Party. These advocate brands of Socialism ranging from State Socialism to revolutionary Syndicalism.

The Social Democratic Federation

The Democratic Federation, founded in 1881 by the late Mr. H. M. Hyndman, mainly as a federation of Radical clubs, with a veiled socialistic programme embracing land nationalization, was the first attempt at a political Socialist organization. In 1889 it became the Social Democratic Federation, avowedly socialistic. Late in 1884 it split into the Socialist League, under Mr. William Morris, pledged to a revolutionary, anti-parliamentary programme; and the Social Democratic Federation, led by Mr. Hyndman. But, captured by anarchists, the Socialist League broke up, many of its leaders rejoining the Social Democratic Federation. The Federation was affiliated to the Labour Representation Committee on the formation of the latter in 1900, but soon withdrew, and in 1908 called itself the Social Democratic Party. It amalgamated in 1911 with a number of local Socialist bodies and changed its name to the British Socialist Party. In 1916 it was affiliated with the Labour Party. Later, in 1916, it declared against the war and pursued a disloyal policy. This attitude, mainly exhibited through its weekly newspaper, the *Call*, led to considerable secessions from the British Socialist Party, and to the foundation by the late Mr. H. M. Hyndman of the National Socialist Party with its weekly newspaper, *Justice*, which, while advocating the establishment of a Socialist Commonwealth on a democratic basis, actively supported the war. On July 31, 1920, the British Socialist Party merged its identity in the Communist Party, pledged to establish Sovietism and the dictatorship of the proletariate.

The Communist Party

On January 29 and 30, 1921, there assembled at Leeds a Communist Conference for the purposes of merging the various Communist bodies into one party. One hundred and seventy delegates took part representing the following bodies:—Communist Party of Great Britain; Communist Labour Party; Communist Party (British Section of Third International); Aberdeen Communist Group; Left Wing of Independent Labour Party; Industrial Communist Party; Jewish Socialist Party; Bolton Communist Group; Croydon Communist Group; Shop Stewards; South Wales Workers' Committee.

Later on, April 23 and 24, 1921, another Communist Conference took place in Manchester to settle the constitution and the rules. The party was called the Communist Party of Great Britain, its ultimate purpose being the establishment of a Communistic Republic and its immediate end the abolition of the wage-system through a social revolution. As a means of furthering a social revolution the party urges the adoption by the workers of a Soviet or Workers' Council system as it exists in Russia, and "for a weapon against the massing of the forces of capitalism" the use of "the dictatorship of the revolutionary masses," This Party applied for affiliation to the Labour Party, but that was refused at the Brighton Conference in 1921 and again at Edinburgh in 1922. It is affiliated to the "Red" or Communist International of Moscow. The best account of the revolutionary organizations in this country is that contained in Dr. Shadwell's *Revolutionary Movement in Great Britain*, Grant Richards, Ltd., 1921.

The Fabian Society

The well-known Fabian Society was founded in January 1884, and has been affiliated to the Labour Party from its inception. It aims at reorganizing society by emancipating land and industrial capital from individual or class ownership and vesting them in the State. It advocates transfer to the community of the administration of such industrial capital as can conveniently be managed socially. As a result of this transfer without compensation, "though not without such relief to expropriated individuals as may seem fit to the community," rent and interest will be added to the reward of labour, and the idle class now living on the labour of others will necessarily disappear. The Society specially tries to influence local authorities so as to impart a socialistic tendency to their administration. The Fabian Research Department has conducted many valuable investigations into industrial questions; since October 1918, it has been known as the Labour Research Department; affiliation with it is open to Trade Unions, Socialist Societies, Co-operative Organizations, Trades Councils, Labour Parties and private individuals. Its object is to co-operate with the Labour, Socialist and Co-operative movements in supplying information upon all questions relating to labour, and it does so most effectively.

The Independent Labour Party

In 1893, the Independent Labour Party was formed. It owes its origin, as has been stated, to the energy of Mr. Keir Hardie. The "I.L.P." was established "to secure the collective ownership of all the means of production, distribution and exchange," and "independent labour representation on all legislative, governing and administrative bodies." Its original constitution stated:

> "That the object of that Party is to establish the Socialist State, when land and capital will be held by the community and used for the well-being of the community and when the exchange of commodities will be organized also by the community, so as to secure the highest possible standard of life for the individual. In giving effect to this object, it will work as part of the International Socialist Movement."

The I.L.P. and its weekly paper, the *Labour Leader*, took up persistently a pacificist attitude throughout the war, especially in regard to compulsory military service. It is represented by four members in the present House of Commons.

The Socialist Labour Party

In 1903, the Socialist Labour Party was established in Glasgow—by secessionists from the Social Democratic Federation—on the lines of the revolutionary American Socialist Party led by Daniel de Leon. It is in close affiliation with the Industrial Workers of the World, and actively agitates to further the Syndicalist conception of industrial Unionism. All candidates for membership must subscribe to "class-war"—no Trade Union official is eligible. The Party propagates revolutionary political action, and also revolutionary industrial action of the extreme syndicalistic type. The Party has between thirty and forty branches throughout the country, owns the Socialist Labour Press, and publishes a monthly paper called the *Socialist*. Although the majority of its members are Trade Unionists, the party refuses to affiliate with the Labour Party. Throughout the recent conflict it carried out an implacable campaign against the war, and impeded in every possible way its successful prosecution.

The Socialist Party of Great Britain

In 1905, other extreme Socialists broke away from the Social Democratic Federation and formed the Socialist Party of Great Britain. Its declared object is to wage war against all other political parties, either "Labour or Capital." It advocates the institution of the most extreme Marxian regime, by means of such revolutionary political action as will secure the "capture" of all the machinery of government whether national or local. It publishes monthly the *Socialist Standard* and is not affiliated to the Labour Party, though it comprises many Trade Unionists.

The National Guilds League

In 1915, the National Guilds League was founded to advocate the cause of Guild Socialism, which has been already described. There are two schools of thought, one which hopes to secure National Guildism by evolving industrial Unionism out of craft Unionism coupled with the Unions securing an ever-increasing control over industry; the other by militant or revolutionary tactics. The National Guilds League has a number of branches throughout the country.

CHAPTER V
THE LABOUR PARTY'S
ADOPTION OF SOCIALISM

3. THE HOME SOCIALISTIC PROGRAMME

It will be sufficient to review the Labour Party's official socialistic policy in regard to home affairs starting from 1918. Previously to that date, a number of resolutions had from year to year been passed, formally as hardy annuals, at the Trades Union Congresses and the Labour Party's Conferences advocating nationalization of land, railways, mines and the municipalization of a number of services of public utility. But from and after 1918 the matter assumes a different complexion.

Nationalization of the Means of Production, Distribution and Exchange

In 1918, at the Nottingham Labour Party Conference a stock resolution was passed in these terms:

> "That the Labour Party press for nationalization of all the means of production, distribution and exchange."

The arguments of the proposer were that because of the existence of landlordism and the power of the landlords, the people had been driven off the land into towns and overseas, with the result that this country had to depend on other countries for food-stuffs. There was no discussion, and the resolution was passed *nem. con.*

The Labour Addendum to the Whitley Report, 1918

The now famous "Committee on Relations between Employers and Employed," known as the "Whitley Committee," which advocated the institution in industries of Joint Industrial Councils, Joint District Councils and Works' Committees, presented the last of their five Reports to the Prime Minister in 1918, dated July 1, 1918 (*Parliamentary Paper* 1918, Cd. 9153). The Trade Union members[4] of the Committee who signed the report appended this note:

"By attaching our signatures to the General Reports we desire to render hearty support to the recommendations that Industrial Councils or Trade Boards, according to whichever are the more suitable in the circumstances, should be established for the several industries or businesses and that these bodies, representative of employers and employed, should concern themselves with the establishment of minimum conditions and the furtherance of the common interests of their trades.

"But while recognizing that the more amicable relations thus established between Capital and Labour will afford an atmosphere generally favourable to industrial peace and progress, we desire to express our view that a complete identity of interests between Capital and Labour cannot be thus effected, and that such machinery cannot be expected to furnish a settlement for the more serious conflicts of interests involved in the working of an economic system primarily governed and directed by motives of private profit."

The Industrial Programme of 1918

The new constitution of the Party which was adopted in 1918 was described as a scheme to secure for the producers by hand or by brain the full fruits of their industry and the most equitable distribution of them upon the basis of common ownership of the means of production coupled with the application to each industry or service of the best system of popular administration and control, and to promote the economic emancipation of the people, especially those who depend upon their own exertions by hand or by brain for the means of life. In explanation of this rather vague programme, the Party stated in a contemporary leaflet, that they intended that the supplies of food and other necessaries of life, especially bread, meat, milk, sugar, butter and margarine, water, coal, light, and transport by rail, steamer, tram and bus, now almost entirely controlled by monopolists, combines, trusts and rings, should be acquired by the State to be administered nationally or municipally solely in the interest of the public and the consumers. In the Party's proposals for reconstruction as contained in *Labour and the New Social Order*, which was finally settled by the Labour Party Conference in June 1918, Labour declared that it stood for:

"The progressive elimination from the control of industry of the private capitalist, individual or joint-stock, and the setting free of all who work, whether by hand or by brain, for the service of the community and the community only," and registered its refusal

"absolutely to believe that the British people will permanently tolerate any reconstruction or perpetuation of the disorganization, waste and inefficiency involved in the abandonment of British industry to a jostling crowd of separate private employers with their minds bent, not on the service of the community, but—by the very law of their being—only on the utmost possible profiteering.

"What the Labour Party looks to is a genuinely scientific reorganization of the nation's industry, no longer deflected by individual profiteering, on the basis of the common ownership of the means of production; the equitable sharing of the proceeds among all who participate in any capacity, and only among these, and the adoption, in particular services and occupations, of those systems and methods of administration and control that may be found in practice, best to promote, not profiteering, but the public interest."

Land Nationalization

At the Southport Conference, 1919, a resolution in favour of land nationalization was formally moved by the Miners' Federation and carried unanimously by the Conference without argument or explanation; it reads thus:

"Seeing that the land alone of all the factors of production is both indispensable to man and incapable of expansion by human agency, it is pre-eminently the rightful property of the nation as a whole. The present system which treats land as private property and prevents free access to it, hampers industry, checks production, crowds the towns by depopulating the countryside, obstructs the provision of good housing, lowers the standard of public health both physical and moral; this Conference strongly urges the Government to bring forward, as early as possible, some scheme for the nationalization of land so as to abolish the present unjust system of land ownership and land leasing. It strongly deprecates the action of the Government in preventing the completion of the valuation of the land, and demands that such valuation shall be completed as early as possible, with a view to the ultimate complete socialization of all land and minerals."

The Control of Industry

In view of divergent proposals and the general lack of any precise information as to the Party's intentions in regard to the control of industry, it is not surprising to find this resolution passed at the Southport Conference, 1919, and, significantly, moved by the British Socialist Party:

"That it be referred to the Executive Committee to consider and report to a further Conference on the arrangements to be introduced into industry in order to provide Labour with facilities to control industry—that is to say, to participate in the promotion of undertakings, the negotiation of contracts, determination of the product, and the selection of markets— and the extent that such control by Labour can be secured, or is desirable, on the basis of the private ownership of land and capital. The Executive shall indicate the distinction between conciliatory Labour and Capital and the actual control of industry by the workers, and to that end is instructed to report on:

"(a) The Industrial Councils and their bearing on the question.

"(b) The co-partnership of Labour and Capital.

"(c) The means to achieve the democratic management of industries in national ownership.

"(d) How far the representation of Trade Unions, through their Executives or by ballot of the members, could ensure participation in actual control, and whether, for effective control, it is not necessary that the employees in the workshop or the pit shall construct an organization, integral to any scheme of democratic management.

"(e) Whether the sole or partial management by Labour of industries in national ownership should be confined to the actual workers therein, or should include workers in other occupations."

The delegate who moved the resolution pointed out that there were different opinions in the Labour Party as to control; one section advocating nationalization pure and simple, another a system of control not necessarily involving nationalization, and that for the guidance of the whole Labour movement an inquiry, as suggested by the resolution, was essential so that "instead of having so many pious resolutions they would have facts and data upon which to build their future policy and activity," The guidance sought has not yet been given.

At the same conference another resolution was adopted as follows:

"That this Conference re-affirms its pledge of nationalization of industry, but, when nationalized, to come under joint control with adequate representation of the workers on the boards."

The mover of it thought the previous resolution might include co-partnership, and to that he objected. In co-partnership, he said, "the workers interested became as great aristocrats as the ordinary employer. Every industry ought to be nationalized and have adequate representation under joint control."

Labour's Report to the Industrial Conference, 1919

In a memorandum by the Right Hon. A. Henderson, Chairman of the Trades Union representatives, which was appended to the Report of the Industrial Conference in 1919 (*Parliamentary Paper* 1919, Cmd. 501) appointed to inquire into industrial unrest, there occur these statements of Labour policy:

"Control of Industry.

"With increasing vehemence Labour is challenging the whole structure of capitalist industry as it now exists. It is no longer willing to acquiesce in a system under which industry is conducted for the benefit of the few. It demands a system of industrial control which shall be truly democratic in character. This is seen on the one hand in the demand for public ownership of vital industries and services and public control of services not nationalized which threaten the public with the danger of monopoly or exploitation. It is also seen in the increasing demand of the workers in all industries for a real share in industrial control, a demand which the Whitley Scheme, in so far as it has been adopted, has done little or nothing to satisfy. This demand is more articulate in some industries than others. It is seen clearly in the national programmes of the railwaymen and of the miners; and it is less clearly formulated by the workers in many other industries. The workers are no longer prepared to acquiesce in a system in which their labour is bought and sold as a commodity in the labour market. They are beginning to assert that they have a human right to an equal and democratic partnership in industry; that they must be treated in future not as 'hands' or part of the factory equipment, but as human beings with a right to use their abilities by hand and brain in the service not of the few but of the whole community.

"The extent to which workers are challenging the whole system of industrial organization is very much greater to-day than ever before, and unrest proceeds not only from more immediate and special grievances but also, to an increasing extent, from a desire to substitute a democratic system of public ownership and production for use with an increasing element of control by the organized workers themselves for the existing capitalist organization of industry."

"(a) A substantial beginning must be made of instituting public ownership of the vital industries and services in this country. Mines and the supply of coal, railways, docks and other means of transportation, the supply of electric power, and shipping, at least so far as ocean-going services are concerned, should be at once nationalized.

"(b) Private profit should be entirely eliminated from the manufacture of armaments, and the amount of nationalization necessary to secure this should be introduced into the engineering, shipbuilding and kindred industries.

"(c) There should be a great extension of municipal ownership, and ownership by other local authorities and co-operative control of those services which are concerned primarily with the supplying of local needs.

"(d) Key industries and services should at once be publicly owned.

"(e) This extension of public ownership over vital industries should be accompanied by the granting to the organized workers of the greatest practicable amount of control over the conditions and the management of their various industries."

"State Control and Prices.

"(a) Where an industry producing articles of common consumption or materials necessary to industries producing articles of common consumption cannot be at once publicly owned, State control over such industries should be retained.

"(b) State control has been shown to provide some check upon profiteering and high prices, and this is a reason why it should be maintained until industries pass into the stage at which they can be conveniently nationalized,"

"Conclusions.

"The fundamental causes of Labour unrest are to be found rather in the growing determination of Labour to challenge the whole existing structure of capitalist industry than in any of the more special and smaller grievances which come to the surface at any particular time.

"These root causes are twofold—the breakdown of the existing capitalist system of industrial organization, in the sense that the mass of the working class is now firmly convinced that production for private profit is not an equitable basis on which to build, and that a vast extension of public ownership and democratic control of industry is urgently necessary. It is no longer possible for organized Labour to be controlled by force or compulsion of any kind. It has grown too strong to remain within the bounds of the old industrial system and its unsatisfied demand for the reorganization of industry on democratic lines is not only the most important, but also a constantly growing cause of unrest.

"The second primary cause is closely linked with the first. It is that, desiring the creation of a new industrial system which shall gradually but speedily replace the old, the workers can see no indication that either the government or the employers have realized the necessity for any fundamental change, or that they are prepared even to make a beginning of industrial re-organization on more democratic principles. The absence of any constructive, policy on the side of the Government or the employers, taken in conjunction with the fact that Labour, through the Trades Union Congress and the Labour Party and through the various Trade Union organizations, has put forward a comprehensive economic and industrial programme, has presented the workers with a sharp contrast from which they naturally draw their own deductions.

"It is clear that unless and until the Government is prepared to realize the need for comprehensive reconstruction on a democratic basis, and to formulate a constructive policy leading towards economic democracy, there can be at most no more than a temporary diminution of industrial unrest to be followed inevitably by further waves of constantly growing magnitude.

"The changes involved in this reconstruction must, of course, be gradual, but if unrest is to be prevented from assuming dangerous forms an adequate assurance must be given immediately to the workers that the whole problem is being taken courageously in hand. It is not enough merely to tinker with particular grievances or to endeavour to reconstruct the old system by slight adjustments to meet the new demands of Labour. It is essential to question the whole basis on which Our industry has been conducted in the past and to endeavour to find, in substitution for the motive of private gain, some other motive which will serve better as the foundation of a democratic system. This motive can be no other than the motive of public service, which at present is seldom invoked save when the workers threaten to stop the process of production by a strike. The motive of public service should be the dominant motive throughout the whole industrial system, and the problem in industry at the present day is that of bringing home to every person engaged in industry the feeling that he is the servant, not of any particular class or person, but of the community as a whole. This cannot be done so long as industry continues to be conducted for private profit, and the widest possible extension of public ownership and democratic control of industry is therefore the first necessary condition of the removal of industrial unrest."

Nationalization of the Coal Industry

As illustrating the position taken up by the Labour Party in regard to the coal industry, the following was the resolution settled by a Joint Sub-Committee representative of the Executive Committee of the Miners'

Federation, the Parliamentary Committee of the Trades Union Congress and the Executive Committee of the Labour Party, which was submitted to, and passed by, all their local demonstrations throughout the country in 1919-20:

"This Meeting declares:—

"(1) That the coal of the country forms an obvious necessity to national life, and that its ownership should therefore be vested in the community.

"(2) That the mines, machinery, and other means for the production and distribution of coal, being essential to the industry, should also be owned by the country.

"(3) That the direction and conduct of the coal-mining industry, being of vital importance to the workers in the industry and the coal-consuming public, should be under the control of National, District and Pit Committees representative of the national Government and the various classes of workers including those engaged in the managing, technical, commercial and manual processes.

"(4) That the objects to be sought by National Ownership and Joint Control on the lines indicated are:—

"(a) To provide the maximum output of the coal consistent with the provision of adequate protection for the workers engaged in this most dangerous employment.

"(b) The introduction of labour-saving appliances on the widest possible scale.

"(c) A more economic working of coal mines consequent on the elimination of the interests of private land and royalty ownership.

"(d) The remuneration of the workers in this industry on a scale commensurate with the dangers endured and sufficient to provide a healthy natural life for all concerned.

"(e) The co-ordination of the distributive machinery of the trade by the elimination of existing private interests and the substitution of municipal and co-operative supplies at prices sufficient to cover costs of production and distribution.

"This meeting therefore calls upon the Government to bring forward legislation for the national ownership of coal mines and minerals on the lines indicated, and in accordance with the recommendations of the Majority Report of the Coal Industry Commission."

On March 11, 1920, a special Trades Union Congress was held in London to consider what action should be taken to compel the Government to nationalize the coal mines, and passed this resolution:

"In view of the repeated refusal of the Government to nationalize the mines, in accordance with the Majority Report of the Coal Industry Commission, and in agreement with the terms of the resolution passed at the Glasgow Congress and the Special Congress held in December last, the Parliamentary Committee suggest the following forms of action as a means to compel the Government to adopt the nationalization of mines:—

"(*a*) Trade Union action, in the form of a general strike;

"(*b*) Political action, in the form of intensive political propaganda in preparation for a General Election;

"In the event of (*a*) being carried, the necessary steps be taken to give effect to it in accordance with the constitution of each Union."

The Congress decided against Clause (*a*) and in favour of Clause (*b*) proposing political action.

At the Brighton Conference, 1921, there was moved by the Miners' Federation and passed unanimously without a debate the following resolution:

"That this Conference views with regret the failure of the Government to introduce legislation for the purpose of nationalizing the mining industry, and reiterates its conviction that this industry will never be placed upon a satisfactory basis in the interest of the community until it is publicly owned and worked between representatives of the State and the technical and manual workers engaged in it, and resolves to continue to educate and organize working-class opinions until the Government are compelled to bring about this fundamental change in the management and ownership of the industry."

The Chairman at that Conference, Mr. Alex. G. Cameron, in the course of his address made these observations:

> "The fundamental truth is that the supporters of capitalism have proved to the world that so long as industry is run on its present lines the workers will have to submit to periods of unemployment and periods of over-employment and that the present capitalist system must go before there can be any permanent solution.

> "The workers, by the strength of their Trade Unions, may from time to time obtain improved conditions of employment, but until they obtain possession of the means of producing wealth, namely, the land, the mines, the railways, shipping, factories and workshops, they will remain dependent on a small section of the community providing them with employment. In other words, they will continue to be at the beck and call of those who own and control the capital of the country. They will, when the capitalists decide, be allowed to apply their labour to the production of wealth, but they will not be permitted to control its distribution.

> "Before the workers will be permitted to control industry effectively, or even the distribution of the products of their industry, they will first require to own the machinery and materials of industry. Such ownership will only be acquired when we capture political power; and political power will come only as a result of hard thinking and intelligent action at the ballot-box. Political power will also enable us to control credit, money, banking and everything which is fundamental to a nation's foreign policy, and is the cause of most, if not all, wars from which the workers of the world have suffered."

The Labour Party's specific proposals for the nationalization of many important industries and "their democratic control" are explained at length in Chapter VIII.

CHAPTER VI
THE LABOUR PARTY'S
ADOPTION OF SOCIALISM

4. THE INTERNATIONAL SOCIALISTIC PROGRAMME

The First International

It is important to note the connection before the war between the Labour Patty and International Socialism. As far back as September 28, 1864, the First International was formed in St. Martin's Hall at the corner of Long Acre and Endell Street, the site now occupied by Messrs. Odhams and used for the publication of *John Bull*. That organization lived under circumstances of great vicissitude as an international centre of socialistic thought until it received its death-blow through the collapse of the Commune In Paris in 1871. Its interesting career is described in Mr. R. W. Postgate's book, *The Workers' International*, and in *The Two Internationals*, by Mr. Palme Dutt.

The Old Second International

The Second International dates from the Paris Socialist Conference of 1889, but was not constituted in its later form of a Central International Socialist Bureau until 1913. In 1914, it included twenty-seven countries with a membership of twelve millions; to it the Labour Party was affiliated. It naturally fell into a state of suspended animation during the war. Unsuccessful attempts were made at Zimmerwald (1915), Kienthal (1916), and at Stockholm (1917), to revive the Second International. Later, a Conference with the same object in view was held at Berne in February 1919, where various Socialist and Labour bodies assembled to further its revival and also to deal with a number of political and industrial questions. This Conference was promoted by Messrs. Arthur Henderson, Emile Vandervelde and Albert Thomas. It passed an important resolution on "Democracy and Dictatorship," part of which was in the following terms:

> "The Conference hails the great political revolutions which, in Russia, Austria-Hungary and Germany, have

destroyed the old regimes of imperialism and militarism and overthrown their Governments.

"The Conference urges the workers and Socialists of these countries to develop democratic and republican institutions which will enable them to bring about the great Socialist transformation. In these momentous times, when the problem of the Socialist reconstruction of the world is more than ever before a burning question, the working-classes should make up their minds, unanimously and unmistakably, about the method of their emancipation.

"In full agreement with all previous Congresses of the International, the Berne Conference firmly adheres to the principles of Democracy. A reorganized society more and more permeated with Socialism, cannot be realized, much less permanently established, unless it rests upon triumphs of Democracy and is rooted in the principles of liberty.

"Those institutions which constitute Democracy—freedom of speech and of the press, the right of assembly, universal suffrage, a government responsible to Parliament, with arrangements guaranteeing popular co-operation, and respect for the wishes of the people, the right of association, etc., these also provide the working-classes with the means of carrying on the class-struggle.

"Owing to certain recent events, the Conference desires to make absolutely clear the constructive character of the Socialist programme. True socialization implies methodical development in the different branches of economic activity under the control of the democracy. The arbitrary taking over of a few concerns by small groups of workers is not Socialism, it is merely Capitalism with numerous shareholders.

"Since, in the opinion of the Conference, effective Socialist development is only possible under democratic law, it is essential to eliminate at once any method of socialization which has no prospect of gaining the support of the majority of the people.

"A dictatorship of this character would be all the more dangerous if it were based upon the support of only one section of the working-class. The inevitable consequence of such a regime would be the paralysis of working-class strength through fratricidal war. The inevitable end would be the dictatorship of reaction....

"It calls upon Socialists throughout the world to close their ranks, not to deliver up the peoples to international reaction, but to do their utmost to ensure that Socialism and Democracy, which are inseparable, shall triumph everywhere."

The International Labour Charter of 1919

The Berne Conference formulated an International Labour Charter which was afterwards submitted to the Council of Versailles for inclusion in the Treaty of Peace, and was, to a considerable extent, incorporated in Part XIII. The preamble of this Charter is important and reads thus:

"Under the wage-system the capitalist class endeavour to increase their profits by exploiting the workers in the greatest measure possible by methods which, if unchecked, would undermine the physical, moral and intellectual strength of the present and future generation of workers. They impede the development and even endanger the very existence of Society. The tendency of Capitalism to degrade the worker can only be completely checked by the abolition of the capitalist system of production. Meanwhile, the evil can be considerably mitigated, both by the resistance of organized workers and by the intervention of the State. By these means, the health of the workers can be protected and their family life maintained. They make it possible for them to obtain the education necessary to enable them to fulfil their duties as citizens in a modern democracy.

"The degree in which Capitalism is restricted varies to a very great extent in the different States. Through the unfair competition of backward countries, these differences endanger labour and industry in the more advanced States. The adjustment of national differences in the legal protection of labour by a system of international labour legislation has long been a pressing need. It has been rendered doubly urgent by the terrible upheavals and awful destruction of the vital forces of the people brought about by the war. At the same time, however, the war is bringing about the possibility of satisfying this need by the formation of a

League of Nations, which now seems certain. The Berne Conference demands that the League of Nations, as one of its primary tasks, shall create and put into execution an International Labour Charter."

At Berne a Permanent Commission was appointed to revive and draw up a new constitution for the Second International. This Permanent Commission, which included Messrs. Henderson, Stuart-Bunning and Ramsay MacDonald of the British Labour Party, met at Amsterdam in April 1919, to continue that work. There was also a "Committee of Action" appointed to deal with certain executive matters, on which Messrs. Henderson, Stuart-Bunning and Ramsay MacDonald were also placed. It was this Committee of Action which went to Paris to interview the "Big Four" on various international questions, including the insertion of the Labour Charter in the Peace Treaty, and issued a manifesto on May 11, 1919, after the Peace Terms were handed, on May 7, to the German delegates, stating that "this peace is not our peace."

The New Second International

At Lucerne, in August 1919, the Permanent Commission finished the drafting of the new constitution of the Second International, and arranged for a General International Socialist Conference to be held at Geneva in 1920, to adopt it. That Conference took place in July of that year. An invitation dated April 10, 1920, was sent out to all Socialist and Labour Parties subscribing to, *inter alia*, the following principle:—"(1) The political and economic organization of the working-class for the purpose of abolishing the capitalist form of society and achieving complete freedom for humanity through the conquest of political power and the socialization of the means of production and exchange, that is to say, by the transformation of capitalist society into a collectivist or communist society." The invitation, after mentioning a number of socialistic questions to which the attention of the Conference at Geneva would be directed, concluded in these words:—"Convinced of the necessity of a great effort to ensure unity on the basis of the traditional principles of the class-struggle and with a view to international action ... we invite you to attend the Geneva Conference."

At the Geneva Conference the constitution of the Second International was fixed; its declared purposes are as follows:

"1. The political and economic organization of the working-class for the purpose of abolishing the capitalist form of society and achieving complete freedom for humanity through the conquest of political power and the socialization of the means of production and exchange, that is to say, by the transformation of capitalist society into a collectivist or communist society.

"2. The international union and action of the workers in the struggle against jingoism and imperialism and for the simultaneous suppression of militarism and armaments, with the object of bringing about a real League of Nations, including all peoples master of their own destiny, and maintaining world peace.

"3. The representation and defence of the interests of oppressed peoples and subject races.

"These principles find three forms of expression in the working-class movement, each at different stages of development, but each necessary; the political, the industrial, and the co-operative. These must, as autonomous bodies, continue to strengthen their national influence and their international unity, and, at the same time, as their ultimate aims are common, and as they are aspects of one great world movement, they should take every opportunity for joint action in an internationalist and revolutionary spirit for the maintenance of the world's peace."

The Geneva Resolutions on Socialism of 1920

A number of resolutions were also passed, and those which relate to "Socialization" are worthy of careful study; they were the draft of the British Labour Party's representatives and were in the following terms:

"Socialization.—By Socialization we understand the transformation from ownership and control by capitalists to ownership and control by the community of all the industries and services essential for the satisfaction of the people's needs; the substitution, for the wasteful production and distribution with the object of private profit, of efficient production and economical distribution with the object of the greatest possible utility; the transformation also, from the economic servitude of the great mass of the actual producers under private ownership, to a general participation in management by the persons engaged in the work.

"The continuous and rapid growth of monopolistic control of industry by Capitalism increases the power of private owners to manipulate the prices of all the necessaries of life, thus reducing consumers to despair. On the other hand, there is the growing unwillingness of organized labour any longer to support a system of production which keeps them in subjection and does not even enable them to raise effectively their standard of life. The consequent intolerableness of Capitalism renders every day more urgent the reconstruction of industry on the lines of Socialization.

"Socialization will proceed, step by step, from one industry to another, according as circumstances in each country may permit. Objectionable as private profit-making enterprise is to Socialists, they will refrain from destroying it in any industry until they are in a position to replace it by a more efficient form of organization. Such a gradual process of Socialization excludes, in general, expropriation of private ownership without compensation; not only because it would be inequitable to cause suffering to selected individuals, but also because a process of confiscation would disturb capitalist enterprise in industries in which Socialization was not immediately practicable. The funds required for compensation will be derived from taxation of private property, including capital levies, income-tax and death duties, and the limitation of inheritances for the benefit of the State.

"In a community of highly developed economic life, with an extensive population largely aggregated in urban centres, Socialization takes three main forms—namely, national, municipal and co-operative.

"For instance, whatever may be provided for the administration of agriculture, the ownership of land should be national, provision being made for the maintenance and security of peasant cultivators, wherever such exist. Other industries of supreme national importance, such as the transport system, the generation of electricity and mines, should also be national. But the management of a large number of industries and services will be in the hands of the municipalities and other local authorities, and federations of these, not only the provision of water and gas and the distribution of electricity, but also, in some countries, the provision of food, clothing and housing. The production and distribution of household supplies of every kind will form, for the most part, the sphere of the consumer's co-operative societies.

"Industries which have not yet arrived at a state of concentration at which they are suitable for Socialization, or in which, for other reasons, Socialization is not immediately practicable, will be subjected to control by the community, with a view to effecting economies and improvements in production and distribution, fixing prices, and ensuring prescribed conditions of employment.

"It is important to notice that, in the large measure of individual freedom that will be characteristic of a Socialist community, the adoption of the principle of Socialization does not include agricultural production by individual peasants of the nation's land, or by independent craftsmen working on their own account, or by artists of any kind, or by members of the brain-working professions—provided always that they do not exploit the labour of other persons. On the other hand, the principle of Socialization excludes the ownership of natural resources or of the instruments of production in the large scale primary industries by individuals or associations of persons of any kind, together with the dictatorship of any person or group over the industry in which they work.

"It is the function of the community as a whole to exercise control over the prices of commodities, and to provide whatever new or additional capital is required from time to time for Socialized industries.

"Administration of Socialized Industries.—A principle of the greatest importance in Socialization is that control must be separated from administration. The control will be exercised by the popularly elected national assembly. The organ of administration in each industry or service must be entirely separate and distinct from those of the political government.

"The National Industries.—Each industry or service will require an organization appropriate to its special circumstances. As a general type it is suggested that a national industry or service should be provided with

"(a) A national board to be composed of representatives of:

"(1) the workers concerned in the industry;

"(2) the management (including the technicians);

"(3) the consumers and the community as a whole.

"(b) Where considered necessary, also district councils for appropriate regional areas, to be similarly composed;

"(c) Works' committees for each factory, mine or other establishment.

"In each national industry there will have to be separate machinery for collective bargaining between the management on the one hand, and each distinct vocation engaged in the industry or service on the other.

"There should accordingly be a Joint Board for each vocation that has separately organized itself, whether in a trade union or a professional association. Each Joint Board should be composed in equal numbers of representatives of the management and representatives of the trade union or professional association concerned.

"The Right to Strike—that is to say, to refuse collectively to continue to serve—cannot be denied to any man or woman consistently with freedom. When it is no longer a question of resisting the profit-making capitalist, but merely of obtaining from the community as a whole equitable conditions of employment and a proper standard of life, it may be expected that the public opinion of the community as a whole will be accepted as decisive.

"Municipal Socialization.—The large part of the industries and services of each community which will be in the hands of the local authorities will be directed by the popularly elected councils of the several localities, with participation in the management of their own services by representatives of the workers by hand or by brain. In municipal administration of industries and services there should be the same kind of machinery of Joint Boards for collective bargaining as in the national industries.

"The Political System of Socialism.—The progressive disintegration of the capitalist system, which has been increasingly taking place during the years of war, and not less during the years of peace following the war, makes it ever more urgent that Labour should assume power in society. In the term Labour we include not merely the manual working wage-earners, but also the intellectual workers of all kinds, the independent handicraftsmen and peasant cultivators, and, in short, all those who co-operate by their exertions in the production of utilities of any kind.

"1. It is an essential condition of this assumption of power by Labour that its ranks should be sufficiently united and that it should understand how to make use of the power in its hands.

"2. Whilst the Congress repudiates methods of violence and all terrorism, it recognizes that the object cannot be achieved without the utilization by Labour of its industrial as well as its political power, and direct action in certain decisive conflicts cannot be entirely abandoned. At the same time, the Congress considers that any tendency to convert an industrial strike automatically into political revolution cannot be too strongly condemned.

"3. The Socialist Commonwealth can come into existence only by the conquest by Labour of governmental power. The main work of a Labour Government will be to adopt, as the fundamental basis of its legislation and administration, both Democracy and Socialization.

"Socialism will not base its political organization upon dictatorship. It cannot seek to suppress Democracy; its historic mission, on the contrary, is to carry Democracy to completion. The whole efforts of Labour, its Trade Union and Co-operative activities, equally with its action in the political field, tend constantly towards the establishment of Democratic institutions more and more adapted to the needs of industrial society, becoming ever more perfect and of higher social value.

"It is to-day the forces of Labour that, in the main, ensure the maintenance of Democracy. Socialists will not allow factitious minorities, taking advantage of their privileged positions, to bring to naught popular liberty. Inspired by the great traditions of past revolutions, Socialists will be ready, without weakness, to resist any such attacks.

"4. The franchise for a Socialist Parliament must be universal, applying with absolute equality to both sexes, without exclusions on grounds of race, religion, occupation, or political opinions. The supreme function of Parliament is to represent all the popular aspirations and desires from the standpoint of the community as a whole. It will deal with defence against aggression from without or within. It will be in charge of the property and also of the finances of the community.

"It will make the laws, and administer the public business. The Ministers in charge of the various departments will be chosen from among its members; and the government of the nation will be its Executive Committee.

"But it will be free to delegate particular powers and duties to any of the other organs of the community hereinafter mentioned, in order to secure the greatest possible participation of those personally engaged in each branch of social life. It will be for Parliament to safeguard not only the interests of the general public of consumers for whose representation on special boards and councils it will provide, but also the interests of the community as a whole in future generations.

"5. It will be for Parliament to determine the general lines of social policy and to make the laws; it will decide to what industries and services the principle of Socialization shall be applied and under what conditions; it will exercise supreme financial control, and will decide upon the allocation of new and additional capital. In the last resort, it will exercise the power of fixing prices.

"6. In the development and expansion of the productive life of the community, a large part will be played by the various organizations formed according to the productive occupations in which every healthy person will be engaged. Thus, provision must be made, in the manner hereinafter described, for the participation in the administration or service of representatives of all the different grades of workers, by hand or by brain, engaged in that particular industry or service. At the same time, each vocation, whether of workers by hand or of workers by brain, desires to regulate the conditions of its vocational life, whatever may be the industries or services among which its membership will find itself dispersed. Each distinct vocation may therefore group itself in a professional association, to which functions of regulation, of investigation, or of professional education may be entrusted by Parliament.

"7. The organizations into which those engaged in the various industries and services will group themselves, whether trade unions or professional associations, may be made the basis of a further organ of social and economic life.

"Alongside Parliament it may be desirable that there should be a National Industrial Council, composed of representatives of the various organizations of trades and professions into which the persons belonging to each occupation may voluntarily group themselves. Such a National Industrial Council would be free to discuss and criticize, to investigate and to suggest, and to present to Parliament any reports on which it may decide. Parliament may, from time to time, delegate to the National Industrial Council the drafting of measures applicable to industry as a whole, or of the regulations to be made under the authority of a statute."

The Second International and Bolshevism

The British Labour Party was asked at the Geneva Conference to undertake the responsibility of inviting all national Socialist and Labour bodies not represented at Geneva to join like itself the Second International. An appeal was sent out signed in December 1920, by Messrs. A. Henderson, on behalf of the Labour Party, J. H. Thomas, and Harry Gosling, on behalf of the Trades Union Congress, and Ramsay MacDonald, as British International Secretary. This letter declared the position of the Second International and also of the British Labour Party in regard to Bolshevism in the following terms:

"The great difficulty which confronts International Socialism, however, is the division of the movement into two camps as a result of the Russian Revolution of November 1918. Bolshevism tried to establish, not only over Russia, but over every other country in the world, the method of seizing political power by armed force, holding that power by the same means and changing the whole economic structure of society by decree and suppression. Since its first success in Russia, it has somewhat modified its position, and at the present moment in this country, it is informing its adherents that those who decry political methods are traitors to the cause of Communism, but that political action should be used solely to prove the abortiveness of the institutions which are to be captured. Obviously, such a compromise with the unclean thing is bound to defeat itself and will only make candidates who pursue such a policy ridiculous in the eyes of electors. It is political and revolutionary futility of the simplest kind. We do not wish, however, to argue out the matter. The policy may be more suitable to some countries than it is to ours, but obviously every Socialist who has any international instinct at all will see that an International based upon Moscow principles can never represent more than the smallest and least influential fraction of the Socialist movement in the various countries. The Second International has, therefore, rejected Bolshevism as the basis of its existence.

"Moreover, the attempts made by Moscow to control national organizations not only in general Socialist policy, but in the details of their own national work, must prevent every such organization with any self-respect and any sense of national freedom from putting itself under such a yoke."

The following statement as to the foundation upon which a Socialist International should be constituted is also important:

"There must be no doubt as to the basis upon which a Socialist International has to be built. It must secure to each Socialist group freedom to work in accordance with its own means towards its Socialist goal; there must be common determination to bring Socialism about; it must be prepared to give international support to all national strivings for liberty and self-government in ways determined by the nations themselves; it must in no way reject (as is now being attempted in some quarters) but unequivocally support the democratic method as that proper to the countries that have already gone through their political revolutions, and that have been put in possession of the political weapon by reason of the insurrectionary movements of their proletariat in days gone by."

The Third or Moscow International

The Second International may accordingly be now regarded as re-established, if not re-created, and the interesting speculation is the extent to which it will secure the allegiance of Socialist parties throughout the world as against the appeals of the Third International or Moscow "Red" International. This latter deserves a short description. In January 1919, just before the meeting of the Berne Conference, and shortly after the Peace Conference at Paris had commenced, a wireless invitation to the first Communist International Congress at Moscow was sent out in the name of the Russian Communist Party, which was the name adopted by the Russian Bolsheviks or Majority Social Democrats after the Revolution of 1917. The Bolsheviks desired to distinguish themselves clearly from Socialist or "social democratic" parties which, in various belligerent countries, had supported their respective Governments. They took the name from the Communist League for which Marx and Engels drew up the famous Communist manifesto which they were commissioned to draw up in November 1847, at the Congress of Communists in London. Lenin, in his book, the *State and Revolution*, draws special attention to the term "communist" as being more scientifically correct than the term "social democrat" and endeavours to prove his point by quotations from the manifesto. Following the lead of Moscow the various revolutionary Socialist parties throughout the world have discarded their Socialist appellations and called themselves Communists. One ought, therefore, to realize that the term "Communism" has now taken on a new and different meaning from its earlier significance. To-day Communism means the principles of Marxian revolutionary Socialism and a scheme of social and industrial organization constructed on those principles which are peculiar to the Bolshevik regime in Soviet Russia. In his admirable little book, the *Two Internationals*, which deals with the complex subject most clearly and with very full documentation, Mr. R. Palme Dutt very properly says that "care must be taken to distinguish this sense of Communism from the sense in which it has been more generally used in this country, namely, (1) the Communist Anarchism of Kropotkin, (2) the conception of the abolition of all personal property, (3) decentralization under a system of loosely associated local communes. Communism corresponds rather to what is often referred to as 'scientific socialism,' only with a special emphasis on its revolutionary aspect."

The First Communist International Congress was held at Moscow in March 1919. It is called the Third International or Communist International; its constitution will be found in the *Labour International Handbook*, 1921, page 190. Shortly stated its purposes are the overthrow of capitalism, the establishment of the dictatorship of the proletariat and of the International

Soviet Republic; the complete abolition of classes and the realization of revolutionary Socialism. Twenty-one conditions of membership, together with instructions for its members, are laid down, some of which are peculiarly illuminating as to Communist principles. Condition 3 says that "the class-struggle in almost every country of Europe and America is reaching the threshold of civil war. Under such circumstances the Communist can have no confidence in bourgeois laws. They should create everywhere a parallel illegal machinery which at the decisive moment will do its duty by the party and in every way possible assist the revolution. In every country where, in consequence of martial law or other exceptional laws, the Communists are unable to carry on their work lawfully, a combination of legal and illegal work is absolutely necessary."

The Communist Party of Great Britain is affiliated to the Third International, but the Independent Labour Party of this country, although it seceded from the Second International, refused to join the Third International, and published a scathing criticism of Bolshevism or Communism which appeared in the *Labour Leader* of December 18, 1919. The Independent Labour Party is affiliated to yet another International, the body known as the Vienna International or the "Two and a Half."

I have set out these details in order to show the nature and the extent of the home and international socialistic programme which the Labour Party has pledged itself, if given the opportunity, to carry into operation.

CHAPTER VII
THE LABOUR PARTY'S
ADOPTION OF SOCIALISM

5. APPROVAL OF DIRECT ACTION

Perhaps the greatest menace to ordered constitutional government is the Labour Party's acceptance of the method of direct action for enforcement of its policy upon an unconforming community. Many distinguished leaders of the Party have declared against the social dangers of wielding such a weapon, but in spite of such admonitions the Party has resorted to it, and created an elaborate machinery for its application; whereupon those distinguished leaders turned round and supported it as forcibly as they previously condemned it. Once any section of the nation becomes addicted to the facile use of such a species of organized tyranny—because it is nothing else—however humanitarian be the alleged aim or purpose, the death-knell of law and order has been sounded.

The Meaning and Qualities of Direct Action

In the revised edition of their *History of Trade Unionism* (1920) Mr. and Mrs. Sidney Webb point out that when they published in 1897 their *Industrial Democracy* the term "direct action" was unknown. In point of fact, this name for the principle or practice of social coercion through economic pressure made its advent into this country from France and the United States of America in 1905. By 1912 it had passed into full currency among advanced sections of organized Labour in Scotland and parts of England, and in practice almost invariably implies either a sectional Strike by a particular group or groups of labour, or a general strike by all groups of labour combined. All strikes are not, however, direct action. Wage-earners reasonably contend that as any individual workman has the right to refuse to enter into or continue under a contract of service, any group of workmen or all groups acting together in a strike are entitled to exercise a like freedom. Mr. and Mrs. Webb are disposed to call such a strike "an economic strike" and to use the phrase a "non-economic strike" to designate a strike undertaken "not for an alteration in the conditions of employment of any section of the trade union world, but with a view to enforce, either on individuals, on Parliament, or on the Government, some other course of action desired by the strikers." It is only strikes of the latter type that they place in the category of direct action; in other words, they make the purpose of the strike the test. That is too limited a definition of direct action, but it would include such a case as the refusal in 1917 of the National Union of Sailors and Firemen to work vessels by which two members of the Labour Party were preparing, at the instance of the Government, to travel on their way to Petrograd; also a like refusal of the same Union in 1918 to carry Mr. Arthur Henderson and M. Camille Huysmans across the Channel *en route* for Paris, the object of the Union being to prevent the organization of an International Socialist Conference. Another case of the same kind was the action of the Electrical Trades Union in 1918 in "calling out" their members engaged in the Albert Hall in London with instructions to appropriate the fuses—which did not belong to them—so as to keep the Hall in darkness and prevent it being used for any purpose, as a reprisal against the proprietors for cancelling the letting of the Hall for a Labour demonstration. Further illustrations of the "non-economic strike" were the threats of the compositors and printers in certain London newspaper offices to cease work during the railway strike in 1919 because of the adverse criticism of the railwaymen by the editorial staff; the threat of the miners to close down the coal mines in 1919 unless compulsory military service was abolished, and unless military and naval action by the British Government against the Soviet Government of Russia was discontinued; the scheme for a strike put forward by the miners in August and September 1920 under the guise of a claim for increased wages, but really for the political purpose of forcing the nationalization of the coal industry.

The very name "direct action" indicates that the action in question is alternative to some other action regarded as indirect, which is invariably the orderly method of procedure, prescribed by industrial agreement, or by the rules of the Trade Union, or by the Constitution of the country. Hence, in my opinion, the fundamental quality of direct action is its anarchic character. Some groups or individuals in the Labour movement resort to anarchic action in preference to orderly procedure, deliberately as recalcitrant minorities, who, bound by the formal agreement of majorities, intend to prevent the view of the majority being carried into effect. Others, impatient reformers who regard orderly methods as too cumbersome and dilatory, and are either not able or not prepared to work for gradual amendment, follow their example. And one further sees direct action adopted with the ulterior object of wrecking existing craft Trade Union organization, as for instance by revolutionary Unionists in old skilled Unions like the

Amalgamated Engineering Union, or by revolutionary Syndicalists who wish to exercise and develop all the latent power of manual workers so that the weapon of the general strike may be sharp and bright on the day when it is to be used to hack down the Constitution, and usher in the social revolution. These, however, are special reasons. In the minds of great and slow thinking sections of Labour, direct action has come to be regarded as the easiest and quickest, sometimes as the only, road to political power. Labour is greedy for political power; it intends to make its political fortune, in the words of Horace, "*Si possis, recte; si non, quocunque modo....*"

The anarchic character of direct action constitutes its real danger far more than its non-economic purpose, if the purpose be non-economic, which it very frequently is not. Just as any anarchic method betokens, so does it beget, a lawless as distinguished from law-abiding quality of mind. Human nature is not lawless in one sphere of its activity and constitutionally minded in another, anarchic, for example, in industrial affairs and orderly in politics. The same strain runs right through; an undisciplined individual makes as bad a citizen as he does a Trade Unionist. It was the anarchic character of direct action that impressed itself most strongly on the writer's mind during the anxious years 1914-1918 before any non-economic strikes such as those described above had occurred.

Direct Action on the Clyde, 1916

Take for instance the strikes of March to April 1916, in the engine shops of Clydeside, which the writer had to handle. The Government had made with the Trade Unions the "Treasury" Agreements of March 1915, providing for the suspension of Trade Union customs in order to accelerate and increase output. The Amalgamated Society of Engineers Executive Council had formally submitted the agreements by ballot to its members, who by a large majority had accepted them. Acting under the agreements the Government proceeded to introduce women into engineering shops throughout the country with the co-operation of the A.S.E. Executive. But on Clydeside members of the A.S.E. refused to allow women to enter the shops on the agreed conditions, or at all.

Many of the shop stewards[5] in the engineering shops on Clydeside were members of the Socialist Labour Party. The principles of the S.L.P., copied from those of the I.W.W., involve class-warfare, the destruction of the official Trade Unions and of all industrial organizations except those of a similar type and creed to the I.W.W. itself, the overthrow of all existing forms of constitutional government and their replacement by a government of manual workers. The method to be employed is direct action. Mr. Beer, in his *History of British Socialism* (Vol. II, p. 393), says: "The S.L.P. theories came nearest to those of Lenin and Trotsky."

On Clydeside in March 1916, the S.L.P. shop stewards saw their revolutionary opportunity. The writer held innumerable conferences with them trying to introduce harmoniously the agreed scheme of dilution of labour, but as fast as he made progress with the assistance of the Executive Council of the A.S.E. and their local Glasgow officials, it was countered by preparations for obstructive direct action. Finally, the direct actionists matured their plans. It is a principle of theirs always to use the sharpest weapons. There was one immediately to hand. The army in France was in dire need of heavy howitzers to smash the system of trenches which the Germans had commenced to consolidate; Mesopotamia urgently required flat-bottomed barges. These two classes of munitions were being manufactured in engineering shops and shipyards on the Clyde. The direct actionists therefore brought out, or tried to bring out, on strike, all employees in every shop and yard where the howitzers or any part of the howitzers or the flat-bottomed barges were in course of construction, with almost complete success, and with disastrous national results. But the Government met direct action by action more direct, and deported from the Clyde the ringleaders, and the strike collapsed. In this direct action strike the purpose was to nullify the agreement between the Government and the Trade Unions as to the introduction of women into the engineering trade, and to destroy the old craft organizations of the A.S.E. and set up a new industrial organization for that trade. The purpose, therefore, was economic, but the method was anarchic.

Subsequently, the Clyde Workers' Committee (a committee of Clydeside shop stewards working in co-operation with the Socialist Labour Party) established revolutionary Workers' Committees in various parts of England, and were behind similar direct action unofficial strikes, repudiated by the Executives of all the Unions concerned, in Barrow-in-Furness in June 1916, on the Mersey in the autumn of 1916, in the engineering shops of England in May 1917, and at other times. These were all economic strikes against trade agreements and arrangements constitutionally concluded between the Government and the Unions. That such anarchic strikes are entirely subversive of all law, order and government in a Trade Union organization as well as in the body politic needs no emphasis. They are just as dangerous to society as any strike regularly declared by a Trade Union for a non-economic purpose.

Conversion of the Labour Party to Use of Direct Action

But to revert to the non-economic strike: Mr. and Mrs. Sidney Webb, who have a wide knowledge of the currents and under-currents of opinions in the industrial world, say on p. 672 of their *History of Trade Unionism* (1920):

> "With regard to a general strike of non-economic or political character, in favour of a particular home or foreign policy, we very much doubt whether the Trades Union Congress could be induced to endorse it, or the rank and file to carry it out, except only in case the Government made a direct attack upon the political or industrial liberty of the manual working-class, which it seemed imperative to resist by every possible means, not excluding forceful revolution itself."

The kind of direct attack by the Government which the writers had in mind was action such as disfranchisement of the bulk of the manual workers, or deprivation of the Trade Unions of their present rights and liberties, or confiscation of their funds. Short of attempted measures like these, it was the considered opinion of those eminently competent writers, looking out over the Trade Union world as recently as the autumn of 1919, that direct action would be rejected by the Trades Union Congress. But the Portsmouth Congress of 1920 was yet to come.

The specific issue of direct action, in connection with the operations against Russia, was brought before the Trades Union Congress in September 1919, but was strategically shelved. Resolutions were, however, passed demanding the cessation of operations against Russia and the nationalization of coal. To enforce these demands, the Parliamentary Committee was instructed in the former case to call a special Trades Union Congress to decide what action should be taken; in the latter to decide "the form of action to be taken to *compel* the Government." This special Congress was held on December 9, 1919—by that time nationalization had become the real issue—but pending the effect of more forcible propaganda, direct action to enforce nationalization was deferred until March 1920. In March, another special Congress was held at which two means of enforcing nationalization were outlined to the Congress—one a general strike, the other intensive political propaganda. Congress decided on a card vote against direct action and in favour of intensive political propaganda in preparation for a General Election.

The solidarity of the Party was seriously endangered by the decision; the direct actionists included influential sections of miners, railwaymen, transport workers and engineers, to many of whom direct action had become an article of belief. Many moderates and extremists, therefore, strove to find an issue on which direct actionists and constitutionalists could be persuaded to co-operate. The production of munitions of war for use in Ireland and against Russia was chosen as the issue. It was cleverly contrived, and at a special meeting of the Trades Union Congress in July 1920, a resolution was passed in favour of a general strike to compel the Government to desist from armed intervention in Ireland and in Russia, and instructing the affiliated Unions to make the necessary domestic arrangements for such a strike. Moderate Labour was thus impaled on the horns of an adroit dilemma, and the more pacificist it was, the more it was impelled to vote for direct action. The Labour Party congratulated itself that it had restored its all-essential solidarity; but the solidarity achieved was more apparent than real—Trade Union domestic arrangements for a general strike progressed with no enthusiasm.

Then came the Polish imbroglio which the extremists exploited to the full in order to establish direct action as the recognized weapon of organized Labour in this country. It is important to follow this development. On August 6, 1920, the Labour Party, without the slightest justification, publicly charged the Government with meditating a war against Soviet Russia in support of Poland, and claimed that the workers would be justified in refusing to render labour services in such a war. A special emergency meeting of the Parliamentary Committee of the Trades Union Congress, the National Executive of the Labour Party, and the Parliamentary Labour Party met on August 9. "It felt certain," so the resolution ran, "that war was being engineered between the Allied Powers and Soviet Russia," and "warned the Government that the whole industrial power of the organized workers would be used to defeat this war." Arrangements were made for a national conference of Labour, and all affiliated organizations were advised to instruct their members to "down tools" on instructions to that effect from the national conference.

Establishment of the Council of Action

On August 13, 1920, the national conference met, 689 representatives of Trade Union executive committees, and 355 representatives of Local Labour Party organizations and Trade councils. Three resolutions were unanimously carried. The first endorsed the creation of the Council of Action which had been formed on August 9 representing the Parliamentary Labour Party, the Parliamentary Committee of the Trades Union Congress and the Executive of the Labour Party. The second continued the Council in being until it had secured: (1) a guarantee there should be no military or naval intervention against the Soviet Government; (2) the withdrawal of all British naval forces "operating directly or indirectly as a blockading influence against Russia"; (3) "the recognition of the Russian Soviet Government, and the establishment of unrestricted trading and commercial relationship between Great Britain and Russia." It also authorized the Council to order any and every form of withdrawal of labour which circumstances might require to give effect to the foregoing policy, and called for swift, loyal and courageous action by every Trade Union official, executive committee, local council of action, and membership in general, in response to such an order. The third resolution authorized the Council to take any steps necessary to give effect to the decisions of the conference, and to "the declared policy of the Trade Union and Labour movement."

The effect of these resolutions was clear. Trade Unions handed over their executive responsibility to the Council of Action, or "Committee of National Security," as one speaker called it. This Council could then impose its will upon the nation through the direct action of seizing it by the throat. That the will may be thought beneficent does not alter in the slightest the anarchic quality of the action. The Chairman of the Parliamentary Committee of the Trades Union Congress, in proposing the second resolution, put it plainly: "Giving effect to this resolution does not mean a mere strike; it means a challenge to the whole Constitution of the country." The report says there were prolonged cheers. He reiterated the same statement at the subsequent meeting of the Trades Union Congress in Portsmouth. The Chairman of the Executive Committee of the Labour Party, in seconding the first resolution, was even more explicit:

> "When the action referred to was taken, if too much interference was attempted they might be compelled to do things that would cause the present authorities (i.e. the Government) to abdicate. They might be forced to tell them that if they could not run this country in a peaceful manner without interfering with other nations, they might be compelled, against all constitutionalism, to chance doing something to take the country into their own hands."

There is nothing confused in this outlook. The speaker regarded direct action as the method by which to achieve his ends. The Labour Party would become the Government without the ordinary preliminary of a General Election. The outsider wonders why the "International," which was sung immediately after the passing of the first and third resolutions, was omitted after the second.

The whole of the Labour argument for this official inauguration of direct action turned on the assumption that the Bolshevik Government was standing in a white sheet and contemplated no ulterior threat to

Polish independence. Labour accepted Bolshevik professions to this effect with credulous alacrity. Then came the amazing *dénouement*. It turned out that, with characteristic Bolshevik duplicity, there had been deleted from the draft of the proposed peace terms, communicated to England, certain vitally important articles going to the root of Polish independence, which, however, were inserted in that presented by the Bolsheviks to the Poles at Minsk on August 19. The doctored English version, after specifying the strength to which the Polish Army was to be cut down, provided that all arms over and above those required for the needs of the army as so reduced, "as well as of the Civic Militia," were to be handed over to Russia. In the Minsk version, the Civic Militia was the crux of the terms; it was to be recruited from one class only, *the workers*; to be in strength four times that of the regular Polish army, and armed; in other words, a Red Army in Poland. This exactly enforced Section 8 of Lenin's Third International Constitution, which stipulates for the "disarmament of the bourgeoisie and the arming of the workers to defend Communism until Capitalism shall finally have been abolished." There was in truth at no time any argument from Poland to support direct action. The reason for its adoption was far more accurately stated by Mr. Robert Williams, the Secretary of the National Transport Workers' Federation, a leading member of the notorious Council of Action. In the *Daily Herald* for August 25, 1920, he is reported to have said as follows:

> "We felt that with the policy of Mr. Lloyd George, which sways to and fro according to events, we were menaced with war from the moment that the Poles were in peril. Together with several friends we drew up a manifesto which even the Conservatives among the Labour leaders signed, because they recognized clearly that they could no longer oppose the advanced elements *which had for so long insisted on the employment of direct action.*"

This recalls Lord Bacon's aphorism on faction: "It is often seen that a few that are stiff do tire out a greater number that are more moderate." The extremists had been struggling for ten years to establish the adoption of direct action under all circumstances as Labour's normal weapon of attack. They succeeded because the chief anxiety of Labour leaders, whether advancing at the head or running at the heels of their flock, is always, at any price, to secure or conserve solidarity.

Setting-up of Local Soviets

Over 350 Local Councils of Action, in many districts called Soviets, were organized to carry out the instructions of the central Council of

Action. Somewhat amusing was it to see how quickly the Council of Action, when it realized that public opinion was setting strongly against it, at once disclaimed any intention of calling a general strike in support of Soviet Russia. All it intended at the utmost "was to veto the manufacture or transport of munitions or equipment for the Poles," The Council quickly appreciated that the nation would not tolerate the application in this country of revolutionary methods. One of the reasons advanced for the formation of the Council of Action was to "prevent interference by the British Government in the affairs of Soviet Russia," No sooner, however, was it formed, than two delegates[6] of the Council went to Paris, there to interfere between the French Government and French Labour. A little logic was infused into them by the French Government, who promptly ordered them out of France.

CHAPTER VIII
THE LABOUR PARTY'S INDUSTRIAL
AND LAND POLICY

1. DETAILS OF THE PROPOSALS

We have already given a general outline of Labour's policy; it now remains to set out its particular proposals in regard to the reconstruction of industry. These we take from *Labour and the New Social Order*, published in 1918. If, as is not unlikely, readers feel aggrieved by want of definiteness, it is not the fault of the author, but of the Labour Party.

The Industries and Businesses to be Nationalized

"The Labour Party stands not merely for the principle of the common ownership of the nation's land, to be applied as suitable opportunities occur, but also, specifically, for the immediate nationalization of railways, mines, and the production of electrical power. We hold that the very foundation of any successful reorganization of British industry must necessarily be found in the provision of the utmost facilities for transport and communication, the production of power at the cheapest possible rate, and the most economical supply of both electrical energy and coal to every corner of the kingdom. Hence the Labour Party stands, unhesitatingly, for the national ownership and administration of the railways and canals, and their union, along with harbours and roads, and the posts and telegraphs—not to say also the great lines of steamers which could at once be owned, if not immediately directly managed in detail, by the Government—in a united national service of Communication and Transport, to be worked, unhampered by capitalist, private or purely local interests (and with a steadily increasing participation of the organized workers in the management, both central and local), exclusively for the common good. If any Government should be so misguided as to propose, when peace comes, to hand the railways back to the shareholders; or should show itself so spendthrift of the nation's property as to give these shareholders any enlarged franchise by presenting them with the economies of unification or the profits of increased railway rates; or so extravagant as to bestow public funds on the re-equipment of privately-owned lines—all of which things are now being privately intrigued for by the railway interests—the Labour Party will offer any such project the most strenuous opposition. The railways and canals, like the roads, must henceforth belong to the public, and to the public alone."

"In the production of electricity, for cheap power, light and heating, this country has so far failed, because of hampering private interests, to take advantage of science. Even in the largest cities we still 'peddle' our electricity on a contemptibly small scale. What is called for, immediately after the war, is the erection of a score of gigantic 'super-power stations,' which could generate, at incredibly cheap rates, enough electricity for the use of every industrial establishment and every private household in Great Britain, the present municipal and joint-stock electrical plants being universally linked up and used for local distribution. This is inevitably the future of electricity. It is plain that so great and so powerful an enterprise affecting every industrial enterprise, and, eventually, every household, must not be allowed to pass into the hands of private capitalists. They are already pressing the Government for the concession, and neither the Liberal nor the Conservative Party has yet made up its mind to a refusal of such a new endowment of profiteering in what will presently be the life-blood of modern productive industry. The Labour Party demands that the production of electricity on the necessary gigantic scale shall be made, from the start (with suitable arrangements for municipal co-operation in local distribution), a national enterprise, to be worked exclusively with the object of supplying the whole kingdom with the cheapest possible power, light and heat."

"But with railways and the generation of electricity in the hands of the public, it would be criminal folly to leave the present 1,500 colliery companies the power of 'holding up' the coal supply. These are now all working under public control, on terms that virtually afford to their shareholders a statutory guarantee of their swollen incomes. The Labour Party demands the immediate nationalization of mines, the extraction of coal and iron being worked as a public service (with a steadily increasing participation in the management, both central and local, of the various grades of persons employed), and the whole business of the retail distribution of household coal being undertaken as a local public service, by the elected municipal or county councils. And there is no reason why coal should fluctuate in price any more than railway fares, or why the consumer should be made to pay more in winter than in summer, or in one town than another. What the Labour Party would aim at is, for household coal of standard quality, a fixed and uniform price for the whole kingdom, payable by rich and poor alike, as unalterable as the penny postage-stamp."

"But the sphere of immediate nationalization is not restricted to these great industries. We shall never succeed in putting the gigantic system of Health Insurance on a proper footing, or secure a clear field for the beneficent work of the Friendly Societies, or gain a free hand for the necessary development of the urgently called for Ministry of Health and the Local Public Health Service, until the nation expropriates the profit-making industrial insurance companies, which now so tyrannously exploit the people with their wasteful house-to-house industrial life assurance. Only by such an expropriation of life assurance companies can we secure the universal provision, free from the burdensome toll of weekly pence, of the indispensable funeral benefit. Nor is it in any sense a 'class' measure. Only by the assumption by a State Department of the whole business of life assurance can the millions of policy-holders of all classes be completely protected against the possibly calamitous results of the depreciation of securities and suspension of bonuses which the war is causing. Only by this means can the great staff of insurance agents find their proper place as civil servants, with equitable conditions of employment, compensation for any disturbance and security of tenure, in a nationally organized public service for the discharge of the steadily increasing functions of the Government in vital statistics and social insurance."

"In quite another sphere the Labour Party sees the key to temperance reform in taking the entire manufacture and retailing of alcoholic drink out of the hands of those who find profit in promoting the utmost possible consumption. This is essentially a case in which the people, as a whole, must assert its right to full and unfettered power for dealing with the licensing question in accordance with local opinion. For this purpose, localities should have conferred upon them facilities:—

"(a) To prohibit the sale of liquor within their boundaries;

"(b) To reduce the number of licences and regulate the conditions under which they may be held; and

"(c) If a locality decides that licences are to be granted, to determine whether such licences shall be under private or any form of public control."

Extension of Municipal Enterprise

"Other main industries, especially those now becoming monopolized, should be nationalized as opportunity offers. Moreover, the Labour Party holds that the municipalities should not confine their activities to the necessarily costly services of education, sanitation and police; nor yet rest content with acquiring control of the local water, gas, electricity and tramways; but that every facility should be afforded to them to acquire (easily, quickly and cheaply) all the land they require, and to extend their enterprises in housing and town planning, parks and public libraries, the provision of music and the organization of recreation; and also to undertake, besides the retailing of coal, other services of common utility, particularly the local supply of milk, wherever this is not already fully and satisfactorily organized by a Co-operative Society."

Control of Capitalistic Industries and Businesses

"Meanwhile, however, we ought not to throw away the valuable experience now gained by the Government in its assumption of the importation of wheat, wool, metals and other commodities, and in its control of the shipping, woollen, leather, clothing, boot and shoe, milling, baking, butchering, and other industries. The Labour Party holds that, whatever may have been the shortcomings of the Government importation and control, it has demonstrably prevented a lot of 'profiteering.' Nor can it end immediately on the declaration of peace. The people will be extremely foolish if they ever allow their indispensable industries to slip back into the unfettered control of private capitalists, who are, actually at the instance of the Government itself, now rapidly combining trade by trade, into monopolist Trusts, which may presently become as ruthless in their extortion as the worst American examples. Standing as it does for the democratic control of industry, the Labour Party would think twice before it sanctioned any abandonment of the present profitable centralization of purchase of raw material; of the present carefully organized 'rationing,' by joint committees of the trades concerned, of the several establishments with the materials they require; of the present elaborate system of 'costing' and public audit of manufacturers' accounts, so as to stop the waste heretofore caused by the mechanical inefficiency of the more backward firms; of the present salutary publicity of manufacturing processes and expenses thereby ensured; and, on the information thus obtained (in order never again to revert to the old-time profiteering) of the present rigid fixing, for standardized products, of maximum prices at the factory, at the warehouse of the wholesale trader, and in the retail shop. This question of the retail prices of household commodities is emphatically the most practical of all political issues to the woman elector. The male politicians have too long neglected the grievances of the small household, which is the prey of every profiteering combination; and neither the Liberal nor the Conservative Party promises, in this respect, any amendment. This, too, is in no sense a 'class' measure. It is, so the Labour Party holds, just as much the function of Government, and just as necessary a part of the democratic regulation of industry, to safeguard the interests of the community as a whole, and those of all grades and sections of private consumers, in the matter of prices, as it is by the Factory and Trade Boards Acts, to protect the rights of the wage-earning producers in the matter of wages, hours of labour and sanitation."

Labour's Agricultural Policy

An official pamphlet called the *Labour Party and the Countryside* states Labour's agricultural policy "as settled by representatives of the Party's 300,000 affiliated agricultural members." With pride it is announced that members engaged in industry and living in towns had no finger in it. It is claimed to be the fruit of practical experience—the conclusion of experts. Endorsed by the National Executive of the Labour Party, it is stated to crystallize the principles upon which the Party will deal with agricultural and rural problems. The basis is to be the non-sectarian principle of "increased production of food stuffs by the employment of more British labour on better cultivated British land." The Coalition Government is charged with repudiating this principle and with having perpetrated in 1921 a shameless and scandalous deceit in "scrapping" the Corn Production Acts, 1917 and 1920.

Abolition of Landlordism

First and foremost, land is to be nationalized. Many evils and much oppression are attributed to private ownership. Landlords have obstructed every measure of land reform; thwarted food production; obstructed housing, small holdings and land reclamation; demanded extortionate prices for land for public needs and appropriated as unearned increment a large part of the value of every tenant's improvement. "For the Labour Party" therefore "the substitution of public for private ownership in land (subject to equitable treatment of each person whose property is required for the public good and to a proper security of tenure for the home and the homestead) underlies in principle all its specific proposals."

Councils for Agriculture

Councils for agriculture are to be constituted for each county, one-third thereof elected by farmers, another one-third by farm labourers and the remaining one-third nominated "by the various public authorities in the county, including the county council, to represent the public interest." Some good work is credited to the existing county agricultural committees, but they are condemned as hampered by their constitution. Members of the councils would receive travelling expenses and payment for time spent on public service. The primary duty of each council would be to supervise farming in the county and secure and maintain an all round improvement in cultivation, an increase in the area under plough and an aggregate increase in the production of food stuffs. In the event of bad farming, councils would have power to take over the land and cultivate it in the public interest. A Central National Council of Agriculture would advise the Minister of Agriculture.

A Legal Minimum Agricultural Wage

A legal minimum wage (whether on a national or district basis is not stated, but presumably the latter) and standard conditions of employment are to be established for every farm, market garden and fruit orchard worker and gardener in domestic employment, to all of whom the National Unemployment Insurance Scheme would be extended. This in the first instance is to be effected by re-establishing the National Wages Board and County Wages Committees of the Ministry of Agriculture, the abolition of which in 1921 is characterized as a "flagrant breach of faith." The fund out of which increased wages are to be paid is to be created out of the profits of better farming, increased production, organized marketing, less costly transport, lower retail prices of farmers' supplies and the elimination of profits now taken by unnecessary middlemen. A national scheme of insurance managed on a co-operative basis by agriculturalists themselves is to be established against the risk of unfavourable weather and sudden falls in world prices.

Workers' Control of Agriculture

"Democratic control" is to be introduced into the agricultural industry as in other industries, "to supersede the economic dependence of the agricultural worker on the farmer for employment and livelihood with the implication of inferiority involved." The operation of the councils of agriculture is to be a step towards that end. But the statement of policy is prudently non-committal and the full meaning of "democratic control" and its implications, so far as agriculture is concerned, receives no explanation.

CHAPTER IX
THE LABOUR PARTY'S INDUSTRIAL
AND LAND POLICY

2. A CRITICISM

We propose now to offer some broad criticisms upon Labour's Industrial and Land Policy.

What Capitalism Is

The primary object, as we have shown, of the Labour Party is to abolish capitalism. What, therefore, do we understand by that? It cannot be better described than has been so admirably done by that distinguished writer, Mr. Hartley Withers, in the *Case for Capitalism*, p. 13:

> "The present system under which we work and exchange our work for that of others is that commonly described as Capitalism. Under it each one, male or female, can choose what work he will try to do and what employer he will try to serve; if he does not like his job or his employer, he can leave it or him and try to get another. He cannot earn unless he can do work that somebody wants to buy, and so he competes with all other workers in producing goods or services that others want and will pay for. His reward depends on the success with which he can satisfy the wants of others. Whatever money he earns in return for his labour he can spend as he chooses on the purchase of goods and services for his own use or for that of his dependents, or he can invest it in opening up a business or industry on his own, account, or in shares and debts of public companies, and debts of Governments or public bodies; these securities will pay him a rate of profit or interest if the companies or debtors prosper and are solvent. Whatever money he earns by labour or by investment he can, after paying such taxes on it as the State demands, hand on to any heirs whom he may name.

"The system is thus based on private property, competition, individual effort, individual responsibility and individual choice. Under it, all men and women are more or less often faced by problems which they have to decide and, according as their decision is right or wrong, their welfare and that of their dependents will wax or wane. It is thus very stimulating and bracing, and might be expected to bring out the best effort of the individual to do good work that will be well paid so that he and his may prosper and multiply. If only every one had a fair start and began life with an equal chance of turning his industry and powers to good account, it would be difficult to devise a scheme of economic life more likely to produce great results from human nature as it now is; by stimulating its instincts for gain and rivalry to a great output of goods and services and by sharpening its faculties, not only for exercise in this purely material use, but also for solving the bigger problems of life and human intercourse that lie behind it."

The capitalistic system dates from the Industrial Revolution (1780-1830), when domestic industry was replaced by factory production. Since those days, as Labour was plentiful and ill-organized and capital more difficult to obtain, the capitalist occupied relatively to the worker a stronger position in industry. This transient incident is what Mr. Sidney Webb in his *A Constitution for a Socialist Commonwealth of Great Britain* describes as "the central wrong of the Capitalist System":—

"But the central wrong of the Capitalist System is neither the poverty of the poor nor the riches of the rich: it is the power which the mere ownership of the instruments of production gives to a relatively small section of the community over the actions of their fellow citizens and over the mental and physical environment of successive generations. Under such a system personal freedom becomes, for large masses of people, little better than a mockery. The tiny minority of rich men enjoy, not personal freedom only, but also personal power over the lives of other people; whilst the underlying mass of poor men find their personal freedom restricted to the choice between obeying the orders of irresponsible masters intent on their own pleasure or their own gain, or remaining without the means of subsistence for themselves and their families."

Our Debt to Capitalism

Labour's proposal, therefore, is to abolish capitalism and replace it by that brand of Socialism known as "nationalization and democratic control." We should first realize what we owe to the capitalism which we are asked to destroy. Our first debt is certainly liberty. This is convincingly worked out by Mr. Harold Cox in his *Economic Liberty*, p. 2. Liberty to possess and use property consistently with the good of the community, liberty to buy, to sell, to work, to strike, in fact complete liberty in all economic relations. This is to be surrendered and replaced by the bureaucratic control of the State Socialist, or the equally autocratic control under the scheme of the Guild Socialist. Liberty is a prize not hastily to be relinquished. This capitalistic system is not the selfish system as described by Labour. It can only exist provided it supplies commodities and services, of which the community stands in need, at prices which the community can afford to pay. That is no light responsibility. One of the necessary consequences of any socialistic organization of industry is that the community must use and pay for such commodities as it is convenient and desirable for industry to produce; under any socialistic regime, therefore, the consumer, instead of being an object of regard, becomes a mere wheel in the mechanism of production.

The capitalistic system develops energy and thrift, though the former has been largely neutralized by the sterilizing effect of Trade Union doctrines against output, and the latter frustrated by the inability of industry as a result of production thus restricted to pay high wages. Under a socialistic regime the worker is to receive not wages but "pay" and whether he works or not. All progress in industry depends upon initiative and enterprise and the readiness to take risks. To-day risks are assumed by the owner of capital and, if they materialize, they are borne by him and not by the workers or the community. It would be ludicrous to say that either the State under State Socialism or industry under any form of democratic control would or could exert the same initiative or show the same enterprise as the private capitalist. Economic history teems with examples of great industries now employing thousands of workers which were originally established by capitalists who, stubbornly persistent, refused to accept failure and by sheer dogged enterprise won through. The world has wonderfully prospered under the capitalistic organization in industry. We see social conditions enormously improved, innumerable social reforms effected, the welfare and well-being of the people prodigiously advanced. Sir Josiah Stamp—an outstanding authority—said in 1921, as a result of a statistical investigation, "the ordinary person of to-day is four times as well off in real commodities as the person in the corresponding stage in the scale in the beginning of the nineteenth century." During this hundred years the population has quadrupled. The lot of the worker steadily progressed from 1800 up till 1900, when, in certain industries, there set in tendencies of retrogression. It has been one continuous record of rise in standard of living, and in wages, both nominal amount and purchasing power, due to improvement in production from the introduction of machinery, development of food production in new countries, and expansion of our export trade. This has been largely the result of the capitalistic organization of industry, and of its ability to meet the demands of the consumer, and of the extraordinary elasticity inherent in the system of adapting itself to varying circumstances.

Without the machinery provided by the much-abused capitalist Labour would to-day be "scratching the ground" to extract a penurious livelihood. The capitalistic organization of industry would never have survived, had it not been in the main economically sound, and, on the whole, a system which made for the good of society. This is the system which is to be wholly destroyed by the Labour Party because of certain alleged defects, and replaced by an untried socialistic regime.

The Alleged Defects of Capitalism

First, it is said that under capitalism the incentive stands ethically condemned in that an employer is actuated wholly by a desire for his own private profit. I fail to see any turpitude in that motive; an employer can only make profit if he succeeds in serving the community. There are, of course, some—I personally have met very few—employers who deliberately try to foist on credulous consumers an adulterated or spurious article. But it is exactly for the same motive, namely, for profit, that the worker serves his employer, or, if that is an unacceptable analogy, that a member of a gang of workers serves his fellow-worker who is head of the gang and employing him. There are just as many workmen, indeed more, who are ready to pass off bad work upon their employer as employers prepared to pass off bad work upon the community.

As against this incentive of private profit the Syndicalists would substitute the imaginary incentive that each worker would work for the good of his own group of workers; the National Guildist that each worker would work for the benefit of his Guild of workers, and the State Socialist that each worker would work for the State. Reduced to its elements, it means that each worker would, in the end, work for what he could get out of it, or if he found that he got the same advantage without working so hard, then he would not work so energetically. The suggestion that workers would work more vigorously for the community or State is so absolutely contrary to my own experience that I find it difficult to treat the suggestion with respect. It was never so during the war—in Government factories, dockyards, arsenals, there was just as much restriction of production as in the works of private employers, and considerably more strikes. In none of our municipal services is it found to be a fact. The railway strike of September 1919, while the railways were under Government control, is only another illustration of the falsity of the suggestion.

It is said that Labour under the capitalistic system is bought and sold as a commodity. That is one of those phrases which expresses more than is meant. The lawyer sells his legal advice, the surgeon his operative skill, the musician his powers of technique, taste and expression just as a person who owns a commodity sells it. I cannot see any moral degradation whatever in the worker accepting wages any more than a private lawyer accepting his salary in a financial house, or a house-surgeon accepting his in a hospital or an organist his in a parish church. All of them are subject to notice terminating their engagements, just as a manual worker—not probably a week's notice, but some longer period. The accusation is put even higher and the capitalist is called a thief, in other words, that he is appropriating in the shape of his own profit something which ought to belong to Labour. This proposition, palpably untrue, is so generally accepted by the workers that it deserves some examination. If a Trade Unionist, say a foreman plater, in one of our large ship repairing centres, works hard and makes, as he does in normal times, a big income, he may do one or two things with it; he may spend it on his own amusements or in wasteful extravagance; on the other hand, he may save and invest it, as I have known many do, in a small industrial concern in his own district. In the first case he is by common consent an honourable, if a foolish, man, in the second he certainly will not be called a thief. He has used by investment a part of his wealth for the ·purpose of producing more wealth, and his resultant increase of wealth is not robbery of the workers in the concern in which his money is invested. But then he is a member of the Labour movement. Between such a case and the case of the financial house which makes a business of collecting the savings or surplus wealth of thrifty persons for investment in industry, there is no difference in principle whatsoever.

Capitalism implies competition, and competition, Labour says, must be eradicated out of social and industrial activity. Why competition should be a good thing in every walk of human life and provide a healthy stimulus, and yet not provide an equally beneficial stimulus in industrial and commercial affairs is hard to follow. What Labour really intends to say is that competition acts so as to depress wages and lower the standard of living of the worker. That is only one side; competition acts so as to increase demand for commodities and the volume of employment, and, if production were not restricted, would increase wages. Then it is said that the capitalistic organization of industry involves economic waste, by which is meant that industry is carried on less efficiently under private management than it would be either under Government or under "democratic control." If there is waste it is the capitalist who suffers, the Trade Unionist always receives his standard rate of wages. If there is waste on the employers' side, as of course there is in some badly organized shops, there is greater waste in the shape of restricted production on the part of the worker. Organization and efficiency are, of course, essential to industrial progress, but to suggest that these essential qualities are better obtained under bureaucratic or democratic control is at variance with our experience during the war and of present conditions in Russia where democratic control has laid the hand of death on industry.

Where Reform is Admittedly Needed

It must not be assumed that the capitalistic system of organization of industry is perfect and needs no reform; unfortunately, it exhibits a number of well-marked deficiencies. First of all, an employer only employs a man as long as he desires or finds he can profitably do so, in just the same way that the workman only works for an employer as long as he finds it suits him and no better job is forthcoming. One defect certainly of the present capitalistic system is the failure of employers in industry as a whole or of each industry in particular to provide against unemployment. On this matter I have a good deal to say in a subsequent part of this book. Again, in the past there was a regrettable tendency which, in recent years, has happily disappeared amongst the best employers, to disregard the human qualities, aspirations, needs and susceptibilities of the worker, coupled with a neglect to provide effectively for his welfare and well-being in the works. This, however, is nothing intrinsic in the capitalistic organization of industry; I have heard equally bitter complaints by the workers when I have been sitting as arbitrator in disputes between employees of the "non-capitalistic" co-operative societies and the societies' democratic managements.

There is, however, a complaint against capitalism which, although it has been very largely remedied in recent years, yet in normal times, immediately prior to the war, certainly existed — that was the insufficient distribution amongst the workers of the product of the industry; capital in many cases received an undue share of the reward. This was a short-sighted policy; for good wages to the workers, provided the workers give good output, results in the workers possessing good purchasing power; and as so many workers are also consumers, this results in a good demand for commodities and so is to the benefit of manufacturers, and the community. But if some employers appropriated by way of profit an unduly large share of the product of industry, the workers did exactly the same if opportunity presented itself. One has illustrations of this in the way in which, by agreement between the building employers and the building Trade Unions, costs were forced up by wage-agreements which largely contributed to the shortage of housing and placed the unskilled builder's labourer in a wage-position substantially higher than that of the skilled engineer tradesman, who normally stands on a higher wage-level.

The Failure of Past Socialistic Experiments

When we are discussing on a priori hypotheses the practical operation of the elemental motives of average men and women, it is wise to learn what experience has to teach us. There have been at least seventy attempts to carry secular Socialism into effect, of which five only survived their fourth year of life. There was the new Harmony Community of Equality, financed and founded in America in 1825 by Robert Owen. One of its articles of constitution provided that "every member shall render his or her services for the good of the whole." It was a disastrous failure. Owen had supplied lands, houses and the use of capital, giving to some persons leases of large tracts of land for 2,000 years at a nominal rent and for moral considerations only. Addressing the settlers in 1827, he said: "I find that the habits of the individualistic system are so powerful that these leases have been, with few exceptions, applied for individual purposes and individual gain." There was also the Brook Farm Phalanx, established in 1842, with which Emerson was associated; the Wisconsin Phalanx, established in 1844, and the North American Phalanx, a few years later.

The leading facts and the history of these Socialistic adventures ought to be read in Mr. W. H. Mallock's the *Limits of Pure Democracy*, Book IV, chap. 2, p. 201, where they are set out with much acute criticism. The last of these great experiments was in 1893, when William Lane established his "New Australia" in Paraguay. In Lane's constitution the workers were controlled and directed by officials of their own choosing. The colony came to sad grief and ultimately decided by vote that every man should be entitled to dispose of the fruits of his own industry. A new grant of land was made by the Government to a large number of the original colonists; they retrieved their failure and became, under the stimulus of each working for himself, successful farmers. The causes of the unhappy end of those great adventures are summed up thus by Mr. Mallock:—"To speak broadly they may be reduced to two, one of them inhering in the nature of all collective industry, the other inhering in the nature of human beings with the sole exception of small and essentially select minorities. The first of these causes was a want of ability in industrial direction. The second was a want of any general sentiment sufficiently strong and persistent to ensure that directions, if given, should be accepted with submission on the one hand and carried out with a diligence punctual and sustained on the other, under a social system the essential object of which was to render the conditions of the worst worker equal to the conditions of the best."

Limits within which Nationalization is Practicable

Labour, of course, will say that these small experiments have no bearing on the question of the nationalization and control of great industries. To some extent they are right. There are, however, certain definite limits to successful nationalization. An industry which is confined to rendering services is a totally different thing to an industry whose business it is to produce commodities. There is nothing like the same severe restrictions on efficiency in the former case as in the latter. The services may indeed be of such a character that they can only be efficiently carried out under the State or under a municipality If the service is one the successful provision of which depends upon a monopoly being preserved, there may be a case for nationalization; as illustrative of this, one may take the case of the Post Office. Again, a comprehensive service may be necessary, in parts of the country where it has to be provided at a loss, in other parts where it can be provided at a profit-the loss in the former case being made good out of the profit in the latter. Under such conditions nationalization may be the only possible procedure. Sometimes continental analogies for nationalization are adduced, but the continental temperament and tradition have been entirely different from those prevailing in this country. There was never in Latin countries the same spirit of private enterprise as with us; in the former, public opinion relied on the State to provide all services in the nature of public utilities. Where there has been an opportunity of comparing the efficiency of services provided by the State with those provided by private enterprise, the comparison is always against the State. One has only to read *German v. British Railways*, by Edwin A. Pratt (P. S. King & Son, 1907), *Historical Sketch of State Railway Ownership*, by Sir William Acworth, K.C.I.E. (John Murray, 1920), to realize some of the drawbacks of nationalization. The Socialist in this country invariably falls back upon the Post Office as a convincing case of the success of State management, but the business community will hardly be prepared to accept the Post Office as a conclusive argument of the efficiency of nationalization.

The Different Schemes of Land Nationalization

What the Labour Party means by "public ownership" of land is not clear. The term "nationalization" is equally vague. In reference to land, it is commonly used to mean some form of "communization," that is to say, acquisition and ownership either by the whole community or a section of the community. The former is true nationalization, i.e. ownership by the nation; the latter is "municipalization," i.e. ownership by a local authority. Municipalization of land has, however, rather disappeared as a proposition.

All land nationalizers assume that ownership embraces two fundamental rights. (1) The right to draw a revenue from the use of the land, i.e. to receive the rent. (2) The right to control the way in which the land shall be used. They describe these two rights as the "right to rent," and the "right of control" respectively. Where land is held in fee-simple the right to rent and the right of control are usually vested in one and the same person, namely the owner. Where, however, the relation of landlord and tenant has been created by a contract of tenancy, the right to rent, when it exists, is usually vested in the landlord. The right of control is vested partly in the landlord and partly in the tenant. The landlord's powers, partial or otherwise according to circumstances, of controlling the uses to which the tenant may put the land, depend upon the contract of tenancy.

Schemes of land nationalization fall into one of three classes according to their effect on the right to rent and the right of control. First, where the whole revenue of the land is ultimately to go to the State, but possession and the right of control of the land is to remain as it is under private ownership. There, transference of land revenues to the State is to be effected by growing national taxation of land values. This is the scheme of the school of land nationalizers who follow Mr. Henry George, and are mainly represented by the English League for the Taxation of Land Values. It is fully explained in Mr. George's book, *Progress and Poverty*, and will be called the "George scheme" or "taxing-out scheme," Second, where the right of control of the land is to be taken from private owners and vested in the State by State purchase, but the owners are to suffer no substantial loss of revenue. They are to receive Government Bonds of such capital value as will produce an annual interest equal to the net rent of the land in question. This is the plan of the Land Nationalization Society, of which the late Dr. Alfred R. Wallace, F.R.S., O.M., was the Chairman. It will be called the "Nationalization Society's scheme" or the "state purchase scheme." Third, where the present owners are to be expropriated, and deprived of the right to rent, and the right of control, and so lose all or a very considerable portion of their income so far as derived from land. Socialists other than the State Socialists who subscribe to the programme of the Land Nationalization Society advocate this policy. Some of them would allow the owners compensation, but nothing like sufficient to maintain their present income. For example, the National Guildists would pay trifling compensation in State Bonds equal in nominal value to the capitalized value of an annuity for two to three years of the same annual amount as the net rent. The Syndicalists, on the other hand, would confiscate the entire private property in land without any compensation whatsoever. These various schemes described under "third" will be called the "socialistic schemes."

The Taxing-out Scheme

Mr. George thus describes his "taxing-out scheme" at p. 288 of *Progress and Poverty*:

> "I do not propose either to purchase or to confiscate private property in land. The first would be unjust; the second needless. Let the individuals who now hold it still retain, if they want to, possession of what they are pleased to call *their* land. Let them continue to call it *their* land. Let them buy and sell, bequeath and devise it. We may safely leave them the shell if we take the kernel. *It is not necessary to confiscate land, it is only necessary to confiscate rent.*"

In regard to the "George scheme," the whole point is whether there is any special justification for confiscating an income derived from land as compared with other incomes.

The State Purchase Scheme

The object of the "Land Nationalization Society's scheme" as published is "to establish public ownership of land by means of fair compensation based on its value as ascertained for purposes of taxation." It is insisted that the State should take possession of agricultural land first and of house property at a later period.

Public ownership, it is claimed, will secure:

(1) That the use of land will be easily obtainable by all classes of the community without being subject to the veto of any landowner.

(2) That the best possible conditions of tenancy will be established so that all State tenants will have the same security as freeholders have to-day and full right to the value of the improvements they make.

(3) That the community will be able to determine in the general interests of all to what uses the land shall be put.

(4) That ultimately the whole value of the land will be secured for the common good.

This, of course, is only a summarized statement of the alleged benefits of State purchase. They are expanded into great detail by the Land Nationalization Society in its various publications.

The Socialistic Confiscation Schemes

The chief characteristic of the "socialistic schemes" is confiscation pure and simple. How exactly that is to be effected depends upon the particular school of Socialism; the constitutionalists say by legislation; the revolutionaries say by direct action culminating in the social revolution.

The Conceptions Underlying Each Scheme

The fundamental conceptions underlying the schemes are as follows:

(*a*) The *Georgites* contend that the bare land was given by God to the human race but was afterwards stolen by robber barons, or taken by wicked kings from the people and handed over on fictitious grounds or nefarious reasons to courtiers who did the royal will.

(*b*) The *Land Nationalization Society* builds up the whole of its case for State purchase upon this basic axiom:

"All men have an equal right to live, and as no man can live without land, it follows that all men have an equal right to the use of the land that is necessary to sustain their existence." Notwithstanding this, land still remains private property; the private owner is supreme in regard to it; he can exclude everyone from it with dire economic results. Only under State ownership, says the Nationalization Society, can this be remedied.

(*c*) The *Socialists*, that is to say, the National Guildists and Syndicalists, found their scheme on both the foregoing assumptions, the Syndicalists in addition claiming that no rent should be paid even to the State, but that the land should belong outright to, and be distributed among, the people.

As a matter of practical politics the State purchase scheme of the Nationalization Society is of chief moment. Although the Georgites and the Socialists are active and vociferous, their respective schemes are of much less relative importance. Even assuming that the land was originally acquired by private persons by robbery or injustice, the best equitable answer to the "taxing-out scheme" is probably that of the Nationalization Society:

> We answer that while the land is *ours* by every moral right, and we propose to assume possession of it by compulsory

process, we recognize that a very large number of honest men (neither robber barons nor their descendants) have invested actual earned money in land, either as individuals or as members of building, insurance and co-operative societies and trade unions.

"Therefore, we do not propose to confiscate that money (i.e. that portion of the rent which represents the value of the bare land) and leave to them what is theirs (i.e. that portion of the rent which represents the value of the improvements)" (*The Land Nationalizer*, May, 1919, p. 5).

The Secretary of the Land Nationalization Society writes thus:

"We who favour compensation justify it on grounds which appear to us to be grounds of equity. We say that the landlords of the present day did not found the system of private property in land, and should not be punished (by spoliation) as if they did. The original wrongdoers are dead and past punishments. Neither are the present landlords alone responsible for the maintenance of the system. That system is supported by the well-to-do classes generally, who look upon land as legitimate private property, and even by the great mass of unthinking landless people who send a majority of landlords and friends of landlords to Parliament at every chance they get. If landowning is a crime, then the majority of the British people are aiders and abettors of it.... We must be prepared to give a fair value for the land whether it be held by a duke or a working man." (*State Land Purchase*, by Joseph Hyder, p. 3.)

The practical answer to the "George" or "taxing-out scheme" is that it is not possible to separate the value of the land from the value of the improvements on it. Anything which mankind has added to the natural land is capital and should, according to the George view, be inviolate. In proposing, as "the George scheme" does, only to allow for "the value of the clearly distinguishable improvements made within a moderate time," capital is being confiscated. That is, something is being confiscated which was not stolen. If one form of capital may be confiscated, why not all forms?

The Land Nationalization Society has formulated many objections to the "George" or "taxing-out scheme" apart from its injustice. They say it would be an interminable process, that it would not be effective—witness the failure of the heavy land taxation in Canada, New Zealand or Australia, to cheapen land or eliminate landlords—that the public would not accept it. So many persons are owners of small pieces of land, it would tend to increase the number of landlords instead of reducing them.

The way in which the advocates of State purchase try to make out their case is very simple, and they do it with great ingenuity. They first endeavour to prove their basic axiom of "the right to live" by appeal to the great English common lawyers, writers on Sociology and authorities on Political Economy. Having done that to their own satisfaction, they proceed to give at length illustrations of alleged despotic and churlish action on the part of landowners. The favourites are the Highland Clearances and landlordism in Ireland. Then in the same vein they bring forward a great collection of cases of alleged refusal of land by landowners for works of public importance, or exaction by landowners of what is said to be (without any evidence) a wholly unreasonable price for land for public purposes (see, for instance, Chapter V, "The Extortion of High Prices for Land" in *The Case for Land Nationalization*, by Joseph Hyder, Simpkin, Marshall & Co.). All these evils are said to be directly due to private ownership in land. These cases, if they ever existed, are amply remedied by recent Acts facilitating the acquisition of land.[7] Having got so far, every hardship or evil to which a farmer or agricultural labourer is subject is likewise under the same chain of reasoning ascribed (without proof) to private ownership in land. If, therefore, the basic axiom is to be vindicated, private ownership must be done away with. There is no logic in such reasoning, even assuming that the basic axiom in its widest extension is sound—as a matter of fact it is not. All these illustrations show is that the present land system may, in certain respects, require reform, not that it ought to be abolished. The argument makes out no case for the complete eradication of the whole landlord system, still less for State purchase. The fallacy lies in the wholly unproved assumption that State ownership is the only alternative to an unreformed land system.

The Disadvantages of State Ownership of Land

It is difficult to state succinctly the many objections[8] to State ownership of land:

(*a*) The first is the incompetence of the State through a rigid bureaucratic administration subject to political pressure to manage efficiently or economically a highly technical industry like agriculture, one whose conditions vary in every district and indeed on every estate (which is admitted by the Labour Party), or indeed the land on which the complex industry directly depends.

(*b*) State purchase would entail an enormous addition to our National Debt which we cannot afford, and for which there is no justification.

(*c*) If landowners were bought out, it is clear that the State would have to make itself responsible for finding annually a vast amount of capital for improvements, and also working capital for the very large number of peasant and other smallholding tenants. It would not, and could not, do it adequately nor as satisfactorily nor to the same extent as existing landowners. If it did, this speculative use of national funds would be quite unjustifiable.

(*d*) If it is desirable to cut up large estates and farms and to establish a vast number of peasant holders in the shape of State tenants, and all the evidence from Ireland and other countries is strongly against the expediency of this course, it can be done without the abolition of private property in land.

(*e*) One thing is certain, that State ownership will not tend to increase production, but will have the opposite effect.

(*f*) It is equally clear that States ownership involves no improvement of the lot of the agricultural labourer, but rather the reverse.

(*g*) There is not the land monopoly alleged. This appears from the fact that over one-half of the cultivated land in England and Wales consists of holdings of comparatively small extent—80 per cent, of the existing farmers farming holdings of under 101 acres.

(*h*) Tenant farmers do not want State purchase.

CHAPTER X
THE LABOUR PARTY'S POLICY
FOR UNEMPLOYMENT

1. WORK OR MAINTENANCE

The Labour Party claims to have foreseen the present prostration of industry, and asserts that it recommended in advance of the disaster complete preventives and remedies which, if they had been adopted, would have neutralized the present world-wide conditions of unemployment. The successive statements of policy issued, and resolutions passed by the Labour Party and the Trades Union Congress since 1917 on the subject of unemployment, disprove conclusively any such claim of prescience.

The Manchester Resolution of 1917

At the Labour Party's Annual Conference in 1917 a resolution asserted that the Government could, if it chose, prevent any considerable unemployment in this country, by maintaining from year to year a "uniform national demand" for labour. This was to be done by co-ordinating the carrying out of public works, and of orders for State Departments and local authorities. "To prepare for the possibility of there being extensive unemployment either in the course of demobilization or in the first years of peace," the Government was called upon to arrange for immediate execution, either directly or through local authorities, of the most urgently needed public works. These were described as housing to the extent of two millions sterling, new schools, roads and light railways, reorganization of canals, afforestation, land reclamations, harbour development, etc. To reduce the risk of adult unemployment it was urged that the school age should be raised to sixteen, scholarships established, and hours of labour shortened for young people, and a 48-hour week introduced generally without reduction of wages. It will thus be seen that Labour, in 1917, in exercise of those powers of prevision now so amply arrogated to itself, thought that unemployment after the war would be so limited in this country that it could be remedied by the adoption of the simple measures mentioned above.

The Memorandum on War Aims, 1917

In London, in December 1917, a *Memorandum on War Aims* was approved at a Special Conference of the Labour Party and the Trades Union Congress, and in February 1918, was accepted by the Third Inter-Allied Conference held in London of Foreign Allied Labour and Socialist organizations. This Memorandum proceeded in the same strain. Section 5 urged the Socialists and Labour Parties of every country to press their Governments to execute numerous public works, roads, railways, schools, houses, etc., at such rate in each locality as would, when superadded to capitalistic enterprise, maintain a uniform demand for labour and so "prevent there being any unemployment." Then followed this fallacious proposition: "It is now known that it is in this way quite possible for any Government to prevent, if it chooses, the very occurrence of any widespread or prolonged involuntary unemployment," and this comment, "if such is allowed to occur it is as much the result of Government neglect as is any epidemic disease."

The Memorandum on Unemployment after the War, 1917

There was also issued, in 1917, a Memorandum called the *Problem of Unemployment after the War*, adopted by the Joint Committee on Labour Problems after the War, representing the Parliamentary Committee of the Trades Union Congress, the Executive Committee of the Labour Party, the Management Committee of the General Federation of Trades Unions and the War Emergency Workers' National Committee. Its proposals for the prevention of unemployment are worthy of analysis. It maintained that unless prevented by concerted action there would be considerable unemployment after the war, and from these specific causes, namely, the discharge of munition workers, delay in works changing over from war to peace production, congestion of ports, demobilization of the Army and Navy, difficulties in securing adequate industrial capital. Again the remedy recommended was the maintenance from year to year of a uniform national demand for labour by the Government and local authorities giving out their orders "in such a way as to make them vary inversely with the demands of private employers." The public works that were to be executed were much the same as before: housing schemes, water and drainage works, parks, schools, public libraries, works planned by the Development Commission and Road Board and held up owing to the war, the development of agricultural and rural industries on a national and co-operative basis, afforestation, and the execution of Government printing postponed during the war. The Government was also pressed to encourage works of which the output, like bricks and cement, were necessary for the carrying on of other work, for example, building.

There could be nothing plainer than this sentence in the Memorandum: "It may be urged that no such action would keep up the demand of other countries for our products, and thus the export trades might fall off; it may be assumed, however, that the principal export trades will certainly be busy (coal, machinery, shipbuilding, constructional iron and steel and all woollen goods) and the home demand for cotton goods is also expected to be brisk." It is obvious, therefore, at this date that the Labour Party never contemplated the present depression in our export trade.

The proposals of this Memorandum were in advance of previous recommendations. To enable local authorities to execute public works, legislation was demanded to facilitate the acquisition of the necessary land. The Government was to use for national purposes the 200 national factories, but for what purpose the Memorandum is eloquently silent. A systematic plan of short-time with full wages was to be introduced for a certain limited period in Government dockyards, arsenals and factories, when the final adjustment to peace-time conditions was taking place. To prevent an overstocked adult labour market there was to be no employment, partial or otherwise, of children under the school-leaving age, which was to be raised to sixteen, and only part-time employment up to a maximum of a 30-hour week for young people between sixteen and eighteen years, the balance of whose normal working week was to be devoted to physical and technical training and education. Twenty thousand additional scholars were to be trained as school teachers, and additional bursaries granted to the secondary schools, universities and technical colleges for pupils from the elementary schools, who would otherwise go into industry. Overtime was to be prohibited, and an 8-hour day to be imposed by statute.

The Memorandum claimed maintenance, apart from the Poor Law, for all persons who were unemployed and for whom no suitable work could be found. Where persons were entitled to unemployment benefit from the Trade Unions they should receive it and in addition be paid unemployment benefit under the Unemployment Insurance Acts; the rate of benefit, under those Acts, to be increased to a sum to be fixed in regard to the prevailing cost of living. Unemployed persons who did not receive benefit under the Acts, and those who had received it, but had run out of it, should be paid maintenance up to a total sum per week fixed in due relation to the cost of living. Trade Unions paying unemployment benefit were to receive a Government subsidy.

In addition the Memorandum called for wide extension of the National Insurance Act, 1911, and for abolition of its restriction to a limited number of trades, and also for amendment of the National Insurance (Part II) (Munition Workers) Act, 1916, which brought in munition workers and persons engaged in metal and chemical industries under the Act of 1911, and created, it was said, invidious distinctions, as for example, between a worker who would be insured if engaged on a particular article needed for use in war, but who would not be insured if engaged on the same type of article when it was needed for ordinary commercial use. The Memorandum also called for amendment of the Act of 1916 in regard to its application to women, and for the extension generally to women of the National Unemployment Insurance Scheme.

The London Resolution of 1918

When one passes to the year 1918, we find no indication whatever that the Labour Party had any premonition of the decline in trade which commenced in the spring of 1920, or were gifted with any widening vision as to the remedies required to meet it. This appears from the proceedings of the Labour Party's Annual Conference in that year, and from the resolution which was passed on the prevention of unemployment. This resolution, after declaring that the years immediately following the war would probably include periods of grave dislocation of profit-making industry, called upon the Government to arrange the carrying out of the next succeeding ten years' programme of national and local government works, including housing, schools, roads, railways, canals, harbours, afforestation, reclamations, etc., in such a way as "any temporary congestion of the labour market may require." This resolution solemnly and without reservation committed the Labour Party to this sweeping generalization:—"Now that it is known that all that is required to prevent the occurrence of any widespread or lasting unemployment is that the aggregate total demand for labour should be maintained year in and year out at an approximately even level, and that this can be secured by nothing more difficult or revolutionary than a sensible distribution of the public orders for works and services so as to keep always up to the prescribed total the aggregate public and capitalist demand for labour, together with the prohibition of overtime in excess of the prescribed normal working day, there is now no excuse for any Government which allows such a calamity as widespread or lasting unemployment ever to occur."

One can thus realize what, up to the end of 1918, were the sovereign panaceas of the Labour Party for the prevention of unemployment after the war. Let us proceed to trace from and after 1919 the recommendations of Labour, which it is now said, had they been adopted by the Government, would have averted the present conditions of unemployment.

The Prevention of Unemployment Bill, 1919

On March 21, 1919, the Labour Party brought to second reading in the House of Commons their "Prevention of Unemployment Bill," which embodied only the old principles that Labour had been advocating since 1900, to meet seasonal and cyclical unemployment. The Bill in no sense met the present abnormal trade depression, and was rejected. It proposed to vest in the Minister of Labour all powers and duties in regard to unemployment insurance, the prevention of destitution, and the relief of the able-bodied poor. It provided that the Minister should advise the Treasury how the various Government works and services should be organized and apportioned over different seasons of each year, and spread over different years, so as "to regularize" the national aggregate demand for employment, including both public and private employment, as between the different seasons of the year, and as between the good and bad years of a trade cycle, and so, by maintaining at an approximately constant level the national aggregate demand for labour both by private employer and by public departments, prevent irregularity of employment. It also put the Minister under an obligation to establish and maintain such institutions as he should deem requisite, in which he was to provide for able-bodied persons entitled to public assistance under the Act, and for whom no suitable situation could be found, such employment of an educational character and such physical and mental and technological training as he should think fit. All persons admitted to such institutions were to be provided by the Minister with proper maintenance. The Bill in addition proposed to constitute as the local unemployment authority, who were to act through an unemployment committee, the London County Council in respect of the Administrative County of London, and the council of every borough and urban district of a population of 20,000 or over, and the county councils in respect of the rest of an administrative county. Each such council, acting through the unemployment committee, was to be bound to organize all work—manual or clerical—under its control, so as to maintain the labour demand in its district at a constant uniform level. In addition, each such council was to be put under obligation to provide every person, for whom suitable employment could not be found, with such maintenance as its medical officer of health might certify to be necessary to maintain such unemployed person and his dependents in a state of physical efficiency. All the expenses of the local unemployment authorities in carrying out the Act were to be met out of the local rates to the extent of a 1*d.* rate; all expenses over the proceeds of a 1*d.* rate were to be recovered from the Treasury. There was no limit whatever to the charge under the Bill[9] upon national funds.

Labour's Recommendations to the Industrial Conference, 1919

The next important declaration in 1919 by Labour in respect of unemployment is contained in the *Joint Report of the Provisional Joint Committee presented to the Meeting of the Industrial Conference, Central Hall, Westminster, April 4, 1919 (Parliamentary Paper, 1920, Cmd. 501)*. It will be remembered that on February 27, 1919, the Government called together, under the shadow of a miners' strike, a Conference consisting of representatives of employers and Trade Unions to consider the industrial situation. That Conference, after expressing its opinion that any preventible dislocation of industry was always to be deplored and in the then existing critical period of reconstruction might be disastrous to the interests of the nation, resolved to appoint a Joint Committee to consider, amongst other things, the question of unemployment and its prevention. A unanimous report was presented by the Joint Committee, signed by the employers' representatives and also by the Trade Unions' representatives, the latter representing all the great Trade Unions, with the exception of the railwaymen, the miners and the transport workers.

In their Report the Committee stated that they had not had sufficient time at their disposal to investigate thoroughly the problem of unemployment, and therefore would only indicate briefly some of the steps which might be taken to minimize it or alleviate it. As aids in this direction they recommended organized short-time, the working of overtime only in special cases, postponement, until bad times, of Government non-urgent contracts, prosecution without delay of a comprehensive housing programme, State development of new industries such as afforestation, reclamations of waste lands, development of inland waterways and, in agricultural districts, the development of light railways and/or road transport. In addition the Committee recommended that the normal provision for maintenance during unemployment should be on a more adequate scale, and be wider in its application than was provided by the then existing Unemployment Insurance Acts, and advocated the extension of the National Unemployment Insurance Scheme to underemployment (i.e. workers on short-time or casual employment for less than a full working week). They also recommended the provision of facilities whereby workers while unemployed and in receipt of unemployment benefit could obtain access without payment of fees to opportunities for continuing their education and improving their qualifications. Child-labour, they advised, should in times of unemployment be limited, and sickness and infirmity benefits increased, the age of qualification for old age pensions reduced and the amount of the pension increased.

The Right Hon. A. Henderson's Addendum

The Memorandum by the Right Hon. Arthur Henderson, on behalf of the Trade Unions' representatives, appended to the Report, dealt further with the question of unemployment. This Memorandum, while in no way disagreeing with the Joint Report which the Trade Union representatives had signed, stated that "the prevention of unemployment and provision against unemployment should have been one of the first thoughts of the Government as soon as the question of industrial reorganization began to be considered. The workers fully understood that steps were being taken to bring into immediate operation, upon the conclusion of hostilities, a permanent scheme both for the prevention of unemployment wherever possible, and for the maintenance of the unemployed where this could not be done." Further, "we are of opinion that the unequal distribution of wealth which prior to the war kept the purchasing power of the majority of the wage-earners at a low level, constituted a primary cause of unemployment." Then followed this finding: "We are of opinion that a general increase in wages by improving the purchasing power of the workers would have a general and permanent effect in the direction of limiting continuous unemployment by bringing consumption up to something more like equilibrium with production."

They accordingly recommended first:—the appointment of a sub-commission to investigate (1) the whole problem of unemployment and especially under-consumption as a cause of unemployment; (2) the allocation of all Government contracts in such a way as to steady the volume of employment, and (3) the co-ordination of orders given by State Departments and local authorities; secondly, the establishment of a comprehensive scheme of unemployment provision extending to all workers on a non-contributory basis, providing for adequate maintenance of all workers unemployed, and for the making up of maintenance pay to workers under-employed. All were to receive a flat rate of benefit with a supplementary allowance for dependent children. The scheme was to be administered directly through the Trade Unions, or, where such were not available, through the Employment Exchanges, which were to be placed under joint committees equally representative of employers and Trade Unions. The Government were to pay to a Trade Union, providing an additional benefit out of its own funds, a subsidy equivalent to 50 per cent. of the amount expended by the Union on unemployment allowances. In addition special provision was recommended for the maintenance of widows with dependent children and for the endowment of mothers "to prevent their being forced into industry against the interest of society."

The Southport Resolution of 1919

In June 1919, the Labour Party again considered at its Annual Conference the question of unemployment, and passed a resolution that full and adequate maintenance should be granted by the Government, through the Trade Unions concerned, for unemployed persons, mothers with dependent children and unable to work, juveniles leaving school and becoming unemployed below the age of eighteen, women receiving training under the Government's training schemes, and women whose out-of-work donation had ceased and who had not secured suitable work from the Labour Exchanges.

The Resolution of September 1919

Again, in September 1919, the Trades Union Congress passed a resolution affirming the right of every member of the community to work or to the receipt of maintenance, and accordingly called upon the Government to regulate national and local authorities' work, and to organize schemes of "socially necessary" work so as to provide employment, and, failing that, to provide adequate maintenance for all workers who could not find suitable employment, and facilities for training while they were out of work. This resolution contained this interesting sentence: "It deplored the inaction of the Government during the past year which had wasted the resources of the nation by allowing hundreds of thousands of willing workers to remain in a state of enforced idleness at a time when the needs of the world called imperatively for increased production."

The decline in trade and failure of demand for commodities first appeared in the summer of 1920, and gradually increased in severity as that year went on.

The Recommendations of the Joint Committee on Cost of Living, September 1920

In September 1920, a Joint Committee on the Cost of Living was appointed by the Labour and Co-operative movements. That Committee made certain recommendations which were not original but a mere reiteration of matters which the Government had previously indicated were of prime importance in connection with the restoration of international trade. The measures which this Committee claimed to be essential for the revival of industry and restoration of trade were as follows:

(1) The re-establishment of international peace;

(2) The definite fixing of war indemnities at reasonable amounts;

(3) Rehabilitation of currencies;

(4) In countries where a return to the gold standard was impracticable, the establishment of a new parity of exchange;

(5) The exchange of goods between different countries by barter pending re-establishment of the machinery of exchange;

(6) An international loan by the League of Nations to enable impoverished countries to resume normal production.

But there was nothing in this programme which was not at this time well under the consideration of the Government.

Vote of Censure in Parliament, October 1920

On October 21, 1920 (see *Parliamentary Debates*, Vol. 133, 1115), the Labour Party unsuccessfully moved a vote of censure in the following terms:

> "That this House views with regret the growing volume of unemployment, and, recognizing the responsibility of the State towards members of the community who are bereft of the means of livelihood, is of opinion that every possible step should be taken to arrest the decline in trade and industry and to provide work or, in default, adequate maintenance for those whose labour is not required in the ordinary market."

The current views of the Labour members in respect of unemployment were very fully stated, and the parliamentary debate should be read. Shortly put, their points were these:

(1) The unemployment problem is a national problem; it can only be successfully solved by the State; it ought not to be left for local treatment by local authorities.

(2) Work should be found by the Government for every workless citizen, willing to work, and, failing that, adequate maintenance.

(3) The volume of agriculture should be increased and smallholdings encouraged.

(4) Trade relations should be established with Russia, Bulgaria, Turkey, and other former enemy countries.

(5) The Government should establish new trades and industries in this country.

(6) Public works should be undertaken, like afforestation, main and other roads.

Critically read, the debate seems strangely barren of any really constructive suggestions by the Labour Party.

Later, on December 16, 1920, the Labour Party sent a deputation to the Minister of Labour to urge him to accept the following propositions in regard to unemployment:

(1) That unemployment insurance is no remedy;

(2) That it is the Government's duty to provide for the unemployed useful work in various Government establishments;

(3) That a grant should be made to the Distress Committees under the Unemployed Workmen's Act, 1905, in order that local schemes for the provision of work might be put in hand;

(4) That the principle of the out-of-work donation granted after the armistice should be restored for the benefit of every unemployed person not covered by unemployment insurance, and that provision should be made whereby persons at present unemployed, but not covered by the Unemployment Insurance Act, would receive benefits under that Act.

This last point was conceded by the Government subsequently in the House of Commons.

Resolution of December 1920

On December 29, 1920, the Labour Party Conference, called to consider the report of the Labour Commission in Ireland, proceeded somewhat inconsequentially to discuss the problem of unemployment in Great Britain and subsequently passed the following resolution:

> "That this Conference, realizing that the growing volume of unemployment and under-employment is due in a large measure to the interruption in world trading following on the war and the defective peace treaties, in addition to the folly of British and allied policy in relation to the Soviet Government of Russia, condemns the British Government for the unwarrantable delay in securing peace and opening trade relationships with the Russian Government.

> "The Conference further condemns the Coalition Government for failing to make provision for the prevention of unemployment and for the proper treatment of unemployed persons; it calls attention to the fact that in February 1920, the Labour Party in Parliament introduced its Bill for the prevention of unemployment, containing

provisions for the maintenance and training of unemployed persons, which the Government refused to accept."

The last paragraph of this resolution is important. It has been customary in recent years for Socialist advocates to assure the workmen that unemployment can never exist under any of the types of socialistic organization of industry, but that it is an evil peculiar to what they call the "capitalistic regime," and that unemployment is merely one of the devices of the employer to break down Trade Union conditions and so lower wages. How exactly the consumer, who, after all, is the person who really controls the production of commodities, is to be persuaded to consume and pay for more commodities under a socialistic organization of industry than under a capitalistic system is not-perhaps wisely so-explained, but the suggestion of the final paragraph is that were the present "pernicious economic system" abolished and the Labour Party in power, then if its Government were unable to provide work it could and would provide maintenance and, the ordinary worker is told, at full Trade Union rates of wages. As to how such scheme is to be financed the resolution is sagaciously silent.

Labour's Refusal to Co-operate with the Government, 1921

In January 1921, the Government decided to set up two Committees on unemployment and invited Labour to join one of the Committees. Labour took the view that the terms of reference were too narrow to serve any useful purpose, whereupon the Government at once expressed its willingness to widen the terms, but on January 11, at a Joint Committee of the Parliamentary Committee of the Trades Union Congress and the Executive Committee of the Labour Party, it was unanimously decided that Labour would not accept the invitation of the Government to join in any inquiry into unemployment. The public resentment aroused by that attitude soon convinced the Labour movement that it had put itself entirely in the wrong, and it tried energetically to put the blame for its decision on the Government. Labour leaders charged the Government with lack of frankness and straightforwardness in regard to the terms of reference, without giving any corroborative particulars whatsoever beyond that unsubstantiated general statement; they contended that co-operation with the Government had never led to anything—forgetting entirely the many benefits which during the war were secured to Labour both in rates of wages and conditions of employment wholly through co-operation with the Government. Truly memories were short. Then finally Labour unconvincingly charged the Government with failing to keep faith, or, if faith had been kept, with keeping it unwillingly and ungraciously, and only as a result of Labour's agitation. The first proof adduced in support of this latter contention was the action of the Government in regard to the Joint Industrial Conference of 1919. The Conference, Labour said, was originally called by the Government; the Joint Committee presented a unanimous report which the Conference accepted; the Government took no action to give effect to the recommendations of the report and the Committee ultimately resigned, and the Conference dissolved. The second case on which Labour relied was that of the Royal Commission on the Coal Industry of 1919; the majority findings recommended alteration of the then existing system of control of the mining industry; "to these the Government refused to give effect." The inaccuracy of this statement will be seen from Chapter XIV. The Government would not accept nationalization. "Labour," so it was declared, "has lost all faith in the good intentions of the Government, and refuses to allow itself to be used once again as a smoke screen."

Labour's Statement of Policy for Unemployment, 1921

As a counterblast to the Government's Committees of January 1921, the Labour Party in that month produced an elaborate programme to deal with unemployment. This will be found in a pamphlet entitled *Unemployment: A Labour Policy*, issued in January 1921. The whole of the suggestions fall under two main heads:

(1) Maintenance of the unemployed and under-employed, and

(2) Provision of work.

The categorical demand was repeated that work should be provided by the Government, and that if work is not, or cannot be, provided, then all unemployed and under-employed should be fully maintained at the expense of the State.

In regard to unemployment benefit, every one for whom no suitable work was available at the Employment Exchanges, or through his or her Trade Union, was to be paid maintenance, which, including benefits under the Unemployment Insurance Acts, should amount at least to 40s. per week for each householder and 25s. per week for each single man or woman over eighteen, with additional allowances for dependants. Increases in these rates were subsequently claimed as the year went on. Neither maintenance nor benefits under the Unemployment Insurance Acts should be limited to any period of time, but should continue as long as no suitable work was available. In the case of under-employment resulting from short-time, the maintenance allowance should be of such an amount as, when added to the actual earnings, would yield a sum equal to the amount of maintenance which the worker would receive if he were totally unemployed.

Training schools were to be provided for women attracted into industry during the war but who, after the war, found themselves unable to secure permanent peace employment. The local educational authorities, assisted by grants from the Exchequer, were to provide courses of training for unemployed male workers. To relieve adult unemployment the Board of Education should be authorized at any time to raise the school-leaving age, and should be restrained from discouraging local educational authorities from making by-laws raising the age of full-time attendance. Local education authorities should be urged to submit fresh schemes for schools, etc., under the Education Act of 1918. Any exemption from school attendance below the age of fourteen to be made illegal; local education authorities to proceed with schemes of "continuation education"; the Government to increase the number of free places in secondary schools and provide maintenance allowances to all free-place pupils in need of them. The number of free-places in all centres of higher education to be increased, maintenance allowances to be given under grant from the Board of Education to persons holding such places; training centres for young persons unemployed to be opened by local educational authorities under grants from the Board of Education.

"Socially necessary" work was to be provided for all. This was to be facilitated by the withdrawal of juvenile labour, and the general introduction of a 44-hour week without reduction of wages, coupled with a drastic regulation of overtime. The work so provided should not be "relief works," but of a "socially productive character" carried out under regular wage-earning employment by workpeople in the appropriate trades. Work merely providing employment for the unemployed without social results was characterized as wasteful for the community and demoralizing to the workers.

The Labour Party tries of set policy to make the Government the scapegoat; so the Report delivered itself as follows:

> "We recognize that the insensate policy of the Government during the last two years both in home and foreign affairs has brought the nation to the point at which wholesale relief is the only alternative to wholesale starvation, and that those who suffer by it must be provided for directly out of the pockets of those more fortunately situated."

In order to increase the volume of employment the Government was enjoined to put in hand, at once, as much as possible of its works programme for the next decade, and cause commodities ultimately needed by the State to be manufactured forthwith; and local authorities and public bodies were similarly called upon to anticipate their requirements. Road improvements were demanded on a much larger scale, and afforestation and foreshore reclamation. Then came the recommendation that the Government should compose its differences with the Building Trade Unions by giving them a guarantee of an adequate minimum housing programme for the next five years, so as to meet "their reasonable claim for safeguards against unemployment"—this to induce the Building Trade Unions, who had more housing work than they could do, to allow unemployed unskilled men, mainly ex-service men, to enter temporarily the building trade! The report alleged that many raw materials and other necessary supplies were being held up by capitalists, for instance, cement, bricks, light castings; to remedy this supposititious state of affairs the Government was urged to take drastic steps to compel the production of these materials in the required quantities. An enormous amount of work in respect of the construction, improvement and repair of railways, roads, waterways and harbours, it was said, ought no longer to be postponed. Schools and other public buildings should be built. The embargoes laid upon borrowing by local authorities should be removed and loans provided for them through the Public Works Commissioners or otherwise by the State to enable them to carry out local public works. The Government was required to resume through county agricultural committees its war-time powers to enforce the proper cultivation of land.

Then follows a series of measures for the restoration of overseas commerce. The root of the problem of unemployment lay, it was said, in the revival of industry and of commerce abroad. "The Government had shirked that duty," and these were Labour's demands:

(a) An end to be put to wars, and all expenditure on armaments and semi-warlike expeditions in this and other countries.

(b) The immediate inception of trade with Russia, and normal political relations with the Soviet Republic. The Russian Government was known to be ready to supply to this country large quantities of timber, hide, flax, platinum and gold in payment of extensive supplies which it needed of railway equipment, means of transport, agricultural machinery, implements of all kinds, clothing, boots, and a thousand and one other commodities. This necessitated and justified the immediate conclusion of an effective trade agreement with Russia.

(c) The restoration of production in, and trade with, other continental countries, but not under the export credits scheme of the British Government—which is "merely an attempt to enable British manufacturers to palm off their surplus goods upon foreign countries instead of supplying the goods to those countries which they really need." The ordinary normal course of international trade is then described, with this naïve observation.

"At present, however, conditions in Central Europe are such that, without further assistance, it is very doubtful if this normal trade transaction would be carried out." The report is most admirable in its modesty as to what "further assistance" it recommends. We may assume that if a recommendation had been available, that would stand criticism, it would have been proffered.

The only proposals which the Report advocated were as follows:

(1) The fixing of the German indemnity at an amount which is both reasonable and practicable in order to end uncertainty and encourage the re-establishment in Germany of normal production.

(2) Credits to be provided for "several European countries" (unfortunately left anonymous), and to be devoted to the production of commodities of which there is no danger of overproduction, and the provision of transport facilities; the granting of these credits to be conditional on the removal by the benefiting-state of all barriers against trade and on rehabilitation of its currency.

(3) All Governments boldly to intervene to arrange on a large scale the barter of whole stocks of surplus commodities. "This, while yielding no profit to speculators, would do much to revive economic prosperity and set going the wheels of industry."

(4) The reorganization of the continental transport systems and the institution of unified control, under the League of Nations, of the railway system between Germany and Russia.

(5) The encouragement and fullest possible use, for trade transactions, of the Co-operative movements of the various nations of Europe.

The Report expressed a halting agreement that large sums of money would be required in respect of the maintenance of unemployed and under-employed, the undertaking of work of social utility, and the financing of schemes for the revival of British industry and the restoration of industry and commerce abroad. It did not attempt to discuss how this money was to be provided; it disposed of the whole question by this facile observation: "We shall be met at once by the criticism that sufficient money cannot be found to meet our demands. We do not believe it. We refuse to be put off during this grave national crisis, imperilling the welfare of the whole population, with pleas of financial stringency." Reference was made to large sums of money which, it was stated, were being spent by the Government on unjustifiable purposes, for example, on expeditions in Mesopotamia, operations in Ireland and in other places. Money, instead of being so expended, should be devoted to the relief of unemployment. If such retrenchment of military and other wasteful expenditure did not yield the total sum required, then, said the Labour Party, "other resources must be tapped," but those resources are not indicated. "While an increasing number of families are daily sinking into starvation, the well-to-do classes have suffered only minor embarrassments. Luxuries must go, if needs be, to provide the means of life and livelihood for those in distress." Hardly a constructive financial scheme.

Manifesto on Unemployment, 1921

The last important announcement was the *Manifesto on Unemployment* issued by the Parliamentary Committee of the Trades Union Congress and the National Executive of the Labour Party after the Trades Union Congress at Cardiff in 1921, "for the information of the Government and the public." It declared, in now familiar language, that unemployment is a national problem, and that the Government is wholly wrong in adopting measures of local treatment. No district, it is asserted, has any control over, or any responsibility for, its unemployment. To make districts responsible is to subject working-class areas of low rateable value to excessive and unjust burdens which they cannot bear and which ought in equity to be spread over the whole country. The Party expressed its strong objection to the limited advances made by the State to the local authorities in respect of relief works, especially to the necessity for so much expenditure being raised by local loans, by that method placing, it was said, the burden upon the backs of ratepayers of the very areas whose affliction was already the greatest. Once again the Trades Union Congress at Cardiff reaffirmed what was described as the fundamental principle—"the duty of the State to provide work or adequate maintenance for every willing worker." Accordingly the Government was required to discontinue countenancing wage reductions, and to stimulate normal production by maintaining the purchasing power of the workers and thereby sustain the whole market. It is also affirmed that sufficient orders for work to relieve unemployment will not be forthcoming except on the basis of national credit. The Government Departments are urged to anticipate, and now place orders for, their future needs, and the Government itself is recommended to place substantial orders for staple commodities with manufacturers, at prices agreed after an examination of costs, and to export these commodities on credit to continental countries needing them, selling them either directly to the Governments of those countries or to Co-operative Societies or other organizations in them, and at the same time to arrange for the sale or other disposal at home of any remaining portions of the stocks of such commodities. In addition a 40-hour working week should be introduced. This, it is said, would result in (i) the maintenance of the morale and efficiency of the people; (ii) the maintenance of machinery in working order pending the return of normal trade; (iii) the maintenance and improvement of the home trade and the stimulation of foreign commerce; (iv) the saving of enormous sums on unemployment benefit and poor law relief. So, it was claimed, the problem of unemployment could be reduced to proportions capable of being adequately dealt with by public works. These formed the next consideration. The Government was requested to prepare a list of schemes of national works in the order of their demand for labour, giving preference to those most calculated to foster the revival of industry, comprehensive housing schemes to be included prominently amongst them. The Government's distinction between schemes of public works as revenue producing and non-revenue producing, it was admitted, was sound, and should be maintained, but in the case of the former, the Government should make a grant of 75 per cent. of the necessary expenditure and lend the remaining 25 per cent. to local authorities free of interest for three years, the rate of interest thereafter being 3 per cent., with arrangements for repayment at stated intervals. In the case of non-productive schemes, the Government to make a grant of 90 per cent. of the necessary expenditure and lend the remaining 10 per cent. to local authorities free of interest for five years, at the end of which time interest and repayment should be the same as in the case of the productive schemes. "If, however, employment is still not forthcoming for all workers, provision for maintenance must be made by means of unemployment insurance benefits on an adequate scale."

In Part II of this book it will be seen how far the Government has gone for the purpose of alleviating unemployment in the directions desired by Labour.

CHAPTER XI
THE LABOUR PARTY'S POLICY
FOR UNEMPLOYMENT

2. ITS IMPRACTICABILITY

The utter impracticability of Labour's principle of "work or maintenance" is almost self-apparent. The primary cause of unemployment is want of work, the result of economic forces, but the cure of unemployment, according to Labour, is to be the provision of work by the Government in the teeth of adverse economic conditions. The work is to be "suitable work," and obviously must be either (1) the production of commodities and services which the consuming public will buy, that is to say, remunerative work, or (2) the execution of public works which, up to that time, have not been constructed, but which, although economic circumstances have not justified their construction before, are deemed proper to be carried out if work has to be found for unemployed persons. Their appropriate name is "relief works." The maintenance is to be such weekly sum as the local medical officer of health deems necessary to maintain each unemployed person and his dependants in a state of physical efficiency. The Unemployed Workmen's Bill, introduced by Mr. Ramsay MacDonald in 1907, was the first Bill enunciating the right to work. In 1908-9 similar Bills were introduced by the Labour Party under the same title. In 1910-11-12, Bills for the same object, called The Right to Work Bill, were introduced by members of the Party.

The Unsoundness of the Right to Work

Attempts were made to describe this principle of work or maintenance as the logical result of the Elizabethan Statutes, under which parish authorities were bound to provide work for the unemployed at wages paid out of a fund collected from persons of substance in the parish, at first voluntarily subscribed, but later raised by tax, and were accustomed to grant "relief in lieu of labour" to persons out of work, for whom work could not be found. Owing to the difficulty of finding work the overseers resorted largely to the latter alternative. The Labour Party's Bill, needless to say, omitted the stern Elizabethan methods provided by law for treatment of the work-shy—whipping, boring through the ear—and for those who ran away, imprisonment for life. The social and industrial abuses to which the system gave rise in the early days of the nineteenth century are well described by Mr. Harold Cox in Chapter 5, "The Right to Work," of his book *Economic Liberty*. It is to be feared Mr. Thomas Pearce, labourer in husbandry, who was examined before the Poor Law Commissioners of 1834, would even to-day experience similar treatment.

> "Asked whether in his parish there were many able-bodied men 'upon the parish,' he replied:
>
> "*Ans.* There are a great many men in our parish who like it better than being at work.
>
> "*Ques.* Why do they like it better?
>
> "*Ans.* They get the same money and don't do half so much work. They don't work like me; they be'ant at it so many hours, and they don't do so much work when they be at it. They're doing no good, and are only waiting for dinner-time and night; they be'ant working, it's only waiting.
>
> "*Ques.* How have you managed to live without parish relief?
>
> "*Ans.* By working hard.
>
> "*Ques.* What do the paupers say to you?
>
> "*Ans.* They blame me for what I do. They say to me, 'What are you working for?' I say, 'For myself.' They say, 'You are only doing it to save the parish, and if you didn't do it you would get the same as another man has, and would get the money for smoking your pipe and doing nothing.' 'Tis a hard thing for a man like me."

The Failure of Work or Maintenance in France

One would have thought the experience of the French Revolutionary Government of 1848 would have been conclusive as to the right to work. Louis Blanc had published, in 1839, his great work, *Organisation du Travail*, in which he preached the right to work and urged on the French Government the advantages of its embarking on industrial production. The Government was to raise a large loan, and with it establish and equip national factories in every branch of industry. Workmen were to be employed, but were to determine by popular election the grades of the different workers. The net profits were to be divided into three parts, one to be distributed equally among the workers, the second to be devoted to the maintenance of the old, incapacitated and the sick, the third to provide capital for extensions and renewals of the industry. The French Government appointed Emile Thomas to set up *ateliers nationaux*, having previously issued a decree that the Provisional Government of the French Republic bound itself to guarantee the existence of the worker by means of work and to guarantee work for all its citizens. The comic and the tragic side of that great adventure are well described in *Histoire des Ateliers Nationaux*, by Emile Thomas, and in *The Right to Work*, by J. A. R. Marriott, M.P., Oxford University Press, and are too well-known to require repetition. They proved a disastrous industrial and economic failure, which of itself led directly to the revolution of June 1848.

Impossibility of Providing Suitable Work

At one time Labour proposed that only work should be provided for every unemployed person, not "suitable work," but the ludicrous absurdity of this proposal became too obvious when it was seen to involve, for example, the transference of the skilled shipwright or boilermaker from the Tyne or the Clyde to work on afforestation in the Highlands of Scotland, or on roadmaking, or some other work of which they had no experience, in another remote part of the country. Now the demand has been modulated into one for "suitable work," which, at any rate, looks more sensible on paper. Whatever chance, however, there may be of finding some work for persons unemployed, there is much less scope for finding suitable work. The lines of demarcation, which confine in water-tight compartments the work of every trade, are so closely drawn, and the determination of every Trade Union is so inflexible as to allow at no time any other person than its own members to engage upon the work of its particular trade, that at times of trade depression it is most difficult to find suitable work. If no suitable work can be found in the district, it can hardly be suggested that in times of depression shipwrights and boilermakers on the Clyde, if they are out of work, should be moved to other places, for example, to the Tyne or the Mersey, where there would be, from the nature of things, local men of their own craft available.

Employment Depends Primarily on Demand

If workers are employed to produce commodities and services, and nobody wants to buy them, it is obviously absurd to place workers on that class of production. On the other hand, if they are called upon to produce commodities and services which people do want and are prepared to buy at a remunerative price, those goods and services can, and ought to, be provided by the ordinary machinery of industry which is normally engaged upon their production; to put unemployed upon that work is merely to compete with, and undercut, those workers who are ordinarily engaged upon that species of output, and throw them out of employment, making the case no better than before. The truth is, as Mr. Harold Cox so forcibly puts it in *Economic Liberty*, p. 74:

> "It becomes clear that we cannot increase the sum-total of paid employment unless we also increase the volume of commodities and conveniences which all men want. None of the schemes ever proposed for State employment for the unemployed do this. They are all designed not to produce things that somebody wants, but to provide an excuse for paying wages to people who cannot find work. In every case the work is made for the sake of the workman, and that very fact implies that the work is not wanted for its own sake."

That brings us directly to the question of "relief works." The only economic justification for them is, that when, on humanitarian grounds, payments have to be made out of public or municipal funds for the maintenance of unemployed persons and their dependants, it is better, instead of giving a dole without requiring any work, to ask for work which may confer some benefit on the community paying wages for it. The irony of the position is that the Trade Unions always ask that the wages paid shall be full Trade Union rates, forgetting entirely that the work is not remunerative work and that it is not at the time wanted by the community, but only provided by the community at an economic loss.

The Farm Colony Fiascos

We have had some experience of attempts to provide "remunerative work."

The Hollesley Bay Farm Colony was established in 1905 by the Central Unemployed Body; the total expenditure on it between 1905 and March 31, 1912, was £178,253, the total realized by sales of produce of the colony during the same period was £41,755, showing a net loss during that time of £136,498. (See *Sixth Report Central (Unemployment) Body*, 1913, pp. 7 and 16.) Mr. John Burns, President of the Local Government Board, speaking in the House of Commons, March 13, 1908 (*Parliamentary Debates*, Vol. 186, 70), said in regard to the Hollesley Bay colony: "The labour and the work of these men is brought into competition with the local market gardeners and farmers, and when I go down to Hollesley Bay I am confronted with small deputations of professional decent agricultural labourers and servants of market gardeners, complaining of the fact that our attempt, well-intentioned, charitably inclined, and fed with State money, on behalf of the unemployed, is dispossessing the decent agricultural labourer." The South Ockenden Farm Colony was established by the West Ham Guardians. Mr. John Burns said, in regard to it: "In the whole time that that colony has been in operation—and no one will but admit that I have given it the most generous and the most fatherly assistance—out of the 790 who have gone through that colony, its object being to train men for the land and to take them back to the land, there is not a recorded instance of the men going back to agricultural work" (*Parliamentary Debates*, Vol. 186, 70). On the same occasion Mr. Burns referred to the Laindon colony established by the Poplar Guardians: "I saw an old agricultural labourer between sixty and sixty-five years old, digging in a field within 200 yards of the colony, getting 15s. or 16s. per week"—Mr. Burns had previously mentioned that the average cost per week per man on the colony was 24s.—"I said to him, 'How long does it take you to dig an acre of land?' He said, 'It takes me a fortnight to dig an acre of that land.' I went across the rail and found on the public works sixty-seven able-bodied men ... taking ten days to dig an acre and a half." Thus, in the colony each man was digging at the rate of one acre in 446 days, while the old agricultural labourer on the adjoining land was digging one acre in 14 days. It will be remembered that the express object of the Central Unemployed Body in setting up these colonies was to provide productive work for the unemployed. No wonder that Mr. Burns, with his great experience, expressed himself in the following terms, July 19, 1906 (*Parliamentary Debates*, Vol. 161, 425):—

> "I believe that relief works ought to be the last resort of any community. They sterilize volition, sap self-reliance, and introduce into industry those very conditions of irregularity and low pay which we are seeking to remove.... If the works are State-aided, charity-fed, tax-founded, or rate-subsidized, they will only be a form of public benevolence that will divert the right money in the wrong way to wasteful ends with demoralizing results. New works unproductive and unremunerative, fed by rates and taxes, are about the worst form of relief that can be imagined."

Mr. Burns's conclusion will be confirmed by every person who has any experience of relief works. The work done is per unit immensely more costly than if it were done under normal industrial conditions; the men know it is not serious work, and therefore do not work.

If relief works have to be provided—and the unemployed cannot be left to starve—what the works shall be, the conditions under which they shall be executed, the extent to which the State ought to go, raise extraordinarily difficult questions calling for the nicest judgment.

It is wholly unnecessary to emphasize the evil of doles, whatever form they take, whether Poor Law outdoor relief or anything else. I have had many cases under my personal notice of men who, being offered work at reasonable rates of pay, refused to take it, stating that they were doing better out of their various payments for unemployment—and they were.

PART II
GOVERNMENT LABOUR POLICY

CHAPTER XII
WAR-TIME LABOUR REGULATION
AND ITS EFFECTS

Many of our industrial difficulties to-day are due to the effect that the war, and especially the measures which it was necessary for Government to take during the war, have had upon the psychology of the workers. To attempt a description of those measures in their entirety would be wholly outside the scope of this book; those who wish to study them will find a full and lucid description in *Labour Supply and Regulation*, by Mr. Humbert Wolfe, C.B.E., shortly to be published by the Oxford University Press. I am only concerned to deal with them so far as they provide guidance for future policy.

Co-operation between Employers and Unions at Beginning of War

The most remarkable feature of the early days of the war was the spontaneous co-operation between employers and workpeople. On August 4, 1914, the Clyde shipbuilding and engineering employers and employees unanimously agreed to recommend their respective constituents to assist in every possible way all firms employed on urgent Government work. On August 10, a similar recommendation was adopted by the shipbuilding and engineering employers and employees on the Tyne. The matter was carried still further; on August 25, at a Joint Committee of the Parliamentary Committee of the Trades Union Congress, the Management Committee of the General Federation of Trade Unions and the Executive Committee of the Labour Party, the meeting resolved that a strenuous effort should be made to terminate all existing trade disputes, and that whenever new points of difficulty should arise during the war, a determined attempt should be made by all concerned to reach an amicable settlement before resorting to a strike or lock-out. The spirit of this resolution was carried into immediate effect.

In July 1914, there were in existence over 100 trade disputes, implicating 72,000 men; this number fell to twenty during August, in which only 9,000 workpeople were concerned; at the beginning of 1915 the number was reduced to ten, and in February 1915, to none at all. The number of fresh disputes which arose between August and December 1914, was very small. That showed the effect that clear appreciation of the national needs had both upon employers and employed.

The Unsettling Effect of Shortage of Labour

This happy state, unfortunately, did not long continue; and looking back the reasons are now quite clear. When the war broke out unemployment was generally feared, so much so that a Government Committee on the Prevention and Relief of Distress was appointed which invited mayors and provosts throughout the country to form local committees to deal with unemployment. The Local Government Board urged local authorities to expedite public work; even the Director of Army Contracts appended to Government contracts a memorandum advising contractors that in executing the work they should arrange for the employment of as large a number of men as possible instead of working overtime. By December 1915, not unemployment, but a grave shortage of skilled engineering workmen proved to be the national difficulty. Various attempts were made to remedy the shortage; first, by transferring skilled men from commercial work to munitions work; next, by obtaining the release of skilled men from the Colours; thirdly, by importing skilled Belgian refugees and mechanics from Canada; fourthly, in some districts, by forming "king's squads" or mobile companies to work wherever they were most needed. All these methods proved quite inadequate and the sole remaining course left open was to make the best use of the skilled men who were actually available, that is to say, to remove them from work on which unskilled men or women could be employed and up-grade them on to the most difficult skilled work which only a tradesman could undertake, or put them as supervisors over the unskilled labour so brought in. This is what was popularly known as "dilution," but its successful introduction involved a definite suspension of Trade Union customs.

In the late autumn of 1914, it was discussed at various conferences between the employers' federations and the unions, but without success. In January 1915, the Government entrusted the problem to the Board of Trade, and in February the Committee on Production under the chairmanship of Lord (then Sir George) Askwith was appointed to formulate a programme for Government action. It is easy, of course, to be wise after the event, but it was an unfortunate circumstance, and deprecated by employers themselves, that it should, in the first instance, have been left to "Capital" to propose to the Trade Unions suspension of customs and practices which the Trade Unions had spent years in establishing, and which were regarded by the average workman as the bulwarks of his trade rights. All these customs, for example, the limitation of apprentices; the restriction on the working of certain machines by skilled men only; the remuneration of overtime; the limitation of output; the exclusion of women and also of men who had not served an engineering apprenticeship, were designed for the purpose of building up a system under which the Trade Union craftsman would have a monopoly of his trade, and be secured as far as possible against unemployment. It was regarded by the men as the natural instinct of every employer to break through these rules, and so, by securing the right to bring in unskilled labour, to reduce the standard of wages of skilled men. In spite of all undertakings by employers that the alterations in working conditions would be only for the period of the war, the workmen were never convinced that such measures were really necessary in the interests of the country or anything but devices of unscrupulous employers. Had Government in the first instance undertaken the negotiation of these proposals, and not left it to the employers, the history of munitions production would have been very different.

The "Treasury" Agreements of March 1915

It was the Trade Unions themselves who represented to the Government that if anything was to be done in the direction of suspending trade customs, the Government would have to take the matter into their own hands. So, in March 1915, a conference was held at the Treasury, when the Cabinet made a direct appeal to the Trade Unions of the country, and concluded a treaty known as the "Treasury" Agreement which, had it been successful, would have secured for the war period a suspension of strikes and of all restrictions upon output. The treaty, however, turned out to be completely ineffective, and the cause is illuminating. At the beginning of March the cost of living had gone up, according to the Board of Trade statistics, to 15 to 20 per cent. above the July 1914 figure. There was a general outburst throughout the country against profiteering; Labour reprinted and circulated Mr. Bonar Law's famous statement that "well-managed ships to-day are making simply enormous profits, and those profits come from the very cause for which the people of this country are making sacrifices in every direction and even giving their lives" (*Parliamentary Debates*, 1915, Vol. 69,793). The result was an immediate increase in strikes. The following were the stoppages of work reported to the Board of Trade:

Number of disputes in progress at beginning of 1915, 10.

During	January	1915	30	fresh disputes.
"	February	"	47	" "
"	March	"	74	" "
"	April	"	44	" "
"	May	"	63	" "

The Limitation of Employers' Profits

The Amalgamated Society of Engineers was represented at the Treasury Conference; its representatives, however, had been instructed not to agree to any scheme until they had reported it to, and obtained upon it the instructions of, their Executive Council. On that becoming known to the Government, the Chancellor of the Exchequer convened another conference on March 25, 1915, at the Treasury with the Amalgamated Society of Engineers, and a further agreement was there signed. At the conference the Amalgamated Society of Engineers insisted that the Government should take steps to regulate employers' profits, arguing that it was unfair to prevent the workman from using his tremendously increased economic power and at the same time leave employers free to use theirs. A supplemental agreement was then made with the Amalgamated Society of Engineers containing this clause: "That it is the intention of the Government to conclude arrangements with all important firms engaged wholly or mainly upon engineering or shipbuilding work for war purposes under which their profits will be limited with a view to securing that benefit, resulting from the relaxation of trade restrictions or practices, should accrue to the State." The national need for limiting employers' profits had been emphasized previously by the Committee on Production. This recommendation had the strong approval of Lord Kitchener; speaking in the House of Lords on March 15 (see *Parliamentary Debates*, 1915, H. of L., Vol. 18,723) he said: "Labour may very rightly ask that their patriotic work should not be used to inflate the profits of the directors and shareholders of the various great industrial and armament firms, and we are therefore arranging a system under which the important armament firms will come under Government control, and we hope that workmen who work regularly by keeping good time shall reap some of the benefits which the war automatically confers on these great companies." Negotiations were undertaken by the Government with various armament and shipbuilding firms with a view to the Government taking possession of them, but these broke down and the Government abandoned the idea. Other negotiations to limit, first, dividends, and then, alternatively, net divisible profits, also collapsed and nothing came of them. The fact that workmen were prevented from forcing higher wages while employers were left free to make higher profits completely nullified the "Treasury" Agreements and something had to be done. On June 9, 1915, the Ministry of Munitions was constituted by Act of Parliament. Immediate steps were taken to draft the Bill which afterwards became the Munitions of War Act, 1915. The Government appreciated the importance of getting the Bill agreed to by Labour, as indeed they ultimately succeeded in doing. The first point on which Labour insisted was the limitation of profits of the employers. This was ultimately provided in Section 5. It only applied to "controlled establishments," and until the later introduction of the Excess Profits Duty the owners of non-controlled establishments were allowed to make such profits as they thought fit. But it was shutting the stable door after the steed was stolen. Throughout the war, Labour never got rid of the notion that the profits of employers were not restricted until Labour had forced the Government to restrict them, and that even then the restriction was on a wholly inadequate scale.

Failure of Compulsory Arbitration

The substantial effect of the Munitions of War Act, 1915, was to give statutory force to the "Treasury" Agreements. The obligations which the Act imposed upon the owners of controlled establishments were substantially the safeguards for Labour contained in the "Treasury" Agreements, and upon Labour the provisions contained in those Agreements preventing stoppages of work. Part I of the Act provided for the settlement of labour differences and in certain cases for the prohibition of strikes and lock-outs, and for compulsory arbitration. It might well be thought that the circumstances of the war provided a unique occasion for the success of compulsory arbitration, but it was a failure, signal and complete. A great many Unions at first acquiesced in arbitration because as long as prices continued to rise, advances of wages were more or less automatically awarded, so as to adjust wages to cost of living. When, however, the Unions refused to go to arbitration, or, if they went, to comply with the award, it was impossible to make them. If 100,000 men cease work it is impracticable to prosecute or fine all of them; to select a certain number soon raises cries of victimization, those prosecuted are made martyrs, and funds are raised by their colleagues for payment of their fines. While the pretence of enforcing awards was maintained for a certain time, everybody concerned in the administration of the Munitions Act knew that compulsory arbitration was a broken reed. This was proved in the very month the Act was passed, namely, June 1915, in the case of the miners' strike in South Wales. But in view of the absolute dead-lock at which collective negotiations between employers and trade unions had arrived by the end of 1914, it was essential for the Government to undertake the general regulation of labour itself, and the powers for doing so were conferred on the Minister of Munitions by the Munitions of War Act, 1915. Much adverse criticism has been levelled at the labour administration of the Ministry, but State regulation was the sole remaining remedy; if this be remembered, it must be conceded that labour was regulated as efficiently as circumstances allowed.

Effect of Relieving Employers of Responsibility for Labour Management

One unfortunate, though inevitable, effect of the Munitions of War Act, and the regulation of labour by the Ministry of Munitions, was the extent to which employers ceased to manage the labour in their own works. Though profits were limited, work was plentiful, and prices ample; they were assured of business without much effort on their part. In addition, many employers resented, and probably not unnaturally, the intervention of the Ministry of Munitions in labour disputes, and when disputes did arise, instead of endeavouring to settle them with the men, contented themselves with reporting them to the Ministry. On the other hand, Trade Unions found it an easier matter to report disputes to, and discuss them with, the Ministry rather than go to the trouble, as before the war, of discussing them with each individual firm. Whatever may have been the real cause, the effect undoubtedly was that the passing of the Munitions Act in 1915, inevitable as it was, has contributed materially to the aloofness which now exists between employers and their workers.

It was not in the normal administration of labour by the Ministry of Munitions that harm occurred—it was when, for political considerations, particular action was forced upon the Ministry by politicians, that real detriment was inflicted upon industry. An example of that is the famous 12½ per cent. bonus. It is well-known that the Ministry and the Admiralty were strongly opposed to that fatal action, but it was thought expedient for Government to try and placate Labour not merely in reference to then existing difficulties, but with a view to possible political developments, and so the bonus was given. As Director of Shipyard Labour of the Admiralty, with over a million men who would be affected by the decision, I strongly protested against it. My protest was registered on the War Cabinet minutes; I stated it would subject the country to an extra annual wages bill of 95 million sterling; I was wrong to the extent of 7 millions, it proved in the end to be 102 millions.

Increases of Wages and Prices

One important question is the position in which the war left the workmen so far as standard of living is concerned; that involves some consideration of wages and prices. It is unnecessary for me to discuss that at length; Professor Bowley in *Prices and Wages in the United Kingdom, 1914-1920*, Oxford University Press, has now most ably dealt with the matter, and reference should certainly be made to that book on this crucial question. In his speech on January 29, 1920, at the Annual Meeting of the London Joint City and Midland Bank, Ltd., the Right Hon. R. McKenna succinctly described how prices rose:

"At the outbreak of war, throughout its course, and right down to the present moment, the Government have been large buyers of commodities, greatly in excess of their normal demands. The first consequence of the immense Government purchases was to stimulate production. Machinery was used to its full capacity; the number of people employed was greatly increased; women took the place of men, and there was a very considerable addition to the total national output. But enlarge the output as we would, it could not keep pace with the nation's requirements. Demand outstripped supply, and, just as it happens when a period of comparative trade depression is succeeded by a trade boom, there was a natural rise in prices. At once more currency was needed, partly to pay the wages of the larger number of workpeople employed, partly because with higher prices shopkeepers keep more money in their tills. To the extent that more currency was issued the spending power of the community was increased. But up to this point the increase was not great. A new condition had to be introduced before any considerable rise could take place. There must be not merely an increase in currency, the total of which, in any case, only represents a small part of the public spending power; but, far more important, there must be a serious addition to Bank deposits. It was not long before this new condition arose. To meet the daily growing expenditure the Government had to borrow freely from the public, from the banks, and from the Bank of England. It is unnecessary to recapitulate the effects of this borrowing. Bank deposits increased enormously. There was no proportionate increase in the supply of goods and the usual consequences followed. Prices began to rise rapidly. The rise in prices was next followed by general demands for increased wages. As these now rose the cost of production rose too, and another turn was given to the screw on which prices were steadily mounting. But higher wages have got to be paid in legal tender money. In the course of the week the bulk of the money paid out in wages comes back through the shops to the Banks, and is paid out by them again to meet the next week's requirements. But, as prices and wages rise, not all of it comes back, and each week a larger amount is retained in the pockets of the people, in the tills of shopkeepers, and in the tills and reserves of the Banks.

"We may stop here to ask, is there any stage in this process at which it would have been proper to limit the issue of currency? The main demand for currency is to meet the weekly wages bill. If wages increase, whether because more workpeople are employed, or because rates are higher, additional currency must be brought each week into circulation. If the supply were cut off, a substitute would have to be found. At the outbreak of war there was not enough legal tender money to satisfy our additional requirements and at once postal orders and even postage stamps were used to make good the deficiency. If men and women are to be employed and paid, means of paying them must be found, and an arbitrary limitation of currency would merely inflict intolerable inconvenience upon the public."

Relation of Wages to Cost of Living

It is customary to measure the cost of living among the working-classes according to the basis of the Ministry of Labour. The Ministry works on an average pre-war working-budget of food, rent, clothing, light and fuel, and miscellaneous items, and ascertains its cost month by month. (See *Labour Gazette*, February 1921.) The cost in July 1914, is taken as 100, the greater cost each month since appearing as 100 and something; this is called the "index-number." What the Ministry does, therefore, is to measure the average increase in the cost of maintaining the pre-war standard of living of the working-classes; it does not, however, take in account any modification of the standard, which, of course, was customary; as for instance margarine used when butter was not obtainable. Lord Sumner's Committee on the Cost of Living to the Working Classes (*Parliamentary Paper*, 1918, Cd. 8980), showed by actual investigation that the index-numbers of the Ministry did not then represent current conditions, but were too high. On the other hand, the Joint Committee on the Cost of Living[10] is of the opinion the figures are under-estimates. All these matters are discussed very fully in the book by Professor Bowley, who gives his own modified index-numbers. Professor Bowley sums it up in these words: "There can be no doubt that some sections, especially the worst paid of the working-classes, were better off in the summer of 1920 than before the war, and it is probable that other sections were worse off. It is not possible to decide whether the average of all wages, measured in purchasing power, had risen or fallen." If, however, one takes the wages in certain trades, for example, railways, mining, and engineering, and compares them with the cost of living since July 1914, they appear in the following relation:

	Ministry of Labour Cost of Living Index.	Professor Bowley's Modified Index	Railway Wages.	Miners' Wages.	Engineers' Wages.	
					Skilled.	Unskilled.
July 1914	100	100	100	100	100	100
" 1915	125	(120)	110	113	110	—
" 1916	145	(135)	120	129	111	—
" 1917	180	(160)	155	136	134	154
" 1918	205	180	195	187	173	213
" 1919	210	185	225	224	199	255
" 1920	252	220	280	260	231	309

CHAPTER XIII
NORMAL GOVERNMENT LABOUR POLICY

Before the creation of the Ministry of Labour in 1916, a general surveillance of labour conditions was maintained by the Chief Industrial Commissioner's Department of the Board of Trade. The Ministry of Labour was formed in 1916 and absorbed the Chief Industrial Commissioner's Department, and took over also from the Board of Trade the administration of Unemployment Insurance, Trade Boards and Labour Exchanges.

Government Departments Concerned

The Statutes under which the Ministry of Labour acts are: Conciliation Act, 1896, and Industrial Courts Act, 1919, in relation to conciliation in, and settlement of, labour disputes; Labour Exchanges Act, 1909—establishment and administration of Employment Exchanges; Unemployment Insurance Acts—insurance against unemployment; Trade Boards Acts, 1909-1918— fixing of statutory minimum rates of wages. In addition, the Ministry has a number of temporary duties such as the training of men disabled in the war and of youths whose apprenticeship was interrupted by war service. Certain other branches of labour legislation are administered by other Government Departments as shown below: (1) The Factories and Workshops Acts and allied legislation dealing with the hours of employment of women and young persons, the health and safety of the workers, dangerous and unhealthy trades, etc., and the Shops Acts, regulating the hours of employment of shop assistants, by the Home Office; (2) Employment so far as dependent on the Education Acts, by the Board of Education; (3) The Mines Acts, regulating the hours and conditions of employment of persons employed underground in coal mines, by the Board of Trade (Mines Department); (4) The Health Insurance Acts, dealing with the insurance of workpeople against sickness, and the Workmen's Compensation Acts, dealing with compensation in the event of accidents arising out of, and in the course of, a workman's employment, by the Ministry of Health.

Conciliation and Arbitration

The general machinery for settlement of industrial disputes in this country by conciliation and arbitration is composed of (1) conciliation machinery within the industry, (2) State machinery. The former consists of voluntary machinery comprising (i) Joint Industrial Councils—these being bodies upon which organized employers and workpeople are equally represented, set up in a number of industries in accordance with the recommendations of a Committee appointed in 1916 and presided over by the Right Hon. J. H. Whitley, M.P., now the Speaker of the House of Commons; (ii) permanent voluntary conciliation boards—an older form of joint body equally representative of employers and workpeople, but differing from the Joint Industrial Councils in that the conciliation boards tend to confine their activities mainly to questions of wages and working conditions while the Councils take into consideration all matters appertaining to the industry; (iii) recognized procedure arranged by organizations of employers and workpeople, not having a formally constituted conciliation board, providing for the discussion of differences as and when they arise.

Whitley Councils

Up to the end of 1921 Joint Industrial Councils had been established in 73 industries and services; 15 are at present in suspense; 1 has been absorbed by another Council. In addition, there are 10 active Interim Industrial Reconstruction Committees in trades to which the Whitley Scheme cannot as yet be fully applied owing to lack of organization. The Joint Industrial Councils and Reconstruction Committees at present functioning cover about 3¾ million workpeople. The Whitley Scheme contemplates the establishment, under the National Joint Industrial Councils, of District Councils—equally representative of employers and employed—and Works' Committees, comprising management and men in equal numbers, and many such bodies have been formed. The activities of Joint Industrial Councils have been directed largely to the settlement of wages claims and the adjustment of working hours, two problems forced into special prominence by the abnormal economic conditions of the past few years. But other questions of working conditions, e.g. overtime payments, payments for holidays, walking-time allowances, out-working and subsistence allowances, fines for late arrivals have also been discussed by the Councils. Some have considered the problem of unemployment and arrangements for contracting out of the National Unemployment Insurance Scheme; others have prosecuted statistical investigations and research into their particular industries; all of them have considered questions of welfare in conjunction with the Home Office; certain of them have considered some commercial matters which affect their industries. The Government agreed to regard a Joint Industrial Council as the Standing Consultative Committee for its industry, and in a number of instances matters such as the foregoing have been discussed on the initiative of the Government. A few Joint Industrial Councils do not deal with wages questions, viz., building, boot and shoe, paper making, printing, and metallic bedsteads, as machinery for the settlement of wages existed in these trades before the Councils were established and it was thought by the industries better to continue such machinery. Certain industries in which organization of employers and employed is well developed, such as iron and steel, coal, cotton, engineering, shipbuilding, have not favoured the formation of a Joint Industrial Council. In them conciliation boards or some well-recognized machinery is in existence for the settlement of disputes.

These facts show the results which have attended the efforts of the Ministry of Labour, acting in tactful co-operation with the employers and employed in various industries, to set up Joint Industrial Councils.

Industry's Own Conciliation Machinery

A unique feature of industrial evolution in the United Kingdom has been the establishment of permanent voluntary Conciliation Boards in very many industries, by agreement between employers and workpeople, unsupported by legal enactment, and depending solely for their success on the goodwill of the parties. Such Boards have existed for many years past. The Board established in the Nottingham glove and hosiery industry in 1860 is probably the first example of permanent machinery in any industry for the systematic treatment of labour disputes. There is a large number of Conciliation Boards in existence. The value of Conciliation Boards (as of Joint Industrial Councils) depends on their ability to prevent stoppages of work rather than on power to settle strikes or lock-outs which may have already taken place. In most cases, the rules of Conciliation Boards provide that no stoppage of work shall be permitted pending consideration of the difference by the Conciliation Board—in some cases, the rules state that, if a stoppage of work has occurred, the Board will refuse to discuss the matter until work has been resumed. The membership of a Board consists usually of equal numbers of representatives of the employers' associations and of the Trade Unions, parties to the agreement establishing the Board. Accordingly, it not infrequently happens that the two sides of the Board are equally divided on the question brought before them, and the efficacy of a Board as an instrument for composing differences depends largely upon the steps normally adopted for resolving such a dead-lock. The rules of some Conciliation Boards contain a clause providing that, in the event of failure of the parties to effect a settlement of a dispute, application shall be made to the Ministry of Labour for the appointment of an umpire, arbitrator or conciliator. The changed conditions during the war, and the special war-time provisions which were necessary for dealing with disputes, had a remarkable effect upon the forms of conciliation machinery in this country, with the result that, in several important industries (e.g. building), the machinery is under revision.

An illustration of the working of Conciliation Boards is afforded by those in the iron and steel industries, which, although now under reconsideration in some districts, have been in existence for many years. In them the remuneration of the majority of the workpeople is regulated by sliding scales under which wages rise and fall in accordance with prescribed advances or reductions in the selling price of the manufactured article, this price being ascertained by accountants at specified intervals. Although the general adjustment of wages is the main object, other useful functions are exercised in these trades by the Boards. Amendments of the sliding scale, alterations in method of working, fixed rates for special classes of work, variation of prices according to difficulties in manufacture, and other similar questions have come under the consideration of the Boards. The Conciliation Boards in the manufactured iron and steel trades show a great similarity in constitution and procedure. They are composed, not of representatives of employers' and workpeople's associations, but of one representative of the workpeople and one of the employers from each of the works affiliated to the Board. Their methods of procedure are alike in affording opportunities for the parties to a dispute to arrive at a settlement by themselves, the services of the Board not being sought until other means have failed. Their rules stipulate that individual causes of complaint must first be discussed between the aggrieved workmen and the employer or his representative. In all cases, except that of the South Wales Iron and Steel Wages Board, the rules provide that, failing a settlement, the question shall then be discussed between the workman, accompanied by his Board representative, and the employer or his representative. In the case of some of the Boards, questions which have passed this stage without a settlement are referred to a Standing Committee, and it is only on the failure of this Committee to effect a settlement, that matters are brought before the Board itself.

For many years the boot and shoe industry has been covered by a series of Local Conciliation Boards existing in all the centres of the industry—questions affecting the industry as a whole being dealt with at National Joint Conferences presided over by an independent Chairman appointed by the Ministry of Labour. Each Local Board appoints a Committee of Inquiry consisting of two manufacturers and two workmen; in case of disagreement, each side of the Board elects an Arbitrator to whom is remitted for arbitration any dispute referred to the Board and which the Board is unable to settle. Should the two Arbitrators not agree the questions are referred to an Umpire appointed by themselves or by the Ministry of Labour. The rules of the Local Conciliation Boards provide that the procedure to be followed in cases of dispute between an employer and his workmen shall be as follows: (*a*) the workmen shall first bring the matter before the employer or foreman; (*b*) should they not be able to agree the representatives of the Employers' Association and the representatives of the Workmen's Union shall endeavour to settle the matter in dispute; (*c*) if these representatives are unable to arrange terms the Secretary of the Board shall forthwith advise the Committee of Inquiry of the dispute; (*d*) in the event of the Committee of Inquiry being unable to settle the dispute it shall be referred to the Board, and, failing a decision, then to the Umpire or Arbitrators, who shall be asked to give their decision within seven days from the date of hearing. This conciliation scheme is the most important of the few to adopt the system of financial penalties.

In addition to the Conciliation Boards, there is a variety of arrangements which, although not coming within the definition of a Conciliation Board, provide definite procedure for the consideration and settlement of differences. Two examples may be given: the highly organized cotton industry has not adopted conciliation board procedure, but the "Brooklands" Agreement, signed in 1893, at the termination of the great contest, provided for many years machinery for settlement of disputes in the spinning branch of the industry. This Agreement has now been superseded by new provisions for avoidance of disputes. As regards other sections of the industry, the principal agreement is that existing between the North and North-East Lancashire Cotton Spinners and Manufacturers' Association and the Northern Counties' Textile Trades Federation. Under this agreement, the procedure is similar to that adopted in the case of the Brooklands Agreement and provides for a meeting of representatives of employers and operatives in the branch of trade affected; if no settlement is arrived at, the dispute is to be brought before a joint meeting of the members of the Employers' Association and the Amalgamated Association of Trade Unions formed in the section concerned; if this meeting fails to effect a settlement, then the matter is to come before a joint meeting of representatives of the Manufacturers' Association and the Northern Counties' Federation. Until all these steps have been taken and have failed, no strike or lock-out notices are to be given. An important feature is a provision that, in cases of stoppages of work, meetings of the representatives of the signatories shall be held at intervals of four weeks in Manchester until the dispute has been settled.

Similarly, Conciliation Boards have not been adopted in the engineering trades. The principal agency for conciliation in these trades is that afforded by the "Terms of Settlement" signed in 1898 on the termination of the great dispute which had commenced in the previous year. This agreement, revised in 1907, provides, *inter alia*, for the discussion of grievances in the first instance by employers and workpeople or their representatives. Should a settlement not be effected by this method, a local conference of employers' and workpeople's associations may then be called to consider the matter, and if the question still remains unsettled, it can be referred to a central conference between the Executive Board of the Employers' Federation and the Executives of the Trade Unions signatory to the agreement. No stoppage of work is permissible until this procedure has been fully carried out. An agreement dated May 20, 1919, amplified the previous agreements by the recognition of shop stewards and the institution of Works' Committees.

This voluntary machinery (i.e. permanent voluntary conciliation boards and recognized procedure for discussion) covers a number of the principal trades of the country, such as building, coal mining, iron and steel, engineering, shipbuilding, cotton, boots and shoes. Before the war, there were some other industries of considerable importance in which Conciliation Boards or other permanent machinery did not exist, presumably owing to lack of organization of the parties, e.g. dockers, carters, seamen, agricultural workers. This has to some extent been remedied during and since the war.

State Conciliation Machinery

Supplementary to the Whitley Councils, voluntary conciliation boards and similar procedure, which are responsible for the settlement of the bulk of the differences that arise, there exists the State machinery—on the one hand, the Industrial Court; on the other hand, the Trade Boards for poorly organized trades. The Industrial Courts Act, 1919 (which for practical purposes embodies the Conciliation Act, 1896), defines the Government's powers of intervention in industrial disputes, such intervention being necessary in cases where the joint machinery is not adequate or where the joint machinery has failed to effect a settlement. The Act sets up a permanent Court of Arbitration,[11] to which recourse can be had by parties to industrial disputes if both parties to the dispute consent. Although permanent provision for voluntary arbitration is thus made by the establishment of the Industrial Court, it has been the policy of the Ministry of Labour, if not always the practice of the Cabinet, that trade disputes should be settled as far as possible by negotiation between Employers' Associations and Trade Unions. When this fails or a Joint Industrial Council, or a Conciliation Board cannot arrive at an agreement, the Industrial Court is an independent authoritative tribunal to which such differences can be referred.

Should the parties so desire, a dispute can be referred by the Minister of Labour under the Act either to a single arbitrator appointed by him or to a special Board of Arbitration composed of members selected by the parties from panels of persons appointed by him to act on these Boards. Reference to the Industrial Court is, however, the normal procedure. A dispute may be referred for settlement under the Industrial Courts Act only after the exhaustion of all available means for conciliation already existing in the trade. Under the Industrial Courts Act, the Minister has power to establish a Court of Inquiry to investigate the causes and circumstances of any industrial dispute, whether the dispute exists or is merely apprehended; moreover, to this course the consent of the parties is not required. These Courts have no power to settle the dispute by arbitration, but are restricted to making a report which serves to put before the public an impartial account of the merits of the case, with possibly a recommendation as to the best course to be pursued to effect a settlement.

The policy of the Ministry of Labour is to place the prime responsibility for the harmonious working of industry upon the employers and employed in each industry, and only to intervene when negotiations between the employers and the Trade Unions have broken down, and then merely for the purpose of bringing them together again and trying to promote a solution of the difficulty acceptable to both sides. Since the armistice, the industrial situation has been peculiarly difficult, and in certain disputes, there has been a political as well as an industrial element which would have made a settlement almost impossible whatever machinery existed, but on the whole it may be claimed that the existing policy of the Ministry of Labour has been fully justified by the results.

Statutory Minimum Wages

Voluntary conciliation machinery can function successfully only in those trades where both employers and workpeople are sufficiently well-organized to enable a collective agreement to be made effective. There must always remain a large section of industry which is poorly organized and for which other means are required for the proper regulation of conditions. State action has accordingly been found necessary to enable the less well-organized trades to fix minimum wages and to enforce proper observance of them; this has been done by means of Trade Boards. The Trade Boards Act of 1909 was passed with the avowed object of eradicating the evils of "sweating"; four trades only were included under the Act, but power was given to the responsible Department (then the Board of Trade) to bring additional trades under the Act from time to time by Provisional Order. In 1918, an amending Act was passed substituting procedure by Special Order for procedure by Provisional Order and modifying the description of the trades which could be brought under the Acts. The Minister of Labour is empowered to extend the Trade Boards Acts to trades to which the Acts do not already apply, if he considers there is no effective machinery in them for the regulation of wages, and that, in view of the rates of wages prevailing in them, a Trade Board is desirable. For this purpose an investigation into the conditions in the industry is first made and, if there be a *prima facie* case for the application of the Acts, the Minister gives notice of his intention to make a Special Order under the Acts. A period of at least forty days must be allowed, in which, if objections are received, the Minister must order a public inquiry to be held by some person not in Government employment, unless he decides to amend or withdraw the order, or unless the objections are merely frivolous. On receiving the report of the inquiry, the Minister then decides whether he should make an Order with a view to establishing the proposed Trade Board or not.

A Trade Board consists of an equal number of representatives of employers and of workpeople in the trade, to whom are added a neutral chairman and two or four persons unconnected with the trade, who are known as "appointed members." Where there is any organization among the workpeople or employers, the Trade Unions and employers' associations are asked to nominate representatives. Where there is no effective organization, the only practicable method is for the Minister to nominate members selected to represent the various types of work done in the trade and the various districts where it is carried on. The number of members varies according to the needs of the trade. Where women are largely employed in the trade, at least one of the "appointed members" must be a woman.

A Trade Board must fix a minimum rate or rates of wages for time-work. Where no other rate has been fixed, piece-workers must be paid at rates sufficient to yield to an ordinary worker at least as much money as the minimum time-rate. It also has power to fix general minimum piece-rates, a guaranteed time-rate for piece-workers, a piece-work basis time-rate on which piece-work prices must be based, overtime rates, and for this purpose the Board has power to declare what is the normal number of working hours per week in the trade. A Board can, if it thinks fit, fix minimum rates of wages for all classes of workers throughout its trade, or, if it chooses, fix only a general minimum time-rate, and leave other rates to be settled between the employers and workpeople themselves. When a rate has been fixed, every employer in the trade must exhibit the Trade Board's notice, giving full particulars of the rate, in his factory, or in the place where work is given out. Any employer who pays wages at less than the minimum rate is liable to a fine of £20 for each offence and to a further fine of £5 for each day after his conviction on which he fails to pay the legal rate. Any worker who thinks he is not receiving the rate due to him may complain to the Minister of Labour or to the Trade Board.

The number of Trade Boards at present in existence is 44. Of these 5 are for England and Wales, 5 for Scotland, and 34 for Great Britain. By May 10, 1922, 30 Boards had been set up in Ireland. These Boards covered in all approximately 3 million workpeople. The Trade Boards are independent bodies, though they are financed and staffed by the Ministry of Labour and though their rates are subject, as described above, to confirmation by the Minister. The Minister of Labour has announced his intention to introduce legislation dealing with the recommendations of a Committee appointed in September 1921, under the chairmanship of Lord Cave, to inquire into the working and effect of the Trade Boards Acts (*Parliamentary Paper*, 1922, Cmd. 1645). A statement of the Government's new policy appears at p. 286 of the *Labour Gazette* for July 1922.

Employment Exchanges

The Ministry of Labour is responsible for the administration of the Employment Exchanges established under the Labour Exchanges Act, 1909, which now number over 400 in Great Britain. The work of the Exchanges falls under two main heads, viz., that of bringing together employers requiring workpeople, and workpeople desiring employment, and that of administering the National Unemployment Insurance Scheme. As illustrating the amount of work performed by the Exchanges during the seven years 1914 to 1920 inclusive, the average number of yearly placings was 1,360,000. The organization of the Exchanges provides a ready means of bringing a demand for labour from any part of the United Kingdom into touch immediately with a supply in any other part. Railway warrants are issued by the Exchanges in necessitous cases subject to a signed undertaking being given, either by the workman or his prospective employer, to repay the amount involved.

Women are dealt with in a separate department of each Exchange, which, in all but the very smallest Exchanges, is in charge of a woman officer and is staffed by women. The administration of unemployment insurance has greatly increased the work of the Exchanges in connection with women. Under the old Insurance Acts about 500,000 women were insured against unemployment, but this number has been increased to 2,750,000 under the Unemployment Insurance Act of 1920. Since the war, in addition to dealing with industrial and commercial occupations, the Exchanges deal with private resident domestic service as a permanent part of their work, and also with applicants who are desirous of obtaining employment overseas. They co-operate with the Central Committee on Women's Training and Employment in selecting women for training courses. In all these matters, and in interviewing and advising unemployed women, valuable assistance is rendered by the Women's Sub-Committees of the Local Employment Committees. Boys and girls under the age of eighteen are dealt with in a special department of each Exchange, except in the case of the smallest Exchanges. In about 250 areas, Juvenile Employment Committees have been set up in connection with Juvenile Departments of Exchanges. These Committees have been appointed under the Labour Exchanges Act, 1909, the Education (Choice of Employment) Act, 1910, or the Education (Scotland) Act, 1908.

During the war, the Exchanges were very largely used by the Government for the purpose of organizing the supply of labour for munitions and essential services. The various measures included schemes for (1) registration and enrolment so that skilled and other essential workers could be removed from one part of the country to another, (2) the temporary release of serving soldiers for munitions and essential work, (3) the supply of substitutes to enable more workers to be recruited in the army from essential industries and services, and (4) the recruitment of women workers for munition work.

The Juvenile Employment Committees consist of representatives of educational and industrial interests in the districts, together with other persons especially concerned in promoting the welfare of boys and girls. In the year 1917, the Minister of Labour decided to associate with each Employment Exchange a Local Employment Committee (at first known as a Local Advisory Committee) to secure for the Exchange the full benefit of local knowledge and to bring it into close touch with employers and workpeople in the district. Local Employment Committees are composed of equal numbers of representatives of employers and workpeople, together with a certain number of additional members (not exceeding a third of the total membership) who are not necessarily connected with industry—among the additional members representation of ex-service men is provided for. The Chairman is nominated by the Minister and the Committee themselves appoint a Vice-Chairman. It is one of the most important duties of these Committees to keep a close watch over the state of employment in their area. Where the local unemployment is severe, it is open to them to urge upon local authorities and private employers the need for widening the field of employment where necessary, and also to advise the Minister with regard to any difficulties which might be removed by departmental action. At the present time the Committees assist in the selection of men from the Exchange registers for employment under schemes devised to relieve abnormal unemployment.

The Work of the Ministry of Labour

The Committee on National Expenditure[12] (see *Parliamentary Paper,* 1922, Cmd. 1581) proposed to abolish the Industrial Relations Department of the Ministry of Labour. They observe that "with the knowledge that, in the end, there will be Government intervention, neither side will have the same incentive to make the final proposals which might lead to a settlement of the dispute." This appears to me an exceedingly hazardous proposal. Anyone with experience of industrial disputes knows that occasions occur when reason disappears, tempers rise and responsibility vanishes, and neither side will meet the other. It is essential in such circumstances for a Government Department to act the go-between if the community is not to suffer. At some time intervention is imperative, and it is a question whether it should be that of the Ministry of Labour working on a consistent policy or of the Cabinet in Downing Street which, lacking the industrial experience of the Ministry, is apt to settle a dispute on any policy, but this question I discuss later at length. The Committee on National Expenditure found that, so long as unemployment insurance is on the present basis, Labour Exchanges are required as agencies for checking payments of unemployment insurance benefits, but not as Labour Exchanges; they recommended that if unemployment insurance by industry could be secured that the Labour Exchanges should be abolished. It is quite clear that that cannot be done, nor does the Committee recommend it to be done while the present National Unemployment Insurance Scheme continues. If insurance by industry is found to be practicable, it may be necessary, from motives of economy, to abolish the Exchanges. Apart from that justification it would be, I think, greatly to the national detriment to do so. While an employer cannot take all his labour through the Exchanges, employers generally learned during the war to appreciate their value. Trade Unions started by being suspicious of the Exchanges, largely because the local delegate of an organized Trade Union regarded it as an important piece of patronage to supply labour of his trade to employers in his district, and he considered the exercise of that patronage as no unimportant factor affecting his re-election. Although in certain districts, no doubt, Exchanges can be abolished, in the main industrial centres their continuance is essential particularly for trades which are ill-organized.

I can say from my own practical experience during the war that the munitions industries could not have been conducted without the expert services rendered by the Labour Exchanges. As Chairman of the Clyde Dilution Commission and of the Tyne Dilution Commission, as

Commissioner for Dilution on the Mersey and in Barrow-in-Furness, as Director of Shipyard Labour, I worked in the closest touch with them. Their officers were invariably men known to, and respected by, local employers and Trade Unions, and possessed a complete grasp of district labour conditions. The work they did in the early days of the war, both in connection with the Ministry of Munitions and the Admiralty, in settling labour differences, is as notable as it is unknown. They formed the nucleus on which the local labour staffs of the Ministry of Munitions and the Admiralty were ultimately built up.

CHAPTER XIV
GOVERNMENT LABOUR POLICY
FOR THE COAL INDUSTRY

Pre-war Conditions

The relationship between employers and employed in the coal industry has been more profoundly modified during the war than in any other great national industry. Before 1914, there existed the Coal Mines Regulation Acts, 1887-1908, and later the Coal Mines Act, 1911, which consolidated and re-enacted with amendments many earlier Acts dealing with employment in mines, payment of wages, and other matters affecting mining. The Act of 1908 limited the hours of work underground to eight per day exclusive of one winding. By the Coal Mines (Minimum Wage) Act, 1912, provision was made for the fixing of minimum rates of wages for miners in each mining district by Joint District Boards of mine owners and miners. Before the war, and indeed up to September 1917, wages were expressed at varying percentages above district basis rates, which had been fixed at various times in the different districts. In one district, Durham, the percentages varied with the selling price of coal. This system was introduced into Northumberland also in 1914. A similar system was at one time in operation in South Wales, but had been abandoned before the war. In October 1912, the Miners' Federation adopted the Nationalization of Mines and Minerals Bill for constituting coal-mining a Government industry to be worked by a Government Department. Then came the war.

The South Wales Strike of 1915

The South Wales miners gave notice to terminate on June 30, 1915, the peculiar agreement under which, since March 1910, their wages had varied within a minimum of 35 per cent. and a maximum of 60 per cent. above the basis rate of 1879, according to the selling price of large coal f.o.b. in Welsh ports. When coal sold between 14s. and 14s. 9d. per ton, wages were 50 per cent. above the 1879 basis, and they were raised or lowered by negotiation for each 1s. up or down in the price. In March 1913, wages had reached the maximum and had remained there. The prices of Welsh coal in 1915 on yearly contracts, on which the bulk of the business was done, were 18s. to 19s. per ton, prices for other coal being up to 35s. per ton. The South Wales miners demanded a new standard 50 per cent. over the 1879 basis; abolition of the maximum; a new minimum 10 per cent. above the new standard to be paid when the average selling price of large coal was at or below 15s. 6d. A selling price of 15s. 6d. meant, under the 1910 agreement, wages 57 per cent. above the 1879 basis—and under the claim meant wages 65 per cent. above that basis. The rest of the miners in Great Britain had claimed a war bonus of 25 per cent. on earnings, and Lord St. Aldwyn had awarded 17½ per cent., which was accepted. The South Wales miners' chief purpose was to establish a higher minimum as against a post-war depression in trade, and to secure during the war higher wages as coal mounted in price. Negotiations between owners and miners broke down—the former agreed to, the latter refused arbitration—the Navy relied on South Wales for coal—a strike was imminent. Mr. Runciman, the President of the Board of Trade, offered the South Wales Miners' Executive generous terms which the Executive accepted "as the basis of negotiations," viz., a new standard 50 per cent. above 1879 provided that the alteration of the standard should not in itself effect an immediate change in wages; abolition of the maximum and minimum of 1910; and the levelling up of rates of certain men. The men rejected these terms—Mr. Runciman very properly would go no further. Mr. Lloyd George then secured the issue of a Royal Proclamation under the Munitions of War Act, 1915, making it an offence punishable under that Act to take part in a strike in the South Wales mining industry, whereupon 200,000 men promptly struck work by way of reply. Mr. Lloyd George himself went to Cardiff and the strike was settled by the Government giving to the miners practically all they had asked, with full indemnity against their breach of the Munitions Act. It was the first time the Government had, measured its strength against organized Labour and the Government's capitulation had a far-reaching repercussion. Compulsory arbitration was discredited and by the Government.

Government War-time Control

The nation's dependence on coal was manifested early in the war; output fell as miners loyally responded to the call for men; prices rose as domestic consumers competed with munition industries for fuel. Early in 1915 exports of coal had to be curtailed by Government—in July 1915, the Price of Coal Limitation Act had to be enacted, limiting the price to be charged for coal at the pit's mouth. Our Allies began to protest against the price charged to them for coal, and coal-owners, exporters and shipowners agreed voluntarily with the Government to limit the price of Ally coal. But that did not go far enough, and ultimately in 1917 under D.O.R.A., powers were conferred on the Board of Trade to regulate prices, and the distribution and transport of coal both for home and Ally use.

Trouble continued to develop in the South Wales mines, and the supply of essential steam coal was in danger. The Government accordingly took over, from December 1, 1916, control of the South Wales coal-field, and as, elsewhere, industrial and transport difficulties were causing great anxiety, they also took over, from March 1, 1917, the rest of the coal-mines in the country, and constituted a Coal Mines Department. The actual management of individual mines was left to their respective owners, the Department directing them how to dispose of their supplies so as best to meet the needs of the country. It was inevitable that as control of the mines had been transferred to the Government, the wages of mine-workers could be a matter no longer for district adjustment but for national settlement by Government, and, since 1917, this was the course adopted. It is unnecessary to go into the question of miners' earnings, they will be found in the volume of Appendices to the Coal Industry Commission's Report (*Parliamentary Paper*, 1919, Cmd. 361, pp. 55 and 109). An admirable comparison as between 1914 and 1920 is contained in Professor Bowley's book, *Prices and Wages in the United Kingdom*. The point to be noticed is that after 1917 wages were paid really out of a national pool consisting of the aggregate profits of the coal industry with the national exchequer behind them. As a result of control, some coal-owners, from their position and circumstances, realized large profits; others suffered considerable losses. To provide compensation for the latter, under an agreement made between the mine-owners and the Coal Controller, scheduled to, and confirmed by, the Coal Mine Control Agreement (Confirmation) Act, 1918, a fund was provided by pooling a prescribed percentage of excess profits. The disparity in the relative profit-making capacity of firms which had always existed was of course materially intensified by control; before the war it had not, however, materially affected industrial conditions. Events soon proved the impracticability of continuing the 1918 compensation provisions. There had existed arrangements for securing supplies of coal to our Allies at prices approximating to those charged in this country for inland consumption—these were terminated in 1919, and the prices of export coal immediately mounted. Some coal-owners, who were granted export permits, realized large profits; others, who had previously suffered loss owing to their being restricted to inland trade, continued to labour under heavy financial difficulties, which were made still more onerous by the reduction of the price of household coal by 10s. per ton in December 1919. To maintain the compensation arrangements of 1918 would have involved the State in heavy subsidies, as a large share of the export profits would have been left in the owners' hands, and loss, for which compensation would have to be paid, would still have been inflicted on collieries producing for the home market. The Coal Mines (Emergency) Act, 1920, was accordingly passed, which repealed the Act of 1918 from April 1, 1919, and provided a new fund from which compensation was to be drawn for collieries working at a loss, but into this fund all excess profits were to be paid, and not a percentage only, as in the case of the 1918 fund.

The Sankey Commission

The shortage of coal, of labour and of transport in 1918, when the German offensive was at its height, led to the rationing of coal, gas and electricity, which continued for about two years. After the Armistice, in November 1918, trade activity increased, the industrial demand for coal grew, and the domestic demand as well, when demobilization was accelerated. The Coal Mines Department only just managed, with the greatest difficulty, to secure an equitable distribution of coal, and this it accomplished with great efficiency. These difficulties were increased by the miners' threat to strike in the beginning of 1919 unless demands for increased wages and reduced hours were conceded. The Government replied by passing the Coal Industry Commission Act, 1919, which set up a Commission under the chairmanship of Mr. Justice Sankey. The Interim Report of the Commission (*Parliamentary Papers*, 1919, Cmd. 84, 85 and 86) recommended a national increase of 2s. per shift to all adult colliery workers, a 7-hour day underground and 46½ hours per week for surface workers as from July 16, 1919. These recommendations were put into operation by the Government. Section 1 (*f*) of the Act required the Commission to inquire into "any scheme that may be submitted to, or formulated by, the Commissioners for the future organization of the Coal Industry, whether on the present basis, or on the basis of joint control, nationalization, or any other basis." On this matter the Commission presented four reports (see *Parliamentary Papers*, 1919, Cmd. 210 and 360): (1) by the Chairman; (2) by the Labour representatives; (3) by the representatives of coal-owners and employers in other industries, except Sir Arthur Duckham, and (4) by Sir Arthur Duckham. Reports (1) and (2) recommended nationalization of the industry; report (3) acquisition of royalties by the State, the continuance of private enterprise coupled with the establishment of Pit Committees representative of management and miners, and District Councils and a National Council representative of coal-owners and miners—for the purpose of discussing working conditions and other questions in the settlement of which both parties are interested; report (4) recommended State acquisition of royalties, the district unification of colliery interests to be worked through District Coal Boards, on which the workers would have some representation, with a Pit Committee at each mine. Each of the four Reports recommended the setting up of a Mines Department.

The Mining Industry Act, 1920

The Government announced, in August 1919, that they could not accept the policy of nationalization, but intimated their readiness to apply the Duckham scheme, but the owners and the miners objected to this. Subsequently, the Government put forward a scheme which was ultimately incorporated in the Mining Industry Act, 1920, providing a compromise mainly on the principles of Report (3)—that of the representatives on the Commission of the coal-owners and employers in other industries. This provided for (1) regulation, for a period not exceeding one year from August 31, 1920, of the export of coal, and of the pit-head price of home coal and bunker coal for coastwise shipping; (2) the future ordering of the industry on a permanent basis, by the co-ordination of all the Government's powers and duties in regard to mines and minerals in the hands of a single Department—the Mines Department of the Board of Trade created by the Act; (3) the grant to the mine-workers of a greater voice in the ordering of the industry by means of representation on Pit and District Committees and Area and National Boards, and (4) the constitution of a fund to be applied for purposes connected with the social well-being, recreation and conditions of living of workers in or about the mines and for research and mining education. The Government also decided that the control of the coal industry, which had been essential as a war-measure, should be removed as soon as export prices fell to something approximating to the inland price. A start was made, in June 1920, in the direction of freeing the distribution of inland coal from restriction by placing it in the hands of local committees of the coal trade.

The Strike of October 1920

Consistently from the beginning of 1920, the Miners' Federation had advanced new wages claims—the complicated details of which will be found in the *Labour Gazette* for August, September, October and November 1920. They contended that their wages had not kept pace with the cost of living—that the coal trade was able to afford the increases claimed—that if wages had been nationally governed by price, as they used to be locally governed, either expressly or virtually, all districts would have received a considerable rise in wages. It was strongly argued that the Sankey National Award of 2s. was intended to improve the pre-war standard of living of the miners, and not to meet war-time increases in cost of living—a contention for which it is hard to see the justification. Negotiations broke down, and a miners' strike began on October 18, 1920, and continued till November 4, 1920, when it was settled on terms agreed between the Government, the Mining Association and the Miners' Federation. The first clause of the Agreement was as follows:

> "(1) Recognizing that on the increased production of coal there depend not only the prosperity of all who are engaged in the coal industry, but also the welfare of the nation and the cost of life of the people, and having in view that this urgent need can only be met if the miners and mine-owners throughout the country work together cordially for this common purpose; and further, having regard to the necessity of setting up machinery for regulating wages in the coal trade so as to get rid of present anomalies and provide against future difficulties,

> "The Mining Association and the Miners' Federation solemnly pledge themselves to make every effort to achieve these objects.

> "To that end they shall:

> "(a) Co-operate to the fullest extent to obtain increased output, and for this purpose will arrange to set up district committees and a national committee;

> "(b) Proceed forthwith to prepare a scheme for submission to the Government at the earliest possible moment, and not later than March 31, for the regulation of wages in the industry, having regard, among other considerations, to the profits of the industry, and to the principles upon which any surplus profits are to be dealt with."

The Strike of April 1921

Prolonged negotiations then took place between owners and men under this settlement. These revealed a fundamental difference: the owners were claiming to return to the old district basis of wages; the miners were insisting on continuance of a national pool and the national settlement of wages as under control. No agreement had been concluded when all remaining Government control was terminated on March 31, 1921, by the Coal Mines (Decontrol) Act, 1921. In spite of failure to agree, both miners and owners indicated their willingness to do all possible to avoid a stoppage. A conference took place, on March 30, 1921, between both sides and the President of the Board of Trade, the miners asking for a continuance of Government subsidy to the industry as long as the then existing depression of trade lasted, but this the Government refused. The owners had previously issued notices terminating contracts of employment on March 31, and indicating the new terms upon which men would be re-engaged. Practically all the men ceased work in accordance with this notice, and refused to resume on the new terms. A stoppage of work took place from April 1 to July 4, 1921. On June 25, terms of settlement were arranged between the Mining Association and the Miners' Federation which were accepted by the votes of a large majority of miners on July 1. This agreement (*Parliamentary Paper*, 1921, Cmd. 1387) was of a remarkable and far-reaching character. By it the miners dropped their claim for a national pool; provision was made for the constitution of a National Board, consisting of equal numbers of persons chosen by the Mining Association and by the Miners' Federation, and of District Boards consisting in equal numbers of persons representing owners and workmen in each district—each Board having an independent Chairman. It was provided that (1) the proceeds in each district of the mining industry should be determined by independent accountants appointed by each side to check by joint test audit, the owners' books; (2) standard wages for each district should be fixed on the basis of the district basis rates of March 31, 1921, plus district percentages of July 1914, plus percentage additions for piece-workers made on the reduction of hours from eight to seven; (3) minimum wages should be standard wages plus 20 per cent.; (4) for each district the total should periodically be ascertained for certain test periods of the standard wages, the cost of production other than wages, and standard profits at the rate of 17 per cent. of the standard wages. This aggregate should then be deducted from the amount of the district proceeds for those periods, and 83 per cent. of the surplus should be applied for payment in the district of an increase of wage above the minimum rates. But 83 per cent. might not be, and indeed in some districts has not been, enough to bring standard wages up to minimum wages. As against this contingency Parliament voted, on July 1, 1921, a subsidy which was not to exceed £10,000,000 to be used to prevent the reduction of adult wages in any district exceeding 2s. per shift during July, 2s. 6d. during August, and 3s. during September. £7,000,000 was actually expended under this arrangement.

The Failure of Part II of the Act of 1920

Difficulties have arisen in connection with the working of Part II of the Mining Industry Act, 1920, relating to the appointment of Pit and District

Committees and Area and National Boards on which owners and workers were to be represented. Section 10 provided that Area Boards should formulate wages schemes, having regard among other considerations to profits of the industry within the area. On the introduction of the Bill for the Act of 1920, the Miners' Federation announced their intention not to assist in working the Act in view of their objection to the settlement of wages on any other than a national basis. Having agreed to a district wages basis in the agreement of July 1921, they decided, in August 1921, to co-operate with the Mines Department in working Part II of the Act. Meanwhile, the owners who originally acquiesced in the terms of the Act, and through spokesmen in Parliament agreed to work it, similarly changed their minds, and the Mining Association announced about the same time that, as the Agreement of July 1921, had in their view achieved the objects aimed at in Part II of the Act, the re-imposition of any measure of Government control over wages and allied questions would be contrary to the best interests of the industry itself and of the community, and through the administration of Part II of the Mining Industry Act would add unnecessarily to the burden of taxation. The correspondence between the Mines Department and the Association is printed in *Parliamentary Papers*, 1921, Cmd. 1551, and 1922, Cmd. 1583, and deserves consideration. In view of the attitude of the owners, the Secretary for Mines made a report to Parliament as required by Section 17 of the Act, and as within thirty days from February 7 no resolution to the contrary was passed by Parliament, Part II of the Act has ceased to have effect. The statutory right on the part of the workers to a voice in the ordering of the coal-mining industry is therefore at an end, and the position is governed by the Agreement of July 1921.

Royalties

Reference is necessary to the State acquisition of royalties, on which there was unanimity amongst the members of the Sankey Commission. One of the principal reasons advanced why the State ought to own the coal was that no unreasonable obstacle should be placed in the way of mining coal, and that due attention should be directed to conserving our principal national asset, which is also a wasting asset. The Government accepted the recommendation, but in the present financial condition of the country it is obviously impracticable to give effect to it.

Summary of Government Policy

Briefly summarized, the Government's Labour policy in connection with the coal-mining industry is as follows:

1. The industry must be worked by private enterprise.

2. The functions of the Government in connection with mining should be centralized in a Mines Department.

3. Such assistance as a Government Department can render in (*a*) the collection and publication of information; (*b*) removing obstacles to production; (*c*) the formulation of drainage schemes; (*d*) preventing wasteful working of a great national asset; (*e*) ensuring the safety and health of the workers, and (*f*) assisting, when asked to do so, in the settlement of disputes, should be rendered through the Mines Department.

4. Providing the means (through the Miners' Welfare Fund) for improving the amenities of mining centres.

5. Encouraging research into the particular problems affecting the health and safety of workers in the industry.

The Mines Department, established under the Act of 1920, is responsible for dealing with one of our most important industrial problems, and the success of its administration up to the present time is full of encouragement for the future.

CHAPTER XV
GOVERNMENT LABOUR
POLICY FOR RAILWAYS

Pre-war Conditions

As Labour proposes on the first opportunity to nationalize the railways, the relationship between the men and the companies is important. Under an Agreement of November 6, 1907, Conciliation Boards consisting of representatives of the companies and the men engaged in the manipulation of traffic had been appointed to deal with questions of hours and wages and working conditions. A railway strike occurred in 1911, and it was stated that one of the reasons for the strike was the dissatisfaction of the railway men with the working of the Railway Conciliation Scheme. The Government then appointed a Royal Commission to investigate the working of the scheme and to report what changes, if any, were desirable, with a view to a prompt and satisfactory settlement of differences. The Royal Commission reported in October 1911, and suggested a new scheme which, with some alterations agreed between the representatives of the companies and of the Unions, was adopted in December 1911. This scheme the Unions gave notice, in December 1913, to terminate at the end of November 1914, at which date they expressed their intention of advancing a national programme for increased wages and a 48-hour week.

Government War-time Control

On August 4, 1914, under an Order in Council made in pursuance of the Regulation of the Forces Act, 1871, the Secretary of State for War issued a warrant—which he renewed week by week, until August 1919, when statutory possession vested in the Minister of Transport under the Ministry of Transport Act, 1919, rendered its continuance unnecessary—authorizing the Board of Trade to take possession of practically all the railways of the country. This was done, but the railways continued to be conducted by their respective managements acting under the instructions of the Railway Executive Committee. On October 1, 1914, a truce agreement was concluded between the companies and the Unions, continuing the 1911 Conciliation

Scheme, but making it terminable on six weeks' notice. Alike with other trades the railwaymen received increases in wages from February 1915, on to November 1918. Up to September 1918, men of eighteen years and over received a war-wage advance of 30s. per week. In November 1918, a sliding scale was arranged under which the war-wage was to rise and fall with the index-number of retail prices as published in the *Labour Gazette*. An additional 3s., raising the war-wage to 33s. per week, was given in November 1918.

The Wage Agreement of March 1919

Following the Armistice, the National Union of Railwaymen gave notice to terminate the truce agreement of October 1914, but early in December 1918, the principle of an 8-hour day[13] was conceded by the Government for all members of the wages staff as from February 1, 1919. In March 1919, an agreement was made between the Government, the Railway Executive Committee and the Unions which provided for increased rates for overtime, night-duty and Sunday-work, but provided for stabilizing other wages till December 31, 1919. An important provision was contained in it providing for a continuance of negotiations to standardize rates so that all men throughout the country doing the same work under the same conditions should receive the same rate of wages. This agreement also provided for the setting up of a joint committee consisting of representatives of the Railway Executive Committee and the two Unions concerned[14] to deal with questions of pay and conditions until "some final arrangement is arrived at in regard to the future position of railways." The agreement stipulated that "when the new Ministry of Ways and Communications is set up it is the intention of the Government to provide in the organization for, and avail itself fully of, the advantage of assistance, co-operation and advice from the workers in the transportation industry." Standard rates were agreed between the Government and the two Unions for drivers, firemen and cleaners by an agreement in August 1919, and negotiations were continued to standardize the rates for other railwaymen.

The Railway Strike of September 1919

The Government's proposals for standardization were rejected by the Unions, who precipitated a strike, on September 26, 1919, on the railways throughout Great Britain. Terms of settlement were signed, on October 5, 1919, providing for standardization at the then existing level of wages up to September 30, 1920, and providing that no adult railwaymen in Great Britain should receive less than 51s. per week so long as the cost of living was not less than 110 per cent. above pre-war level. Work was resumed on October 6. Subsequently an agreement was made between the Government and the two Unions that, apart from the wage negotiations then in progress, questions of wages and conditions of service should, during the remainder of the period of control under the Ministry of Transport Act, be dealt with by a Central Board consisting of five railway representatives and five representatives of the two Unions. Failing agreement by the Central Board, disputes should be referred to a National Wages Board consisting of four railway managers, four railway workers or their representatives, and four users of railways, one nominated by the Parliamentary Committee of the Trades Union Congress, one by the Co-operative Union, one by the Federation of British Industries, and one by the Associated Chambers of Commerce, with an independent chairman appointed by the Government. The agreement also provided for Local Committees, to which matters of local importance would be referred. The Railway Executive Committee became unnecessary in view of the Ministry of Transport Act, 1919, and a new Advisory Committee was set up, consisting of twelve general managers and four representatives of the workers.

The Wage Agreement of March 1920

As a result of the negotiations, an agreement was completed on March 20, 1920,[15] providing for standardization of rates of pay, for wages to rise and fall according to cost of living, and for a standard rate below which wages should not fall. This is one of the most important industrial agreements. The principle of the arrangement was as follows. There were many classes of men on different railways graded by different names and receiving different rates of pay although doing substantially the same work. These various classes were reduced into a small number of specified grades. Further, in regard to certain grades, the country was divided up into sections, for example: (1) London area; (2) provincial, industrial and mining areas and large towns, and (3) rural districts. Then, on a system of averages, the mean pre-war weekly rate of pay of the men of a particular grade on all the railways in a particular section of the country was ascertained; to that a sum of 38s. as war-wage was added. This combined sum was to form, as from January 1, 1920, the wage to be paid as long as the cost of living remained at 125 per cent. above pre-war cost of living. For every five points rise or fall in the cost of living there was to be an increase or reduction of 1s. per week. Standard or minimum rates were fixed representing generally 100 per cent. increase on the average pre-war rates of the respective grades. These were rates below which wages would not fall, however much the cost of living might go down. This agreement provided on a more fully developed basis for a Central Wages Board of ten members, five representing railway administration and five the Unions, and for an appellate or National Wages Board of twelve members, four representing the railway companies, four the Unions and four the users of the railways, with an independent Chairman appointed by the Government. In promulgating the settlement the Government made this announcement: "In dealing with questions of wages it has been kept clearly in view by the Government that some addition to railway wages was due before the war, and that the claims of the railwaymen to a higher standard of remuneration were only then postponed because of the country's necessities." After this agreement certain claims for improvements in pay and working conditions were submitted by the Unions to the Central Wages Board, and, on the latter's failing to agree, referred to the National Wages Board. The Board by a majority agreed that certain advances of wages should be given, but they said they could not be justified on the ground of increase in the cost of living as that was provided for by an automatic advance under the sliding scale. The Government agreed to the advances being given.

The wages, therefore, of railwaymen in the conciliation grades consist of certain rates agreed upon in March 1920, which represented the average pre-war weekly rate of pay of the men in any grade or group of grades, plus 38s. per week, together with further increases ranging from 2s. to 7s. 6d. per week, or 2s. to 8s. 6d. in the case of signalmen, granted in June 1920, by the National Wages Board, the whole being subject to variations under the sliding scale, whereby there is a reduction or increase of 1s. per week for every fall or rise of five points in the cost of living as shown in the figures published by the Ministry of Labour. Adjustments in the bonus due under the sliding scale are considered by the Central Wages Board. A difference arose in regard to the operation of the sliding scale, and a *modus operandi* was agreed on by the Central Wages Board which is described in the *Labour Gazette* of April 1921.

The Railways Act, 1921

On August 19, 1921, the Railways Act, 1921, was passed, and Section 62 provided that, as from the date when the railways ceased to be in the possession of the Minister of Transport—which was August 15, 1921—and until otherwise determined by twelve months' notice, such notices not to be given before January 1, 1923, all questions of wages, hours and conditions of railway servants should, in default of agreement between a company and the Unions, be referred to the Central Wages Board, or on appeal to the National Wages Board. The Act reconstituted both Boards, and provided that the Central Wages Board should consist of eight representatives of railway companies and eight representatives of the railway employees—four appointed by the National Union of Railwaymen, two by the Associated Society of Locomotive Engineers and Firemen, and two by the Railway Clerks' Association. The National Wages Board was provided to consist of six representatives of the railway way companies, six representatives of the railway employees—two appointed by the National Union of Railwaymen—two by the Associated Society of Locomotive Engineers and Firemen, and two by the Railway Clerks' Association—and four representatives of the users of railways—one appointed by the Parliamentary Committee of the Trades Union Congress,[16] one by the Co-operative Union, one by the Associated Chambers of Commerce, and one by the Federation of British Industries, with an independent Chairman nominated by the Minister of Labour. The Minister has nominated Sir Wm. Mackenzie, K.B.E., K.C.—the President of the Industrial Court.

The Railway Conciliation Machinery of 1921

The Act further provided that councils on the lines of the Whitley Councils should be established for each railway company on the general basis of schemes to be prepared by a committee consisting of six representatives of the General Managers' Committee of the Railway Clearing House and six representatives of the National Union of Railwaymen, the Associated Society of Locomotive Engineers and Firemen, and the Railway Clerks' Association. These schemes, which have now been prepared, provide for: (1) local consultation; (2) local departmental committees; (3) Sectional Railway Councils, and (4) Railway Councils. At stations or depôts with a number of employees in a department or group of grades less than seventy-five, such employees are to be entitled to appoint representatives to discuss local matters with the Company's local officials. At stations or depôts where the number exceeds seventy-five, a committee is to be set up, consisting of not more than four elected representatives of the employees in the department or group of grades concerned, and not more than four representatives of the company. The objects of the local committee are to provide a recognized means of communication between the employees and the local officials, and to give the employees a wider interest in the conditions under which their work is performed. A local committee is to discuss: (a) suggestions for the satisfactory arrangement of working hours, breaks, time-recording, etc.; (b) questions of physical welfare; (c) holiday arrangements; (d) publicity in regard to rules; (e) suggestions as to improvements in organization of work, labour-saving appliances and other matters; (f) investigation of circumstances tending to reduce efficiency, and (g) the correct loading of traffic to ensure safe transit and the reduction of claims. Before a matter is discussed by a local committee it must first be submitted by the employees to the officials of the company in the ordinary manner, but, failing a satisfactory reply within fourteen days, it may be reported to the secretary of the employees' side of the committee. The company in the same way must exhaust the constitutional machinery.

Sectional Railway Councils

Sectional Railway Councils will consist of not more than twelve elected representatives of the employees, and not more than twelve appointed representatives of the company, and not more than five Sectional Councils are to be established on any railway. Each side will have its own secretary, who will have the right to take part in the proceedings. If one takes a railway on which the whole staff of the company is divided into the usual five sections, viz., (1) clerks, station-masters, supervisors, etc.; (2) locomotive men; (3) traffic department men; (4) goods and cartage staff, and (5) permanent way department men, platelayers, etc., each section will elect representatives to the Sectional Council, and the number of representatives of each section will be according to the proportion of the employees in the groups of the grades in the section. In addition, the number of representatives elected to each group of grades will be distributed as nearly as possible by districts. Sectional Councils will deal with: (a) local application of national agreements relating to standard salaries, wages, hours of duty and conditions of service other than subjects submitted directly to the Central Wages Board by railway companies or the Trade Unions; (b) suggestions as to operating, working and kindred matters; (c) other matters in which the company and the employees are mutually interested, such as co-operation with a view to securing increased business, greater efficiency and economy, the well-being of the staff, recruitment and tenure of service, etc.; (d) subjects remitted by the Railway Council to a Sectional Council.

Railway Councils

For each railway a Railway Council is to be appointed consisting of not more than ten representatives of the company and ten representatives of the employees. The representatives of the employees will consist of two members of each Sectional Council; each side will have a secretary with power to take part in the proceedings. The Railway Council will deal with all matters with which a Sectional Council can deal, and which are of common interest to two or more sections, but it can deal with no matter before a Sectional Council has had an opportunity of considering it. If a Sectional Council is unable to agree on any matter, the employees' side may refer it to the Trade Unions concerned, or the Council may, by agreement, refer it to the Railway Council. If a Sectional or a Railway Council cannot agree on any question of the local application of national agreements in regard to rates of pay and conditions of service, the matter of difference may be submitted by the employees' side to the Trade Unions concerned, who take it up with the Company, and, failing agreement, may refer it to the Central Wages Board. Before employees can submit any question to a Sectional or Railway Council they must first submit it to the company to consider in the ordinary way, but, failing a satisfactory answer within twenty-one days, the facts may be reported to the employees' secretary of the Council concerned, and the company itself must proceed in the same way. The working of the Railway Councils and Committees will be followed with the greatest interest by all concerned in the development of industrial conciliation machinery.

CHAPTER XVI
GOVERNMENT LABOUR POLICY
FOR AGRICULTURE

Government War-time Control

The necessity during the war of encouraging the production of food at home led to the Corn Production Act, 1917, which provided for control by the Ministry of Agriculture of cultivation, the constitution of an Agricultural Wages Board to fix minimum rates of wages for persons employed in agriculture, and for guaranteed minimum prices for wheat and oats. Minimum rates were fixed, and from time to time varied. Although the Board did not wipe out wholly the pre-war county agricultural wage-differentials, they very largely reduced them—the final percentage of increase varying from about 110 per cent. to 230 per cent. over pre-war. After the Armistice, the Government wisely realized it would be a mistaken policy to try and continue to fix minimum prices for oats and wheat, or to control cultivation and regulate wages. When wholesale prices broke in 1921, and the community became unable to pay the minimum prices, the Government decided it would be unsound finance to maintain prices and wages out of a national subsidy. In war-time it may be right to compel farmers to grow wheat and oats because of the country's needs—it is wholly wrong to do so in peace-time—the right policy is to leave them to cultivate their land as they, in their own interests, think fit.

Government's New Policy in 1921

The Corn Production Acts (Repeal) Act, 1921, was thereupon passed. That Act abolished minimum prices and wages, created a special fund of £1,000,000 for agricultural development, and provided that the Minister of Agriculture as respects England and Wales, and the Board of Agriculture for Scotland as respects Scotland, should be empowered to take steps to secure the voluntary formation of local Joint Conciliation Committees, representative of persons (whether owners or occupiers of agricultural land) employing persons in agriculture, and of agricultural workpeople, for the purpose of dealing with rates of wages, hours of work and conditions of employment. The Act provides that a rate of wages agreed upon by a Joint Conciliation Committee, and on the Committee's application, confirmed by the Minister and duly advertised, becomes the wage legally payable in the area, unless the Committee certifies that under the special circumstances of a particular case it is satisfied that a contract for a lower rate is fair and reasonable, or, in the event of the Committee refusing so to certify, the Court in which proceedings are taken for the recovery of the rate agreed by the Committee is so satisfied.

The Establishment of Joint Conciliation Committees in England and Wales

As the Ministry of Agriculture's function is confined to moral suasion, the task of getting these Committees established is a difficult one, and the Ministry is to be congratulated on the progress it has made. Many farmers are still incensed at the repeal of the Corn Production Act, and the resulting loss to them of a substantial subsidy on wheat and oats, and are inclined to resent any action by the Ministry. The leaders of the workers are equally incensed at the abolition of the Agricultural Wages Board with its compulsory powers, and demand its re-establishment. The scheme of Conciliation Committees, moreover, was launched at an unpropitious time. Prices were falling rapidly, and farmers, after having cultivated their crops throughout the year on the basis of a fairly high cost of production with wages at a high level, found themselves compelled to sell their produce at prices less, in many cases, than half those of the previous year. In consequence they pressed for substantial and immediate wage reductions. From the workers' point of view the autumn of 1921 was equally inopportune for initiating a new system of settling wages, as, owing to the favourable summer, work on the farm was well advanced and farmers were in a position to reduce their staffs. In addition, the growing amount of unemployment materially weakened the workers' bargaining power.

The Work of the Conciliation Committees

The greatest tact and discretion was, therefore, necessary to avoid any appearance of undue interference by the Ministry, and at the same time powerful persuasion had to be exercised to induce both sides to come to an agreement. The officers of the Ministry (assisted by officers appointed for the purpose by the Minister of Labour) have, notwithstanding all these difficulties, succeeded with signal ability in embedding already the roots of the scheme deep down into the agricultural industry. In the short time which has elapsed since the passing of the Act of 1921, 61 Committees have been established, covering the whole of the country, and of these, 54 have made agreements, though in some cases they have only been for short periods. In the remaining 7 areas, although efforts to agree have been made, no agreement has yet been reached.

The rate of wages which is now being paid generally for male agricultural workers is about 30s. to 32s. for 48-50 hours, and many Conciliation Committees have agreed on these rates. In the north of England the rates are usually somewhat higher, while in East Anglia and in several counties where no agreements have been reached the employers refuse to offer more than 30s., a rate which the workers equally refuse to accept. These rates compare with the Wages Board rate of 46s. for 48-50 hours, which was in force up to the beginning of September 1921. The Wages Board at their last meeting reduced this rate to 42s., which was the rate in force when the Conciliation Committees came into being. There was a fall in October 1921, to 36s. per week, followed by a gradual diminution to the rates mentioned above. Long period agreements running up to the beginning of October 1922, were successfully concluded in several counties with the assistance of representatives of the Ministry of Agriculture, at 32s. for 48 hours up to the beginning of March 1922, and 31s. for 50 hours over the remainder of the period. These long term agreements are a hopeful feature. The farmer gets a settled rate of wage when farm operations are in full swing, including both hay and corn harvest; the labourer gets a certain minimum wage, under which he will benefit by further falls in the cost of living during the currency of the agreement. At the same time, the rates now operative make full allowance for the changes to date in the cost of living. Taking the pre-war average cash wages at 16s. 9d. per week, the comparative figure based on the cost of living index number for June 1, 1922, of 80 per cent. over July 1914, would be 32s. 2d., and it is probably true to say that the agricultural labourer has experienced, since October 1921, a greater reduction in wages than most other trades. From the farmers' point of view, however, the fall in wages is more than justified by the drop in prices, which has been appreciably more rapid than the fall in the cost of living.

One most encouraging circumstance is the extent to which concluded agreements are faithfully observed by the farmers. The Committees have no direct power to enforce their decisions; they may send their agreements to the Minister of Agriculture for confirmation and then under the Act payment of the agreed rates becomes recoverable at law. As yet five Committees only have asked for confirmation of their agreements. On the whole, employers are opposed to confirmation, and the workers do not demand it. Although the agreements are in the main observed by employers, the workers' representatives complain that this is not so in every case. If there were any serious tendency towards non-observance the employers on the Conciliation Committees would agree to submission of agreements for confirmation; they would not allow some employers to evade payment of the agreed rates while others paid. The absence of any such general demand indicates that, substantially, the agreed wages are being paid.

Agriculture and Unemployment Insurance

The Labour Party makes the singularly disingenuous complaint that the Government does not apply the National Unemployment Insurance Scheme to persons engaged in agriculture. The true facts are that on December 2, 1920, the Agricultural Wages Board appointed a Committee, under the chairmanship of Sir Henry Rew, K.C.B., comprising representatives of employers and also representatives of unions whose members were engaged in agriculture, to report upon the extent to which the Unemployment Insurance Acts could practicably, and with benefit, be applied to agricultural workers. The Report of the Committee (*Parliamentary Paper*, 1921, Cmd. 1344) was unanimous, and to the effect that there was general opposition both by employers and workers to the inclusion of agriculture under the provisions of the Unemployment Insurance Scheme. One of the workers' representatives, a signatory to this finding, appended a note to say that he believed in some districts there was an undoubted desire of the agricultural workers to be included under the Act—notwithstanding that, neither his finding nor that of the other workers' representatives recommended the extension of the Unemployment Insurance Acts to agriculture.

No one who is aware of the difficulties, especially in the agricultural industry, of successfully introducing methods of collective bargaining, could fail to appreciate the soundness of the policy of Joint Conciliation Committees, or fail to rejoice at the steady progress which the Ministry of Agriculture is making.

CHAPTER XVII
GOVERNMENT POLICY FOR UNEMPLOYMENT

Unemployment is to-day a burning question; it will always be in industry an outstanding difficulty. The main lines of Government policy are, therefore, important; they are of comparatively recent date. From 1890, and indeed before, Metropolitan borough councils and their predecessors, the vestries, and the principal provincial local authorities had been in the habit of providing relief works every winter for the unemployed, each on its own method and without investigating the necessitous circumstances of applicants for work. Local Labour bureaux—really Labour Exchanges—had been established in London by some vestries and metropolitan borough councils without statutory authority. Their establishment was formally authorized by the Labour Bureaux (London) Act, 1902. In 1905 Lord (then the Right Hon. Walter) Long, when President of the Local Government Board, inaugurated a voluntary scheme consisting of central and district committees in London to collect funds and provide work to deal with distress arising from unemployment. The practical operation of this scheme was deemed sufficiently successful to warrant the passing of the Unemployed Workmen's Act, 1905, which provided for establishment, by order of the Local Government Board, of a statutory Central Unemployed Body and metropolitan Distress Committees in London, and outside London, of Distress Committees with central and local powers in each municipal borough or urban district with a population of not less than 50,000, and for the rest of a county, of Central and Local Committees. Then, as has been described, the State Labour Exchanges were authorized in 1909. Their establishment was the first attempt of Government to deal with unemployment on a considered policy.

1. STATE UNEMPLOYMENT INSURANCE

The next deliberate step was the scheme of State insurance against unemployment instituted by Part II of the National Insurance Act, 1911. It applied compulsorily to about 2½ million workmen in building, shipbuilding, engineering, construction of works and vehicles, iron-founding, and, to an extent, saw-milling, but not to non-manual workers.

The contribution per week was: employers, 2½d.; workmen, 2½d.; State, 1⅔d., the State contribution being thus one-fourth of the whole. The benefit assured was 7s. per week for fifteen weeks, but nothing during the first week of unemployment, and, when payable, only at the rate of one week's benefit for every five contributions paid. In 1916, the National Insurance (Part II Amendment) Act, 1914, brought in under the scheme a further 1¼ million workpeople employed in certain trades, principally metals and chemicals, and engaged in the manufacture of munitions of war. At the Armistice, the scheme therefore only covered some 3¾ million persons. This provision was wholly inadequate to meet the unemployment which ensued. A scheme of free out-of-work donation was instituted by the Government for both civilian workers and for men and women discharged from the Forces. This scheme remained in operation from November 1918, until November 1919, for civilians, and until March 1921, for ex-members of the Forces, and, in a few special cases, somewhat longer.

The Present Scheme of 1920

It was plainly necessary to make further provision, so a Bill for the extension of unemployment insurance was introduced in the House of Commons, first in December 1919, and again in February 1920, and passing into law in August as the Unemployment Insurance Act, 1920, came into operation on November 8, 1920. It is the statute under which the permanent National Unemployment Insurance Scheme is regulated—by it all previous enactments relating to unemployment insurance are repealed. This Act brings into insurance practically the whole industrial population, and also non-manual workers whose remuneration does not exceed £250 per annum. It excludes, however, agriculture and private domestic service, and empowers the Minister of Labour to grant certificates exempting the permanent employees of certain public undertakings, but, save in the case of railway servants, the numbers engaged in such specially excepted employments are not large. The total number of workpeople insured as the result of this Act is about twelve millions. The contributions prescribed by the Act of 1920 (since temporarily increased) are as follows:

	Employer's Share.	Employee's Share.	State Contribution.
Men	4d.	4d.	2d.
Women	3½d.	3d.	1⅔d.
Boys (over 16 and under 18)	2d.	2d.	1⅓d.

Girls (over 16 and under 18)	2d.	1½d.	1d.

The scheme is mainly worked through the Employment Exchanges. An unemployment book is issued to every insured worker, and, on obtaining employment, he is required to lodge it with his employer, who keeps it while the employment lasts, and when paying wages must affix to it a stamp of the value of the combined contributions of himself and the worker.

The books are valid for twelve months, from the beginning of July in one year to the beginning of July in the following year—a period known as the "Insurance Year." Every July the books are exchanged. Employers usually lodge the books of their workers in bulk at the Employment Exchanges, where fresh books are written up for the ensuing year, but a workman has the right to take his old book himself to the Exchange and obtain his new book for the ensuing year.

Workmen are also entitled to receive from the Department, on application, a statement showing the condition of their accounts.

The stamps representing contributions are sold at Post Offices, and the proceeds of sales are paid over weekly by the General Post Office to the Ministry of Labour. The remittances are placed to the credit of the Unemployment Fund established under the Act, and the State contribution is added to the amounts so received, and similarly credited to the Fund. When the Fund is in credit, i.e. when the revenue is more than sufficient to pay the benefits accruing due, any surplus moneys are handed over to the National Debt Commissioners for investment on behalf of the Fund. Owing to employment being exceptionally good immediately before and during the war, the Fund accumulated a considerable surplus, which amounted, in November 1920, when the Act of that year was passed, to about £20,000,000.

The benefits prescribed in the Act of 1920, which were afterwards temporarily varied, are 15s. a week for men and 12s. a week for women, with half-rate for boys and girls. Benefit was provided to be payable after the first three days of unemployment, afterwards permanently increased to six by the Unemployment Insurance (No. 2) Act, 1921, which constitute a "waiting period," and for a maximum of twenty-six weeks in any "insurance year." It was fifteen weeks in the Act of 1920, but this was increased to twenty-six by the Unemployment Insurance Act, 1921. The amount of benefit must not in any event exceed the proportion of one week's benefit for every six contributions paid, i.e. one day of benefit for each contribution. This limit is in certain cases temporarily suspended by the Unemployment Insurance Act, 1921.

The conditions for the receipt of benefit are that a prescribed number of contributions have been paid, viz. a minimum of twelve under the Act of 1920—in certain cases temporarily relaxed by the Unemployment Insurance Act, 1921; that applications for benefit have been made in the prescribed manner; that the contributor proves that since his application he has been continuously unemployed, capable of, and available for, work, but unable to obtain suitable employment, and that he has not exhausted his right to benefit. The workman is disqualified[17] from benefit if his unemployment is caused by a stoppage of work due to a trade dispute at his place of employment, or if he has lost his employment through misconduct or by voluntary resignation without just cause. Nor is benefit payable while the workman is an inmate of a prison or a workhouse or any other institution supported out of public funds, nor whilst he is resident outside the United Kingdom. Should he be in receipt of sickness or disablement benefit under the Health Insurance Acts or of an old age pension, he can claim no benefit.

Once an insured worker becomes unemployed, the employer must return to him his unemployment book, which he must lodge at the Employment Exchange, where he may claim benefit. When a claim is made, an inquiry is addressed by the Exchange to the last employer of the workman as stated by him on the claim form, in order to ascertain whether the conditions for the receipt of benefit are satisfied, and whether any of the disqualifications apply. During the currency of his claim, an unemployed insured worker must attend at the Exchange as evidence that he is unemployed. There he signs a declaration during the normal working hours of his trade that he is unemployed and unable to obtain suitable employment. In normal times, the frequency with which unemployed insured workers have to attend for this purpose is as follows: If the worker lives within two miles of the nearest Exchange, he is required to attend daily; if he lives between two and four miles from the Exchange, he attends every other day; between four and six miles, he attends once a week, and furnishes a declaration signed by two persons that he is unemployed; if he lives more than six miles from the nearest Exchange, he is not required to attend there personally for the purpose of giving evidence of unemployment, but may forward a certificate signed by two persons as to the continuance of his unemployment. Claims for benefit are adjudicated upon, in the first instance, by officers appointed under the Act known as insurance officers. The manager of the Exchange acts as an "insurance officer" and authorizes payment of obviously valid claims. Those as to which doubt arises are sent to the Chief Insurance Officer in London for adjudication. If the insurance officer's decision is unfavourable to the claimant, the latter has a right of appeal to a Court of Referees, consisting of an independent chairman, a representative of employers and a representative of the contributors. The chairman and the panels are appointed by the Minister of Labour. Either the insurance officer, or the Trade Union to which the claimant belongs, or the claimant himself, if leave is given to him by the Court, has a further right of appeal from the recommendation of the Court of Referees to an umpire appointed by the Crown, whose decision is final and conclusive.

While all claims to benefit have, in the first instance, to be made at an Employment Exchange—where benefit is in general paid—power is given to the Minister under Section 17 of the Act of 1920 to enter into arrangements with associations of contributors (practically all Trade Unions) under which members of such associations may prove their unemployment and receive their benefit through the machinery of the association. Before such an arrangement can be made, the Minister has to be satisfied that the rules of the association provide for payment out of its own funds of unemployment benefit to its members, and that the association has in operation a system for obtaining notification of opportunities of employment and of placing its members in employment. State benefit paid out by associations under this arrangement is subsequently repaid to the association from the Unemployment Fund. The associations are further entitled to a grant-in-aid of their administrative expenses not exceeding 1s. for every week of State benefit paid to their members under the arrangement. Shortly before the decline in trade, which began in the autumn of 1920, arrangements were completed or were in course of completion under Section 17 with nearly 200 associations having a membership of nearly 4,000,000 persons. Owing, however, to the increase of industrial depression and the consequent strain on the financial resources of the associations, a number of these arrangements were either terminated or not completed. The number of arrangements in operation on July 31, 1922, was 145, covering a membership of rather more than 1,000,000.

A new and important provision of the Act of 1920 was the right given to industries to contract out of the State scheme and institute special schemes of compulsory insurance for their own workers. Before a special scheme can be approved it has to be submitted by a Joint Industrial Council or an association fully representative of the majority of employers and employed in the industry. The Minister has to be satisfied that insurance against unemployment in the industry can be more satisfactorily provided by a special scheme than under the general scheme of the Act. The special scheme must cover all the employed persons in the industry, and the benefits must be not less favourable on the whole than the benefits provided by the Act. The industries which might naturally be disposed to contract out of the general scheme are those in which unemployment is less than the average rate of unemployment in all the industries included in the general scheme. In other words, only those industries might be expected to contract out which could, by reason of their lower rate of unemployment, provide greater benefits for the same rate of contribution as under the general scheme, or the same or a slightly better rate of benefit for a lower contribution. As against this, the rate of State contribution payable to a special scheme is reduced to a sum not exceeding three-tenths of the contribution which would otherwise be paid by the State in respect of contributions from the industry if the employers and employed persons in the industry remained in the general scheme. Only one special scheme has, so far, been approved, viz. that for the Insurance business, which covers about 80,000 persons. In view of the temporary emergency provisions made in the Unemployment Insurance Act, 1921, and the Unemployment Insurance (No. 2) Act, 1921, to meet the abnormal amount of unemployment, it became necessary to suspend the right of additional industries to contract out until the Unemployment Fund again attains a position of solvency.

A feature of the State scheme which is open to criticism is the right of insured persons to receive a refund in respect of their contributions. This provision follows generally the lines of Section 95 of the Act of 1911. The refund made is the excess of the employed person's share of the contributions paid in respect of him, less any benefit he has received. Refunds are not payable unless the employed person has reached the age of 60 and has paid in the aggregate a specified number of contributions.

Emergency Provisions

Owing to the acute industrial depression, it has been necessary to add to the permanent scheme a number of temporary provisions. It was realized, when the Act of 1920 was being framed, that special provision was required to meet unemployment occurring immediately after the passing of the Act amongst persons who were being brought into compulsory insurance for the first time. Accordingly, Section 44 of the Act of 1920 provided that, for twelve months after the commencement of the Act, i.e. up to November 8, 1921, eight weeks' benefit might be drawn if four contributions had been paid. Between the passing of the Act on August 9, 1920, and its commencement on November 8, 1920, the industrial situation materially worsened, and when the Act came into operation considerable numbers of workpeople were unemployed who had not paid even four contributions. The Unemployment Insurance (Temporary Provisions Amendment) Act, 1920, was accordingly passed in December 1920, providing that if an unemployed person could show that, although no contributions had been paid in respect of him under the Acts, yet he had in fact been employed in an insurable occupation in each of ten weeks since December 31, 1919, or of four weeks since July 4, 1920, that would count as equivalent to payment of four contributions under Section 44 of the Act of 1920, and eight weeks' benefit might be paid to him.

Temporary Act of March, 1921

Unemployment continued to grow, and early in 1921 it was apparent that many persons, who would normally have paid contributions and so qualified for benefits under the Act of 1920, were disqualified because, owing to the exceptional industrial position, they had not been in a position to pay contributions. The Unemployment Insurance Act, 1921, was therefore passed in March, 1921, which came into force immediately, and made special provision for the payment of unemployment benefit to persons who were not qualified for benefit by reason of not having paid contributions. Under the Act of March, 1921, it was provided that during each of two special periods, the first from March 3, 1921, to November 2, 1921, the second from November 3, 1921, to July 2, 1922, unemployed persons might draw up to a maximum of sixteen weeks' benefit provided they showed:

(1) That they had been employed in each of not less than twenty weeks since December 31, 1919 (ten weeks for ex-members of H.M. Forces).

(2) That they were normally employed in an insurable occupation.

(3) That they were genuinely seeking whole-time employment but unable to obtain it.

The decision whether applicants for benefit satisfy the special conditions prescribed by the Act of March, 1921, rests with the Minister, but was given the power to refer questions relating to compliance with the requirements to the Local Employment Committees. This power has been freely exercised, and in practice the recommendations of the Committees in regard to cases submitted to them for consideration are usually accepted by the Minister.

The Act of March, 1921, increased the rates of benefit to 20s. a week for men and 16s. a week for women, with half-rates for boys and girls. Arrangements were also made for an increase in the rates of contributions as from the beginning of the next ensuing insurance year, viz. July 4, 1921, but these were again increased by a subsequent Act. Notwithstanding the special provision of benefit made by the Act of March, 1921, large numbers of persons who remained unemployed and had exhausted their rights to benefit in July 1921. It was, therefore, decided to introduce fresh legislation, making further provision for this class of case.

Temporary Act of July, 1921

The solvency of the Unemployment Fund had been impaired by the Act of March, 1921, and at the same time distress from unemployment was increasing. The Unemployment Insurance (No. 2) Act was, therefore, passed on July 1, 1921, which gave power to the Minister to extend the maximum period of benefit which might be drawn in each of the two special periods prescribed by the Act of March, 1921, by six weeks, making the maximum period of benefit twenty-two weeks, instead of sixteen. A great number of six-week extensions were granted, dating from February 22, 1922, which expired on April 5, 1922. At the same time the rates of benefit were temporarily reduced to 15s. a week for men and 12s. a week for women, with half-rates for boys and girls as long as the "deficiency period" lasts, i.e. (Sect. 16) until the Treasury certifies that the Unemployment Fund is solvent; and the waiting period of three days in the Act of 1920 was permanently raised to a week as under the original Act of 1911. The contributions payable from July 4, 1921, were increased under the Act of July, 1921, to the following amounts:

	Employer's Share.	Employee's Share.	State Contribution.
Men	8d.	7d.	3¾d.
Women	7d.	6d.	3¼d.
Boys	4d.	3½d.	1⅞d.
Girls	3½d.	3d.	1⅝d.

These rates of contributions were payable until July 1, 1923, or the expiration of the deficiency period, whichever is the later, after which the rates prescribed in the Act of 1920 were restored.

It has to be borne in mind that the provisions made by the Unemployment Insurance Acts of December, 1920, March, 1921, and July, 1921, are temporary only, and not part of the normal State scheme. The Act of March, 1921, authorizes the Treasury to advance moneys to the Unemployment Fund up to ten million pounds; this was increased to twenty million pounds by the Act of July, 1921. It has been necessary for the Treasury to make advances to enable the Fund to pay the benefits: the amount owing by the Fund to the Treasury on December 31, 1921, was approximately eight million pounds.

Temporary Provision for Dependents' Act of November, 1921

As part of the temporary emergency programme of the Government to alleviate the abnormal unemployment existing in the autumn of 1921, the Unemployed Workers' Dependents (Temporary Provision) Act, 1921, was passed on November 9, which made provision for the payment of allowances to the wives and dependent children of unemployed workers who were in receipt of benefit under the Unemployment Insurance Acts. This provision, as made by this Act, was for a period of six months only— to end on May 7, 1922. The Dependents Act provided that persons who were liable to be insured under the Unemployment Insurance Acts and their employers should, for a period of six months from November 7, 1921 (which period might be extended in the event of any deficiency occurring in the Fund) pay additional contributions for the purpose of creating a Fund separate and distinct from the Unemployment Fund, out of which allowances for dependents would be paid. To the contributions of employer and employed, the State made an addition.

	Employer's Share.	Employee's Share.	State Contribution.
Men	2*d.*	2*d.*	3*d.*
Women			
Boys	} 1*d.*	1*d.*	2*d.*
Girls			

Grants were made at the rate of 5*s.* per week for a wife and 1*s.* a week for each dependent child.

Temporary Act of April, 1922

Yet still further emergency legislation has been necessary to meet the continuance of unemployment. On March 13, 1922, there were in Great Britain 1,690,000 insured persons registered as wholly unemployed and 225,000 as on short-time. Of these, large numbers began to run out of benefit on April 5, the date at which expired the six weeks' extension of benefit under the Act of July, 1921, each subsequent week adding to this number. On July 2, 1922, the whole of the emergency or "uncovenanted" benefit provided by the Temporary Act of March, 1921, would have wholly expired. In addition, on May 9, 1922, the Unemployed Workers' Dependents (Temporary Provision) Act, 1921, came to an end. The Government accordingly passed the Unemployment Insurance Act, 1922, which came into operation on April 6, 1922. The effect of its complicated provisions can be shortly summarized. It terminated the second special period under the Act of March, 1921, at April 5, 1922, instead of July 2, 1922, as by that Act provided. It then prescribed a third special period and a fourth special period, the third from April 6, 1922, to November 1, 1922, the fourth from November 2, 1922, to July 1, 1923. During the third special period, insured persons no longer entitled to benefit under the permanent insurance scheme will be allowed to receive "uncovenanted" benefit for an aggregate of fifteen weeks, increased to twenty-two weeks by the Unemployment Insurance (No. 2) Act, 1922—passed July 20, 1922. As this fifteen weeks' benefit had to cover thirty calendar weeks, it was divided up into three periods of benefit with a gap between each of five weeks, reduced to one week by the Act of July 20, 1922. During the fourth special period, twelve weeks' benefit will be paid, with two possible further extensions of five weeks each. The insurance benefit remains, under the Act of April, 1922, at the same level as before, namely 15s. per week for the men and 12s. for the women, with the additional benefit provided by the Dependents' Act of November, 1921, 5s. per week for the wife, and 1s. per week for each child. The rates of contributions by employed persons, employers and the State are the totals of the contributions under the Act of July, 1921, and the Dependents' Act of November, 1921, and are, therefore, as follows:

	Employer's Share.	Employee's Share.	State Contribution.
Men	10d.	9d.	6¾d.
Women	8d.	7d.	5¼d.
Boys under 18	5d.	4½d.	3⅞d.
Girls	4½d.	4d.	3⅝d.

These will be the contributions until the end of the deficiency period as defined in Section 16 of the Act of July, 1921.

From June 1921, to March 1922, the Unemployment Insurance Scheme was continuously carrying an average of 1¾ million persons, and 53½ million pounds of benefit were distributed; the Government's estimate is 1½ million persons wholly unemployed from April 1922, to June 1923. These figures will involve the payment of sixty million sterling in benefit for those fifteen months; of this amount the State will ultimately contribute one-quarter of the whole as against one-fifth under the permanent scheme of the Act of 1920, and the liability of the State will continue at the higher figure until the end of the emergency period. For the financial year 1922-23, the estimates provided for £12,196,130 as the State's contribution to the Insurance Fund and £551,760 to the Dependents' Fund, making a total of £12,747,890. In April fourteen millions of the twenty million borrowing powers conferred on the Minister of Labour by the Act of July, 1921, were exhausted, and it was estimated that the whole twenty millions would be exhausted by July 1922. The Act of April, 1922, therefore increased the borrowing powers of the Minister from twenty millions to thirty millions sterling.

The Efficiency of the State Scheme

This was investigated by the Committee on National Expenditure (*see* First Report *Parliamentary Paper*, 1922, Cmd. 1581, p. 144). They recommended, and properly so, that the question should be carefully explored of placing unemployment insurance on the basis of insurance by industry. They also urged an investigation by a committee of experts of the administration of the State scheme with a view to its improvement. Very considerable simplification and improvement would appear to be possible judging from the report of Sir Alfred Watson, the distinguished Government Actuary. The cost to the taxpayer of Unemployment Insurance and Employment Exchanges since 1912-13 is stated in the Report of the Committee on National Expenditure to be as follows:

	Administrative cost (gross).	Appropriation from Unemployment Fund.	Net Charge to Exchequer on account of Administration.	Government Contribution to Fund.	Total Charge to Votes.
	£	£	£	£	£
1912/13	640,000	151,000	489,000	378,000	867,000
1913/14	769,000	246,000	523,000	602,000	1,125,000
1914/15	764,000	227,000	537,000	546,000	1,083,000
1915/16	834,000	231,000	603,000	538,000	1,141,000
1916/17	905,000	329,000	576,000	746,000	1,322,000
1917/18	1,168,000	445,000	723,000	1,007,000	1,730,000
1918/19	1,950,000	455,000	1,495,000	994,000	2,489,000
1919/20	3,613,000	459,000	3,154,000	912,000	4,066,000
1920/21	4,593,000	1,115,000	3,478,000	2,200,000	5,678,000
1921/22	6,039,000	3,250,000	2,789,000	6,720,000	9,509,000
1922/23	5,020,000	4,150,000	870,000	8,231,000	9,101,000

The above figures do not include the cost of the Unemployed Workers' Dependents Act, which is financed independently of the Unemployment Fund and which imposes on the Vote charges of £2,192,000 in 1921/22 and £670,000 in 1922/23.

In my judgment, one thing is certain: if the National Unemployment Scheme had not been administered, as it has been, by the Ministry of Labour through the past and present dark days of depression, there would have been a serious upheaval in this country. The very fact that a worker could go and discuss his position with a sympathetic official of the Labour Exchanges helped to soothe his feelings of resentment against his unhappy lot. The receipt of benefit over the counter of a State institution encouraged him to believe that the State took an interest in the welfare of himself and his dependents. Whether, therefore, unemployment insurance by industries as a whole or each industry separately may or may not be arranged in the future, it would be exceedingly ungrateful of the people in this country to overlook the national work that has been performed by the Ministry of Labour and the officials of the Employment Exchanges under most difficult circumstances.

2. CONSTRUCTION OF WORKS OF PUBLIC UTILITY

Unemployment Grants Committee

In December 1920, the Government decided financially to assist local authorities to enable them to put in hand works of public utility in order to relieve unemployment, and appointed the Unemployment Grants Committee, under Lord St. Davids as Chairman, to receive applications for grants, examine schemes and allocate funds.

The Scheme of 1920

The Committee was instructed to observe, amongst others, these general principles:

1. Works were to be approved only in cases where the Ministry of Labour certified that serious unemployment, not otherwise provided for, existed in the area administered by the local authority undertaking the work.

2. The works were to be such as would be approved by the appropriate Government Department as suitable works of public utility.

3. The grant was not in any case to exceed 30 per cent. of the wages bill of additional men taken on for the work.

4. Preference in employment was to be given to unemployed ex-Service men.

The powers of the Committee were subsequently extended as follows:

(i) The grants could be increased from 30 per cent. to 60 per cent. of the wages bill.

(ii) The Committee was authorized to assist, in addition to local authorities, (a) "public bodies"—being any board, commission, rating authority or trustees, or other body or persons who manage or undertake works in pursuance of statutory powers, not being a body trading for profit, and (b) through the local authority—boards of guardians, distress committees and voluntary agencies.

A sum of £2,000,000 was placed at the Committee's disposal for the financial year 1921-22, and a further sum of £630,000 for 1922-23. All this money has been allocated, though not spent (see Table), and has provided, or is providing, direct employment for approximately 110,000 men for varying periods. Nearly as many more are indirectly employed in the preparation of materials for use on the approved works in factories, workshops, quarries, etc. Almost 3,000 applications from local authorities have been considered in detail, of which over 2,000 have been granted. The total capital cost of the works so financially assisted is estimated at approximately £9,000,000.

The Extended Scheme of 1921

In September 1921, the Government directed the Unemployment Grants Committee to undertake the administration of a further scheme for the relief of unemployment through local authorities. The new scheme provided for giving to local authorities, who put in hand works of public utility for the relief of unemployment, financial assistance on the following basis:

(a) *In the case of revenue-producing works*: Grants equivalent to 50 per cent. of the interest for five years on loans raised for a period of not less than 10 years in order to meet expenditure oil approved schemes.

(b) *In the case of non-revenue-producing works*: Grants equal to 65 per cent. of the interest and sinking fund charges on loans, raised to meet expenditure on approved schemes for a period of half the term of the loan, subject to a maximum period of fifteen years' grant. Both classes of grants were conditional on the work being commenced before January 1, 1922, and completed before March 31, 1923. The commencing date was, however, subsequently extended. A provisional limit of £10,000,000 was originally fixed as the total capital value of the approved works to which these two grants were to be applied. Local authorities, however, took up the Government proposals with so much enthusiasm, and the work of examining and approving the Schemes was accomplished so expeditiously, that by the end of 1921 schemes to the capital value of nearly £10,000,000 had been approved, and many others were under consideration.

The Government accordingly decided, in December 1921, to increase from £10,000,000 to £13,000,000 the capital value of the works which might be approved for these grants; and on the further development of the work, in January 1922, again extended the limit from £13,000,000 up to £18,000,000. Works up to the limit are certain to be approved. Up to May 31, 1922, the capital value of the works approved was:

Revenue-producing works	£4,587,005
Non-revenue-producing works	12,655,358
Total	£17,242,363

(For details, *see* Table)

The amount of direct employment which it is estimated will be given by these works is 629,113 men-months. The amount of employment indirectly given in the preparation of materials will probably amount to as much more. The cost to the Exchequer of the national financial assistance afforded to these works must necessarily at the present time be somewhat of an estimate, as the loans raised by the assisted authorities are for varying periods, with the result that the grants vary from periods of two-and-a-half up to fifteen years. The burden to the State is a diminishing one, and is spread over a period of fifteen years, but the total amount of the burden so distributed will probably amount to about £8,700,000.

The work done by the Unemployment Grants Committee has been of an extraordinarily difficult and complicated character and most capably directed. It has been no easy task to exercise a wise and statesmanlike discretion, amid the welter of proposals, the pressure for financial assistance and the stringent limitation on the latter. So far as it is possible to administer relief works on a sound basis the Committee has achieved it.

Analysis of Approved Schemes Assisted on the
Basis of 60 per cent. of the Wages Cost.

Up to May 31, 1922.

Nature of Scheme.	Amount. £	Percentage.
Roads	1,002,284	36.0
Parks, recreation grounds, cemeteries	623,604	22.3
Gas, water, sewerage and sewage disposal	474,650	17.0
Tramways	201,721	7.2
Painting	200,053	7.2
Docks, harbours, quays	92,235	3.3
Land reclamation	57,303	2.0
Electricity	48,675	1.8
Miscellaneous	90,093	3.2
Total	£2,790,618[18]	100%

Analysis of Approved Schemes Assisted on the Basis of Grants of Interest and Sinking Fund.

Up to *May 31, 1922.*

Non-Revenue Producing.		
Class of Work.	Value of Loan Sanction. £	Percentage of Total.
Roads	6,948,969	54
Sewers	3,585,239	29
Parks	758,997	6
Water (Scottish)	498,860	4
Sea defence	484,536	4
Public Instns.	267,063	2
Miscellaneous	111,694	1
Total	£12,655,358	100%

Revenue Producing.		
Class of Work.	Value of Loan Sanction. £	Percentage of Total.
Electricity	1,976,614	43
Water	1,334,097	29.5
Tramways	916,562	20
Gas	145,365	3
Cemeteries	51,942	1
Miscellaneous	162,425	3.5
Total	£4,587,005	100%

All Schemes.		
Class of Work.	Value of Loan Sanction. £	Percentage of Total.
Roads and footpaths	6,948,969	40.5
Sewers, sewage disposal	3,585,239	20.3
Electrical undertakings	1,976,614	11.6
Water undertakings	1,832,957	10.6
Tramways	916,562	5.4
Parks and Recn. Gds.	758,997	4.5

Sea defence and river embankments	484,536	2.8
Public Institutions	267,063	1.6
Gas undertakings	145,365	.8
Cemeteries	51,942	.3
Miscellaneous	274,119	1.6
Total	£17,242,363	100%

N.B.—The roads assisted by the Unemployment Grants Committee, while distinct from the Expedited Road Schemes of the Ministry of Transport, nevertheless were all examined by the latter Ministry before approval by the Committee.

3. EXPEDITED ROAD SCHEMES

To meet the extension of unemployment, in the autumn of 1920, the Government created a special fund for expediting the construction of new arterial roads and the improvement of existing roads of importance. The fund amounted to £10,400,000, consisting of: (1) £4,000,000 to be contributed from the Road Fund (established under Sections 2 and 3 of the Roads Act, 1920, from the proceeds of the duties on mechanically propelled vehicles and horse-drawn carriages and drivers' licences, less £600,000 payable to Local Taxation Account); (2) £1,200,000 to be contributed by the Treasury, and (3) £5,200,000 in loans from the Treasury to local authorities. The scheme provided for a grant from this fund to local authorities who expedited road works approved by the Ministry of Transport, of one-half of the cost, and if the local authorities were not able to find the other half, for a loan for that amount repayable within five years, at Treasury rate of interest. A condition was that one-half of the cost of the work should be labour cost; if the latter fell below one-half, the grant would be proportionately reduced. In addition the Government passed the Unemployment (Relief Works) Act, 1920, on December 3, 1920, which by the Expiring Laws Continuance Act, 1921, is continued in force till December 31, 1922. This Act expedites and simplifies the procedure for compulsorily acquiring and entering into possession of land for works of public utility intended to mitigate unemployment.

The 1920-21 Programme

On March 31, 1921, the commitments on this special fund, in respect of road works commenced to relieve unemployment, were as follows:

	No. of Schemes.	Grant. £	Loan. £	Total. £
Metropolitan area	23	1,200,000	623,000	1,823,000
Remainder of England, Wales and Scotland	130	1,762,000	1,255,000	3,017,000
				£4,840,000

A description of the schemes will be found in the "Report on the Road Fund for 1920-21," *Parliamentary Paper*, 1921, Cmd. 245.

The 1921-22 Programme

The continuance of unemployment necessitated still further efforts, and in the autumn of 1921 the Government, with the assistance of the Ministry of Transport, again took action. It was decided to allocate a further sum of £2,000,000 from the Road Fund for road works in areas in which the Ministry of Labour certified that serious unemployment existed, for the relief of which no other provision was available. This sum of £2,000,000 was allocated as follows:

(1) £1,000,000 to special road schemes estimated to cost £2,250,000 in Essex and Kent to be carried out by unemployed labour resident within the County of London, the Government undertaking to provide the difference between the cost of the works £2,250,000 and the £1,000,000 contributed by the Road Fund, viz., £1,250,000 less such contributions as could be obtained from the local authorities in whose districts the roads were situated.

(2) £1,000,000 to road works in the provinces other than the schemes referred to under (1).

The allocations for the unemployment road programmes of 1920-21, and the above for 1921-22 overlapped; a readjustment was necessary. The present readjusted allocations are now as follows:

1.	1920-21 Programme.	£
	(1) London (Arterial Roads)	1,139,364
	(2) Metropolitan Area	96,437
	(3) Provinces	2,260,093
	(4) Reserve	489,106

		£3,065,000 Road Fund.
	£3,985,000	£920,000 Exchequer Contribution.

(The £920,000 Exchequer contribution represents the authorized total of commitments against the £1,200,000 provided in Sub-head B. of the Road Grants (Unemployment Relief) Vote, 1921-22; the balance viz., £280,000, has been surrendered.)

2.   1921-22 Programme.

(1) Special London Schemes:

(a) Road Fund	£1,000,000	
(b) Ministry of Health (U.R.) Vote	£1,250,000,	less local authorities' contributions.
(2) Other Schemes (Road Fund)	£1,935,000	

Loans to Local Authorities under

3.   Sub-head A. of Road Grants—Unemployment Relief-Vote.

(1) In respect of the schemes under the 1920-21 programme, as above, up to a total of	£3,985,000
(2) in respect of schemes to be transferred from the 1920-21 programme to the 1921-22 programme up to a total of	402,671
	£4,387,671

The total commitments, therefore, in respect of road works to relieve unemployment are £12,557,671, less the local authorities' contributions under 2 (1) (b) above.

By the end of February 1922, the funds had been fully allocated to particular schemes, although in a few cases the details had not been completely settled nor the grants finally made.

The Special Metropolitan Schemes

Following the practice of 1920-21, a separate allocation was made in 1921-22 for dealing with unemployment in the Metropolitan Police Area. The distress in that area is relatively so serious that special steps had to be taken to cope with it. The conclusion, without doubt rightly come to by the Ministry of Transport, was that it was better to carry out schemes in Essex and Kent on which a large number of men could be employed than road works in the built-up metropolitan area on which only a small number could be usefully engaged. The labour engaged on these works is obtained through the Labour Exchanges in London.

The special London Schemes are as follows:

(1) Widening and improvement of the London-Tilbury Road, including new by-passes at Rainham and Purfleet.

(2) Construction of new road 21 miles in length from Tilbury to Southend in continuation of the Greater London "Eastern Avenue" already in progress.

(3) Widening and improvement of existing trunk roads in North Kent:

(a) Erith-Dartford Road.

(b) London-Folkestone Road.

(c) London-Dover Road.

(d) Watling Street (Dartford-Strood).

The Provincial Schemes

In the provinces so large a number of schemes have been put in hand that only a few typical cases can be mentioned.

Wallasey is widening her principal exit to the Wirral area and Birkenhead.

Middlesex County Council is undertaking the widening to 60 feet of Kingsbury Road, which connects Kingsbury, Hendon and Harrow.

Lancashire County Council is constructing a new road so that through traffic between Preston and Liverpool may "by-pass" Ormskirk. They are also improving the road from Liverpool to Prescot, parts of the existing road being widened, and the line and width of the remainder being improved by new construction.

Glasgow has widened an existing road and constructed two sections of new road, thus affording a connection between her principal south-western exits, and has also widened the road to the south-east. In addition, a commencement is now being made upon the widening to 80 feet of the road to Milngavie and Paisley.

Bolton has taken in hand the widening to 60 feet of Wigan Road.

Coventry is constructing a new road which will connect two of her north-western exits, and is widening to 50 feet Barker's Butts Lane, which will afford an additional convenient outlet in the same direction.

Norwich is constructing a section of a ring road round the city, including the erection of three new bridges.

Redcar and Eston are constructing a new road between Redcar and Grangetown, part of a scheme for providing better communication between Middlesbrough and Redcar.

Neath Rural District Council is constructing a new road through the Dulaid Valley, which will be a great improvement upon the winding, narrow and steep road that has hitherto been the only route through this industrial area.

Plymouth has widened the main road from Devonport to the north, and another road which will afford a less congested route from Plymouth towards the west.

Birmingham has in hand several extensive road widenings, forming part of her town planning scheme.

Southport is constructing a section of new road to enable traffic to and from Liverpool to avoid an exceedingly narrow portion of the existing road.

Durham County Council is constructing a section of new road from Easington towards Hartlepool which will provide a much shorter route for East Coast traffic.

Conditions Attaching to Grants

Since the initiation of the 1921-22 Roads Programme, the following conditions have been attached to all grants made from the Road Fund towards the cost of road works started with a view to relieving unemployment:

(a) Unskilled labour to be employed to the fullest extent practicable.

(b) All unskilled labour for a probationary period of six months to receive a rate of wages not in excess of 75 per cent. of the local authority's rate for unskilled labour. This requirement of a lower rate of wages than the prevailing local rate does not apply in cases where the work is carried out by contract.

The reduced rate of 75 per cent. does not apply to skilled men, employed in their trade, nor to properly qualified navvies.

In cases where the men are employed for not more than three days in the week the reduced rate applicable is increased from 75 per cent. to a maximum of 87½ per cent.

The probationary period may include the time during which the man has been employed on Government-assisted works under previous schemes.

The reduced rate (for the probationary period) must be calculated to the nearest farthing per hour.

(c) All unskilled labour to be obtained through the Employment Exchanges, which give preference to ex-Service men, and do not submit unskilled men for engagement unless they have been registered at an Employment Exchange for at least seven days.

4. POOR LAW RELIEF

In this country the traditional method of alleviating distress resulting from unemployment has been by Poor Law relief administered by Boards of Guardians. During 1920 and 1921, many persons who were uninsured and faced with destitution, and many persons who, though insured, found the benefit insufficient for the maintenance of themselves and their families, came to the Guardians for relief. There were three times as many people in receipt of out-door relief during the winter of 1921-22 as there were in 1915, and two and a half times as many as in 1910. This has necessitated the raising of large sums by Guardians and heavy increases in the Poor Law element in local rates. The administration of out-door relief under circumstances such as the present is a matter of the greatest difficulty. Guardians are, not unnaturally, disposed on humane grounds to give relief on as generous a scale as possible, which varies according to the Guardians' views and the district. On the other hand, this results in heavy charges on ratepayers, and a preference in many of the able-bodied recipients for doles instead of work, and possibly thereby an aggravation of unemployment. The general supervision of the work of the Guardians falls to the Ministry of Health, and that Department has undoubtedly discharged that invidious duty with judgment and efficiency.

Principles Governing Administration of Relief

By a circular letter dated December 29, 1920, the Minister of Health directed the attention of Guardians to the fact that under Article 12 of the Relief Regulation Order, 1911, they could not grant outdoor relief on a wholesale scale, or depart from the standard prescribed by that article unless under special circumstances—they were, therefore, bound to examine into the special circumstances of each particular case, and report to him any departure from the ordinary practice. This was a most necessary admonition in view of the amount being distributed from State funds in the shape of out-of-work donation and pensions. Again, by Circular 240 dated September 8, 1921, the Minister of Health reverted to this important matter and indicated the rules which, in his opinion, and that of the Association of Poor Law Unions, should govern the administration of relief. The first was that as Poor Law relief should be restricted to what was necessary to relieve distress, the amount thereof should be calculated on a lower scale than the earnings of the independent workman maintaining himself by his own labour. I need hardly stop to criticize the Labour contention that the relief should be of no less amount than the full Trade Union rate of wages of the recipient—it would be as demoralizing to the recipient as it would be disastrous to the community. The second rule was that no relief should be given without full investigation of the circumstances of each applicant, obtaining from the latter a signed statement of the total income of the household from all sources. The third rule was that the greater proportion of the relief granted should be given not in money but in kind, i.e. goods supplied on presentation of an order drawn on the Guardians' own out-relief distribution stores or on local tradesmen. Guardians were further urged to make, by way of loan, all relief given to or on account of any person over twenty-one, or to his wife or any member of his family under sixteen, in cases where there was a reasonable prospect of the recipient being able to repay within a reasonable period.

Ascertainment of Applicant's Income

A very important scheme for the voluntary registration of income from public sources such as pensions, allowances or grants from the Ministry of Pensions, or Local War Pensions Committees, unemployment benefit under the Unemployment Insurance Acts, dependents' allowances under the Unemployed Workers' Dependents (Temporary Provision) Act, 1921, and from other sources, was put into operation with great success in certain local districts under the auspices of the National Council of Social Service, which pressed the general adoption of the scheme upon the Government. A somewhat analogous scheme was later outlined by the Minister of Health for districts where such voluntary registration schemes were not in operation, which is described in Circular 261 dated November 23, 1921, and provided that similar information should be communicated by the Government Departments concerned to Boards of Guardians. At the same time, the Minister warmly endorsed the principle of voluntary registration. Guardians ought, of course, before giving out-door relief, to ascertain the weekly income of all the members of an applicant's household. The only sources of income which are not to be included are the first 5s. received from a Friendly Society as sick pay (Outdoor Relief (Friendly Societies) Act, 1904) and the first 7s. 6d. of sickness benefit (National Insurance Act, 1911, as amended by the National Health Insurance Act, 1920). On the other hand, Section 6 of the Unemployed Workers' Dependents (Temporary Provision) Act, 1921, suspended during the currency of that Act (i.e. up to May 10, 1922) the provisions of the Unemployment Insurance Act, 1920, forbidding Guardians to take account of the first 10s. of unemployment benefit. Section 14 of the Unemployment Insurance Act, 1922, made this suspension permanent and further enables benefit due to any person in respect of any period to be paid to the Guardians, if and so far as they have given that person out-door relief which they would not have given if the benefit had been punctually paid.

Assistance to Guardians to Carry out Works

In a number of cases the Minister of Health has facilitated the undertaking by Guardians of works of excavation, road improvement and the like for the provision of employment, and has allowed a variation of the regulations in force so as to enable Guardians undertaking such works to employ direct labour upon them instead of, as in the ordinary course, resorting to a contractor. In this way Guardians are enabled to select the labour from the ranks of those already destitute. In other cases in which Guardians have themselves been unable to provide any work, arrangements have been made by the Minister of Health by which works, which could not ordinarily be undertaken under the scheme of the Unemployment Grants Committee, are put in hand by the sanitary authorities, the labour engaged being supplied by the Guardians, and, in view of the importance of providing work rather than relief, the Minister has undertaken to give any sanction necessary to cover the contributions made in this connection by the Guardians to the sanitary authorities executing the Works, so long as the poor-rate does not incur a charge greater than the cost of relief which, but for the works, would have had to be given.

Funding of Cost of Relief

The cost of relief is normally a charge upon the current rates. There have been cases where the unexpected increase in the cost of relief resulting from unemployment upset the estimates of annual expenditure made by the Guardians and placed them in serious financial difficulties; and again, others where this annual cost is so heavy as to place an unreasonable immediate burden upon the ratepayers. To meet these abnormal cases, power was given by the Local Authorities (Financial Provisions) Act, 1921, to fund the cost, and for that purpose to authorize the raising of temporary loans for a period not exceeding a maximum of ten years. Temporary loans amounting, up to the middle of July, 1922, to £6,204,776 have been sanctioned by the Minister of Health under this Act, the usual period allowed for repayment being two years, though in several cases as much as five years has been allowed.

Help to Poorer Metropolitan Unions

Poor Law relief in London is always a matter of exceptional difficulty, and there has, since 1867, been a Common Poor Fund, through the agency of which certain Poor Law expenses are pooled and charged to the whole of the unions in London. During the war, this Fund was placed on a stereotyped basis, but with the rise of prices and with the growth of unemployment relief, hardship was caused to the poorer unions. An emergency arrangement was accordingly made for placing this Fund on an unstereotyped basis, much to the advantage of the poorer unions. Later, by the Local Authorities (Financial Provisions) Act, 1921, certain additional expenses in each union, and particularly the cost of out-door relief, so far as this was given within a scale and subject to conditions prescribed by the Minister of Health, were added to the expenses of a union chargeable on London as a whole. By this Act the burden of out-door relief in boroughs such as Poplar has been very greatly lightened by being spread over the wealthier boroughs like Kensington and Westminster. The Minister of Health, by Statutory Rules and Orders 1922, No. 3, prescribed the scale. It is, of course, within the power of Guardians to exceed the scale to meet exceptional needs in any particular case, but not at the cost of the Common Poor Fund.

Assistance to Guardians to Raise Loans

In cases where a Poor Law authority is in danger of being brought to a standstill by inability to raise from other sources loans sanctioned by the Minister for current expenditure, the Minister is empowered himself to advance the necessary money, on such terms and conditions as may be recommended by a Committee established under the chairmanship of Sir Harry Goschen, K.B.E. Up to the middle of March 1922, it had only been necessary to place three applications before this Committee.

CHAPTER XVIII
GOVERNMENT POLICY FOR UNEMPLOYMENT

5. GUARANTEE OF LOANS

The Trade Facilities Act, 1921, represents the most important of the constructive proposals which resulted from the conferences held by the Prime Minister at Gairloch in the autumn of 1921. The general opinion of the experts summoned to those conferences was that a large amount of new constructional work (extension and electrification of railways, construction of docks, extension of manufacturing works, etc.), which would normally have taken place during the war, still required to be carried out, but that such work was being held up by the high costs of manufacture and the high rates which had to be paid for money. It was felt that although much of this work was urgently needed for the proper service of the public handling of trade, the placing of orders might be deferred indefinitely in the hope of a fall in prices, and meanwhile the Government would be compelled to go on paying unemployment doles. If, however, cheap money could be provided, one at least of the main obstacles would be overcome, and this might in many cases afford sufficient inducement to commence the works immediately.

The Trade Facilities Act, 1921

Under the Trade Facilities Act, the Treasury is empowered to give a guarantee of principal and/or interest on a loan to be raised "by any government, any public authority, or any corporation or other body of persons," the proceeds of which loan are "applied towards or in connection with the carrying out of any capital undertaking or in, or in connection with, the purchase of articles, other than munitions of war, manufactured or produced in the United Kingdom required for the purposes of any such undertaking, provided that the aggregate capital amount of the loans, the principal or interest of which is guaranteed under this section, shall not exceed the sum of twenty-five million pounds." An Advisory Committee— Sir Robert Kindersley, G.B.E., Sir William Plender, G.B.E., and Colonel Schuster, M.C.—was appointed to recommend to the Treasury, the cases in which, in its opinion, a guarantee should be given.

The Committee's power is limited in two ways. In the first place it can only recommend a guarantee on a loan (i.e. it cannot guarantee an issue of shares). In the second place, the Committee has no power to recommend a guarantee "except for the purpose of a capital undertaking"(i.e. it cannot guarantee "working capital"). Many manufacturers in the country have orders on hand from foreign purchasers which they are unable to execute because they cannot finance themselves for the period between the date on which the orders are put in hand and the date on which payment is received from the foreign purchaser. Cases of this sort come under the Export Credits Scheme, and not under this scheme. The Act empowers the Committee to recommend a guarantee of a loan by a foreign Government, municipality or company, even though the articles (e.g. steel rails) manufactured with the proceeds of the guaranteed Joan were to be erected or used outside this country, provided always that the proceeds of the guaranteed loan itself were spent on goods manufactured in the United Kingdom.

The Trade Facilities Act thus enables new works to be undertaken which would otherwise have been postponed indefinitely. This on the one hand provides work directly and indirectly, and so avoids the demoralizing influence of the dole. On the other hand, if the scheme is wisely administered, no liability should fall on the Government, that is to say on the individual taxpayers. An assurance as to the wisdom of its administration was afforded by the composition of the Committee itself, combined with the pledge given by the Chancellor in the House of Commons that the Government would not interfere with the Committee's discretion. It was thereby made certain that sound business considerations rather than political expediency would be the guide to the Committee's activities.

Policy of Advisory Committee

While the greater part of the guarantees are given to companies and undertakings operating in Great Britain, the Committee considers that (subject, of course, to the material being bought in this country) it would help to advance general economic restoration if part of the fund were allotted to enterprises abroad, e.g. in the extension and improvement of foreign railways. By that means the foreign country's productive and purchasing power would be increased and she would resume her place as a supplier of the world's necessities and as a purchaser of the world's—and Great Britain's—manufactured goods. The difficulty, however, of dealing with foreign loans is that the countries which chiefly require assistance are those suffering from a heavily depreciated currency, and accordingly the service of a sterling loan would place so onerous a burden on them that it would be more than doubtful whether they could bear it and meet their obligations. To find adequate security in such cases is, therefore, a great difficulty, to which there is added the unwillingness of such countries to pledge even the inadequate security which it is within their power to give, and the record of many of these countries as regards their past obligations has not been such as to inspire confidence. The Committee keeps always before it the fact that it is a custodian of the Public Purse, and that much more harm than good would be done by recommending guarantees in cases in which the risks are greater than the principles of sound commercial prudence would accept.

The principles on which the Committee acts are these:

First, that its principal duty is to assist in the extension of sound undertakings with proved good management which are deferring well-thought-out plans of extensions or new works owing to the difficulty of raising money on reasonable terms under present abnormal conditions. It does not feel that it is called upon to recommend a guarantee in cases of a speculative nature for which, even in normal times, the promoters would have found difficulty in raising money. Nor does it think that it ought to recommend guarantees to relieve undertakings from financial embarrassments incurred through lack of ordinary commercial foresight on the part of those responsible for their management. A guiding rule is that the Government's liability should be as small as possible, and that a good commercial Security should be obtained in every case. In the second place, the Committee, realizing the gravity of the unemployment problem and the demoralizing effect of the continued receipt of doles, prefers those schemes which can be put in operation immediately rather than schemes which would take some considerable time to mature. In the third place, the Committee favours schemes of public utility. These fall into two classes. In the first place, there is a public utility undertaking as ordinarily understood, i.e. a corporation working under statutory powers and not trading for profit. In the second place are the companies, such as railway companies, which carry out an indispensable national service, and which in actual practice cannot earn excessive dividends for their shareholders. The reason for this preference has been partly the direct benefit to the general community from the improved facilities for the public thereby rendered possible, and partly the feeling that the guarantee could more properly be given to undertakings in respect of which it was unlikely that Government assistance would result in the earning of a large profit for private promoters and shareholders. In the fourth place, the Committee insists that all contracts must be on the basis of competitive prices. It feels that it would be wrong for the Government guarantee to be given in any case in which an unreasonably high price was going to be paid for the materials. Not only would such a course be unjust to the taxpayer by making the Government responsible for money going, not into wages and materials, but in paying high profits to manufacturers; it would be against the best interests of the country as a whole, since it would be impeding the return to a level of prices on which this country could meet foreign competition.

Difficulties of the Committee

The Committee has encountered many difficulties. The most important of these has been the lengthy negotiations necessary in every case. Frequently, the application when submitted is not on lines which the Committee feels justified in approving, and protracted discussions are required to reduce it to a business-like and acceptable form. The Committee in fact has been in the position practically of an issuing house which had to issue £25,000,000 worth of securities of every possible kind and variety in a very short time. Every one with experience of this class of business will realize what that means. As the Committee's power is limited to recommending the guarantee of loans, it has found a difficulty in the fact that many companies, at the time of making their application, have not possessed the necessary borrowing powers. Meetings of shareholders and debenture holders have frequently been necessary in order that these powers might be sanctioned. In other cases, the companies have required Parliamentary approval for an increase in their loan capital. All of these difficulties have taken time to surmount, but the Committee has always instructed applicants to start the preliminary work of obtaining their tenders, etc., as soon as it has decided the broad lines on which a guarantee could be given, so that real work can be commenced and men employed from the very moment that the necessary formalities are completed.

Guarantees already Given

Guarantees have been given in numerous cases. Work which otherwise would not have been done has been provided in the shipbuilding and repairing business, in the construction and improvement of docks and canals, in the extension of railways, in the electrification of railways, and in the extension of a number of electrical undertakings. This has facilitated the employment of direct labour in a number of places, and in addition, orders for the manufactured goods, principally cement and iron, have been placed in the manufacturing towns of the North and Midlands. To take a concrete instance, a guarantee has been given to the London Underground Railways for extensions. This means an immense amount of direct employment; it entails the placing of large orders for new locomotives and rolling stock. The men for whom employment has been found would otherwise have been living on the dole. Not only is their moral improved, but their purchasing power is increased, and the prosperity of industries as a whole has been fostered. Further, new tracts of country will be opened up for the Londoner and an impetus given to the construction of houses in suburban areas. This example, which is chosen at random from a number of others, shows the beneficial effect for the community as a whole, of the guarantees which have been given under the Trade Facilities Act.

Two White Papers (1922)—62 and 121—state that up to June 29, 1922, the Treasury has stated its willingness to guarantee principal and interest on loans of an amount of £17,042,143 for periods of years varying from four to twenty-five in respect of a number of enterprises of which the following are typical: Harland & Wolff (£1,493,345), ship repairing works on Thames and dock and wharf on Clyde; South Eastern & Chatham Railway Company's Managing Committee (£6,500,000), electrification of suburban lines; London Electric Railways Company (£6,000,000), enlargement of tunnel of City and South London Railway, and extension of London Electric Railway from Golders Green to Edgware; Calcutta Electric Supply Corporation (£500,000), purchase of generating and transforming plant and cables; Rhymney Valley Sewerage Board (£250,000), sewage disposal and sewerage scheme for urban districts in Rhymney Valley.

6. THE EXPORT CREDITS SCHEME

Under the Overseas Trade (Credits and Insurance) Act, 1920, the Overseas (Credits and Insurance) Amendment Act, 1921, and the Trade Facilities Act, 1921, the Government has done much to relieve unemployment by assisting the manufacturer to export his goods from the United Kingdom. The Government's plan is known as the "Export Credits Scheme"; it is administered by the Department of Overseas Trade. Its main essential is that the Government will guarantee bills drawn by United Kingdom exporters on customers abroad as against shipment of goods exported from the United Kingdom, when such bills are submitted through the exporter's banker with the banker's recommendation for guarantee attached, and the circumstances are such as bring the case within the scheme. The goods must be commodities (other than arms and ammunition) wholly or partly produced or manufactured in the United Kingdom, and include coal; but the Government will not assist to finance goods to be shipped on consignment, or the carrying of stocks either in the United Kingdom or elsewhere. The sum of outstanding credits must not at any one time exceed twenty-six millions sterling. The sum now outstanding is sixteen millions.

A lucid statement of the history, nature and working of the scheme by Sir Philip Lloyd-Greame, M.P., the Parliamentary Secretary to the Department of Overseas Trade, appears in the *Accountant* for February 4, 1922. The scheme does not supplant, but supplements, the ordinary commercial machinery of finance by providing credit in cases where, although the trade involved is inherently sound, bankers and financial houses are not disposed, or in a position, to supply the necessary accommodation. The closest co-operation is maintained with the banks. By letter of October 14, 1921, from the Bankers' Clearing House to the President of the Board of Trade, which appears in the *Accountant*, the Committee of London Clearing House Bankers expressed their willingness "to take all such steps as lay within their power to encourage the operation of the scheme, especially having regard to the object which the Government had in view, that of ameliorating the present conditions of unemployment." The Department of Overseas Trade is assisted by an expert and experienced business committee representative of the Joint Stock Banks, the Eastern Banks, the Accepting and Discount Houses, and manufacturers and merchants.

The scheme now applies to all countries in the world, but not to British India, Ceylon and the Straits Settlements, where there are large unabsorbed stocks and in respect of which adequate banking facilities exist, nor to Russia. New credits may be granted up to September 8, 1923, but all credits must be liquidated by September 8, 1927. Credits of two kinds are granted—"specific credits," and "general credits." The former are given in respect of particular transactions, for example, the completion of a large engineering or constructional contract abroad; the latter are credits up to specified amounts for specified countries and for specified periods in respect of goods not necessarily sold at the time the credits are given, and are intended to meet the convenience of merchants doing business abroad on short term credits. A United Kingdom merchant selling small quantities of commodities abroad through some travelling representative finds it quite impossible to submit each transaction to the approval of the Export Credits Department. The merchant can thus enter into transactions abroad up to the amount of the general credit without any reference to the Department, while the latter undertakes to guarantee the bills drawn within the agreed period for the goods that are shipped. The bills carrying the Department's guarantee are regarded in the discount market as "first-class bills." The Department prefers that the bills should be of as short duration as possible, but permits renewals provided that the credit is not extended beyond twelve months. With the Government guarantee that the bill drawn by the foreign customer or his agent will be met, the United Kingdom exporting merchant can thus borrow on the security of the bill at the ordinary market rate in the customary way.

Specific Guarantees or Credits

In case of specific credits the Department will guarantee up to 100 per cent. of the bills drawn against the shipment where the credit does not exceed twelve months, and up to 85 per cent. in cases where the credit exceeds twelve months. Two bills, in the latter case, are usually drawn, one for 85 per cent. of the transaction which is guaranteed for the full amount of the draft, and the second for the balance of 15 per cent. which is not guaranteed. The Department does not require a bill to be accepted before guaranteeing it. If security is to be deposited by the importer, the Department requires a letter of guarantee from the importer's bank, which must be an approved bank, that the bill will be accepted and that approved security will be deposited immediately upon the first presentation of the documents to the importer, and the Department assesses the value of the security so deposited. If no security is to be deposited, the Department requires a similar letter of guarantee, or some other satisfactory evidence that the bill will be accepted.

In case of default by the importer to accept or meet the bill when due, the Government has no recourse against the United Kingdom exporter where the importer, in the first instance, deposited security assessed as sufficient by the Department to cover the whole amount guaranteed. The importer may, however, have put up some security, but security not deemed enough by the Department to cover the whole amount guaranteed. In that event, the Department retains recourse against the United Kingdom exporter for 50 per cent. (when 85 per cent. or less of the bill has been guaranteed), or for 57½ per cent. (when 100 per cent. of the bill has been guaranteed) of the difference between the amount guaranteed, on the one hand, and, on the other, the total of the amount (if any) paid by the importer, plus the amount which the security was accepted as sufficient to cover or which the security, when realized, yields, whichever is the greater. When the importer puts up no security the Government retains recourse against the United Kingdom exporter for 50 per cent. of the difference between the amount guaranteed and the amount (if any) paid by the importer, where 85 per cent. or less of the amount of the bill has been guaranteed; where 100 per cent. has been guaranteed—for 57½ per cent. of that difference.

General Guarantees or Credits

In the case of general credits, when the Government accedes to an application made through a bank, say, to guarantee for six months bills up to a sum of £10,000 drawn by some particular United Kingdom exporter as against shipment of goods to Rumania, the Government would guarantee each bill up to its total value at such rate of commission as the Department may fix. At the end of the six months, if the amount of the guaranteed bills totals up to, say, £9,000, that represents the liability of the Government. When afterwards the bills fall due, and there is any loss, the Government has recourse on the United Kingdom exporter for 57½ per cent. of the ultimate loss. The Government does not require that any security shall be put up by the importer, but is prepared to consider the offering of special terms when security is put up.

The Government is also prepared to make arrangements with approved banks, banking houses, and credit associations under which, for an agreed premium, the Government will assume responsibility for a share not exceeding 70 per cent. of any loss incurred by such banks, etc., in respect of transactions carried through by them for United Kingdom exporters, which comply with the same conditions as to the nature of the goods as those prescribed under the Export Credits Scheme.

7. OTHER MISCELLANEOUS SCHEMES

Money has been allocated by the Government to assist schemes of land improvement, drainage and farm water-supplies so as to provide employment for agricultural workers, also forestry schemes and light railways:

	£
Ministry of Agriculture:	
Land Drainage	388,000
Of this £113,000 is recoverable from drainage boards and landowners.	
Farm water-supplies	9,600
The balance of cost, £18,600, is borne by landowners.	
Scottish Board of Agriculture:	
Land Drainage (half cost of schemes)	21,000
Forestry Commission:	
Unemployment schemes in addition to the normal estimates	206,000
Additional expenditure thereon by landowners and local authorities	141,000

In the sum of £5,500,000 set aside during the winter 1921-22 for general unemployment relief, provision was made for assistance to approved light railway schemes. Up to June, 1922, two such schemes had been approved for grants from the Treasury equal to half the total cost, subject to maximum grants of £162,500 in all.

From time to time steps have been taken to assist in relieving the situation by special measures operating in Government industrial establishments. A short-time system was introduced into War Office and Admiralty establishments to spread employment. The highest number of additional men thus engaged was 9,900. No additional men are now employed. Alternative work, e.g. waggon repairing, manufacture of medals, coin-blanks, locomotives, new wagons and miscellaneous articles for the Post Office and for private firms, has been carried out in War Office and Admiralty establishments. The highest number of men employed thereon was 8,800. The Office of Works undertook an emergency programme of decorative and repair work in Government Departments during the winter 1920-21, when the highest number of additional men thus engaged was 2,600. During the winter 1921-22, this Department also undertook relief work in the Royal Parks, the highest number of additional men employed on this work being 390. The expenditure in both classes of scheme was about £127,000. The sum of £563,000 was also set aside during the winter 1921-22 for accelerating Government contracts whereby employment was found for some 600 men.

Summary of National Expenditure

As between the Armistice and May 19, 1922, there has been devoted to the relief of unemployment out of public funds the total sum of £281,216,460, under the following heads:

			£
1.		*Granted by Government:*	
	(1)	Unemployment Relief Works	26,819,600
	(2)	Out-of-Work Donation and Unemployment Benefit	144,000,000
	(3)	Resettlement Training	} 31,972,000
		Civil Liabilities	
		Overseas Settlement	
	(4)	Export Credits Scheme	26,000,000
	(5)	Guarantee of Loans	25,000,000
	(6)	Accelerated Government Contracts	563,000
	(7)	Land Settlement of Ex-Service Men	1,523,860
	(8)	Loans to County Councils for Small Holdings for Ex-Service Men	12,269,000
			268,147,460
2.		*Appropriations from Non-Government Sources:*	
	(1)	Contributions by Local Authorities to 1 (1) above	12,694,000
	(2)	Contributions from National Relief Fund to 1 (3) above	375,000
			£281,216,460

In addition, local authorities have initiated, without Government assistance, relief works on which, between the commencement of trade depression in September 1920, and May 19, 1922, an aggregate of wages of at least £450,000 has been paid. Guardians have during the same period expended at least £60,000,000 on out-door relief. The above figures exclude the temporary loans by the Ministry of Health to embarrassed Guardians.

The really critical time in regard to unemployment will be the forthcoming winter, 1922-23. Trade Union out-of-work benefits have shrunk and dwindled through lack of funds. Homes and furniture, utensils, etc., with two winters' hard times have wasted down to the bare bone, clothing is worn out, and there is little or no reserve of resources; in some districts conditions fill one with apprehension. Added to the natural gravity—social and economic—of the situation, is the quite definite attempt of the Communists to exploit subterraneously these unhappy circumstances for revolutionary purposes.

PART III
THE TRUE LABOUR POLICY

CHAPTER XIX
THE OUTLOOK OF THE WORKER

My endeavour, henceforward, will be to state, as concisely and clearly as the subject permits, the main principles of policy which, in my judgment, should be applied to industry and its problems. As a necessary preliminary one must indicate the characteristics of the worker, his sentiments and aspirations, his defects, his virtues. After years of continual intercourse with labour, I confess my failure to meet in the flesh the workers as depicted in current revolutionary publications; nor have I succeeded in discovering among them that alien race with sympathies and sensibilities different from those of the rest of the community, ever moved by materialistic motives, always pursuing some irrational course of foolish selfishness as described in another type of literature. Against the unwarranted accusation that the British working-man in his opinions, feelings and sentiments is at all a different person from the ordinary British citizen, I have never ceased to protest. That he often suffers from a limited outlook, reacts to prejudice, and cherishes at times a grudge against society, I am not going to deny; but after working among workers, and, later, spending a great part of the war-period in controlling one million workmen of every description, and meeting in familiar intercourse their Trade Union executives, their district committees and their own deputations in numerous shops and yards, I can truthfully say that I generally found the worker a human being who is open to reason and to acceptance of a view substantially fair and just, once his ignorance is dissipated, his prejudices removed, and his humanity recognized. He has, however, no patience for humbug, rhetoric or cant. The trouble is that he has not been treated in the past as a sentient and rational person by politicians, or even his own Trade Union leaders — the main cause of our present industrial difficulties.

Ignorance about Industry

When in retrospect I recall my impression of the outstanding characteristic of the British working-man as I knew him in the workshops, I unhesitatingly fasten on his appalling ignorance of economic matters. Few of the "rank and file" have any conception whatsoever of the factors and forces which constitute that type of economic activity known as industry, still less of the contribution of industry to our national prosperity. And in regard to commerce and its part as the handmaiden of industry, their ignorance is even more profound. There never plays upon their imagination the least glimpse of the wonderful complexity of the mechanism of finance nor of the amazingly intricate organization of buying and selling. Who can blame them—they have never been told. I have kept a meeting of workmen keenly interested for an hour, after the conclusion of some official business, in a simple explanation of the functions played by finance in industry, and of the various kinds of financial operations entailed in the marketing of the product of their particular factory. Workmen respond to sympathetic education with cheerful alacrity. One of the expedients to which the Department of Shipyard Labour resorted was the institution of talks with workmen in various ship-repairing districts of the rôles being played in the stirring circumstances of the times by naval and merchant ships which were in dry-dock in local shipyards for reconditioning or repair. It had a most stimulating effect; men found themselves no longer sluggishly working upon an uninspiring metal hulk, but upon a living ship redolent with stirring associations, engaged in performing for the nation functions and duties which they could readily understand. There was less time lost, less sleeping on night-work, fewer stoppages of work; greater expedition, larger output.

Misconceptions as to Wages

The rate of wages is a matter ever present to the mind of the worker. It is the question of most general discussion in normal times; but at all times there is a strange failure to appreciate the true facts of the position. The average workman thought, before the war, that his employer was always able to raise his rate of wages, if not to the particular level demanded, at any rate sufficiently to afford a substantial increase, and that only the employer's selfishness stood in the way of this being done. Such most certainly was the opinion generally entertained by Labour when, during the war, the State became virtually the employer. Time after time bodies of workmen told me in perfect good faith that there was no difficulty whatever in the Government paying the rate of wages which they claimed. It seemed to them wholly immaterial that they were being paid, not out of the product of their work, but out of money borrowed by the State, with all the consequent inflation of currency and rise of prices. While, at the end of the war, many of the more enlightened Labour leaders appreciated, and a few, whom I honour, publicly denounced, the futility of the mad race of wages after prices, the average workman never was able to grasp it. There was a simple way, he thought, of compensating him for increased prices—merely to raise wages. Much of our industrial trouble to-day is due to the spurious appearance of prosperity which was caused by the high nominal wages of the war-period, and to the notion engendered in the mind of Labour that the Government could now, by resorting once more to war-time methods of controlling industry, create the same prosperity as existed immediately after the war. There is a foolish belief even among moderate men that the Government refrains from doing so in the interests of employers, in order to bring about a reduction of wages and a retrogression in conditions of employment, and to weaken the power of the Trade Unions.

Discontent and its Causes

One who moves among the workers cannot fail to be struck with the discontent which permeates them. Some people call it "industrial unrest," and condemn it as a menace to society; they forget that discontent with existing conditions is an essential element of progress. Society advances, not by uniform and rhythmic strides in a fixed direction, but by convulsive movements which, if plotted on a plan, would present the appearance of gyrations to right and left of the axis of progression, but generally register a forward march. In our democratic organization of society, where the mutual relations of constituent elements of the community are so generally governed by common-sense compromise, no section that was passive could ever hope to better its social conditions.

There are several causes for the prevalent dissatisfaction, of which probably the most potent is the increasing standard of education. Those who take the trouble to compare the education of our industrial classes of to-day with the lack of education of the workers at the beginning of the nineteenth century, as described in some of the first Factory Inspectors' reports, cannot fail to realize what enormous progress has been achieved; and this progress has—and happily so—given birth to a new vision. One of the first effects of education is to stimulate aspirations for improvement of material conditions, and the social observer generally finds that the first aspirations created in this direction by education are frequently not kept within the bounds which a fuller education and a wider experience ultimately impose.

Effect of Bad Environment

As, during the decades immediately before the war, the outlook of the workers widened under the influence of education, and especially as a result of the facilities for travel from the towns into the country for holidays and recreation, there has arisen an increasing dissatisfaction with industrial surroundings and home conditions. Nor is that surprising. Owing to the aggregation of factories during the industrial revolution, as near as possible to the centre of towns, and the huddling of houses in crowded, fetid and ill-built courts, as near as possible to the factories, a condition of things grew up, and indeed in many large towns still continues, more than sufficient to cause industrial discontent. Men are told by Socialist proselytizers the plausible story that such a state of things is one of the inevitable concomitants of the capitalistic organization of industry—a statement quite untrue. What caused it was the impotence of municipal organization in those days to control town planning or regulate the construction of streets and erection of houses, and the insufficient development of the social conscience as to the things which ought to be done for the good of the community. Some of our successful leaders of industry have conclusively demonstrated, by the most convincing of tests—viz., the commercial success of their venture— that there is no necessary connection whatsoever between bad industrial environment and the prosperity of their "capitalistic" works. Take for example Lord Leverhulme's beautiful garden village at Port Sunlight, and many similar model villages connected with other industrial undertakings. Nothing more conduces to industrial contentment than a comfortable home; no one can expect contentment in the occupants of many of the old houses which still disgrace some of our industrial centres, with their leaky roofs, rotten floors, muddy backyards and general structural decay, in which it is impossible to keep things nice, or children tidy, or household effects clean. Our municipalities are doing great work in sweeping away dwellings of this kind. Their final disappearance is a matter of expense and rates, for removal is costly. Local authorities are performing wonders in keeping, so far as they can, old buildings fit for human habitation, but there is a limit to the process of patching up ancient and dilapidated houses.

Fear of Unemployment

Another active cause of industrial discontent is insecurity of employment. If this week a man is in work and has no certainty of work next week—a condition even in normal times of large numbers of the industrial population—he is persistently oppressed by a desolating fear. Want of work is the menacing spectre which haunts the background of every working-class home. Intermittent employment produces serious decay of human fibres and moral degeneration—an inevitable result of the discouragement caused by fruitless seeking after work, and of the shifts to find food for wife and family. The inability to organize any uniform routine of living leads straight away to improvidence: when a man is in work one week, he spends all he has, relying on continuance of the work; next week, if unemployed, he has nothing except perhaps some unemployment pay or benefits. It is systematically rubbed into him by exponents of Socialism that unemployment is solely caused by the capitalistic organization of industry, that there can be none under the Socialists' regime, as if any socialistic scheme for the reorganization of industry is going to compel the consumer to buy more commodities and services than he would be prepared, or able, to buy under capitalistic production.

Dissatisfaction with Status in Industry

A contributing cause to industrial discontent of growing moment is what the worker describes as the denial to him of a human status in industry. He complains, especially in the matter of being taken on or discharged or put on overtime or night-work, indeed, with respect to the whole conditions of his employment, that little or no regard is paid to him as a human being. He is content to accept the theory of the Labour intellectuals—it is certainly not his own conception—that he is a wage-slave taken on and discharged just as it suits his employer's interests, and that his labour is bought and sold on the same principles as any other raw material in industry. The old paternal relation of employer and employed, unfortunately much weakened by the introduction of the factory system, has undoubtedly disappeared with the conversion of family businesses into vast joint-stock company concerns; personal touch between the master and his men no longer exists. There is, however, no ground for suggesting—as Socialists are fond of instilling into the minds of the workers—that this is still another inevitable result of the capitalistic organization of industry. In some of the largest and greatest of capitalistic works, workers can be, and to my knowledge are, treated with consideration and sympathy. Their human values can always be respected and full human status accorded to them if only the right spirit prevails between employers and employed, and proper machinery exists for its infusion into workshop life.

Belief in Agitation

Discontent, expressed in constant agitation, has unfortunately been of practical value; that is one reason why it is so rife in industry to-day. No substantial increases in wages or improvement in working conditions have, in the past, been conceded voluntarily by employers, but only after pressure by the Unions, subject, of course, to considerable qualifications in special cases. It is more or less inevitable that it should be so, having regard to the way in which the machinery of collective bargaining has been operated by both sides. Every time, when an increase of wages, or an improvement in conditions is demanded and refused, and then ultimately given under threat of a strike, it feeds the springs of future discontent and confirms in the workers' minds the efficacy of agitation. In the latter days of the war the unsettled condition of industry was largely due to the fact that in the earlier days wage-increases had been refused and then conceded by the Government under pressure of strikes and threats of stoppages by the workers. Each time such capitulations took place it seriously ministered to the spirit of discontent.

Desire for Improvement

When one turns to other forces now commencing to pulsate through Labour, one is impressed by the increasing general desire for mental and cultural improvement, at times pathetic in its search for simple gratifications. Some persons scoff at this seeking after higher things by the working-classes; their scorn is ill-timed, and their irony misdirected. There is rapidly developing, I am glad to say, an increasing movement in this direction. Those engaged in social work in our great industrial centres can testify to the innumerable ways in which this aspiration is finding healthy expression.

More than one foreign observer has recorded his opinion that the stability of the British Constitution is materially due to the strong attachment to, and sentiment for, family life that prevail in this country. No member of the community is a stronger supporter of family life than the British working-man; no one is prepared to make more substantial sacrifices for its maintenance and preservation, no one more frequently has to make them. In this respect the British worker is one of the greatest living individualists, and the strength of his family individualism will never let him be converted into a thoroughgoing Communist. Theorists may talk to him till tired of working for the State and the community—I had to use that argument in war-time—he will answer them, as I have been answered on the Clyde: "I work for the wife and bairns."

Low Conception of Work

In regard to his conception of work the British working-man is hopelessly wrong in his outlook. Some find pleasure in work; the manual worker is not one of them. He has come to regard work as a species of thraldom, instituted, not for his profit or improvement, but solely for the maintenance of his employer and the swelling of his profits. This, of course, is merely a weak dilution of the Marxian fallacy. The modern manual worker, because he has never been taught to look upon work as a moral duty or upon industry as one of the highest forms of national service, sees no dignity in work, and is sensible of no obligation incumbent on him to work to the best of his ability or even for the duration of the working day. The number of expedients to which I have known manual workers resort— in other respects honest, upright men—in order to scamp the job, or cut time, would be perfectly surprising to those not conversant with industry. To-day the moral obligation to work seems inverted into a duty to do as little as possible for the wages. Sometimes the motive is to make the job last longer, at other times, to assist unemployment by making work go round, and, where remuneration is based on payment by results, for less altruistic reasons, to force up the prices paid for the job. But although the Marxian doctrine—that the more work an employee does the more he contributes to the betrayal of his brother workers by assisting the employer to amass illicit gains out of their exploitation—explains much of the work-shyness and "ca-canny" of to-day, there are other reasons. One is the extent to which work is subdivided in modern factory organization. In an engineering shop, a job done thirty or forty years ago by a skilled man on a general purpose machine is now subdivided into a large number of constituent operations. These will be performed by different workers on different semi-automatic machines, and the finished part will be assembled by another set of workers into the final product. In the old days the tradesman saw the finished article gradually taking shape under his creative craftsmanship; to-day no worker sees anything but the single operation which he performs. As a result, there is little to minister to the instincts of a craftsman. The workman employed on such repetition work becomes quickly apathetic, his interest relaxes, his inventiveness atrophies, his initiative dies, he degenerates into a cog, and, being human, into an inefficient cog, in the vast mechanism of industry. These methods of mass production are quite inevitable in modern efficient practice, and the only antidote is to encourage the workers to acquire a wider interest in industry, and in the prosperity of the works in which they are employed, and to cultivate a spirit of culture so that their minds may be filled with other things which satisfy their human aspirations, and replace the noble satisfaction which a tradesman used to feel as the creation of his handicraft grew beneath his skill.

Suspicion of Employers

If asked what was the strongest sentiment I found permeating the workshops, I should answer, suspicion of employers. In some districts it is worse than in others; in some works it is worse than in other works in the same district. Many reasons have been advanced for its existence, but the real explanation is simple. Between the fifties and the eighties of last century, when the machinery of collective bargaining was coming into operation, the principle of action adopted by many employers was "enlightened self-interest"—the individualistic theory that an employer best served his own interests, and, automatically by so doing the best interests of the country, by furthering on all occasions his own advantage. To call this greed or selfishness is wrong. It implied no callous disregard of the rights of the workers, but it did involve such a bias of mind that the interests of employees were subordinated in the scheme of industry to those of the employers. In the course of collective bargaining, of manœuvring for position, of higgling, many managements contracted the habit of seizing upon any circumstances which might enable them to cut piece-rates and time-allowances, bring down wages, revise conditions of employment, and adopted the invariable attitude of resisting all the demands of their employees. Such employers have disappeared, but "the evil that men do lives after them." Not unnaturally, the workers learned to decipher some hostile motive behind each action of their employer, however apparently beneficent, and regarded everything he did with unalloyed suspicion, and as calling for the closest scrutiny. This is the cause of the want of confidence in the industrial atmosphere to-day. While it continues so charged with mistrust, confidence between all persons concerned in industry, which is necessary for production and essential for smooth running of the industrial machine, can never flourish. All employers unreservedly now deprecate this unhappy condition of things, many have gone to exceptional trouble to dissipate the blight on industry of such distrust, but memories are long, industrial prejudices tenacious, and it will take time and much effort to forge a bond of trust.

The Worker and his Trade Union

The attitude of the British worker to his Trade Union reflects the British temperament. Abroad one sees the workers follow their Unions in matters both industrial and political; in this country there is no such general surrender of individual judgment. So far as industrial questions are concerned, with the exception of some smaller Unions whose members seem always in a seething condition of revolt, and certain revolutionary elements in some of the great Unions, the majority of Trade Unionists will follow their own

Union leaders. That, however, is a very different thing from following the general lead of the combined Trade Unions as expressed through the Trades Union Congress or the Labour Party. As one result of the craft organization of industry in this country, which at times during the war showed signs of disintegration but now seems more firmly established than ever, the Unions are almost as suspicious of one another's motives—a result of the fear of one trade invading the other's work—as Labour in the mass is suspicious of the employers. Where, however, a question is, rightly or wrongly, represented to involve a principle directly affecting the common interests of all workers, the Trade Unionist has been so well drilled in the virtue of solidarity that he will, generally, range himself under the banner of organized Labour. In regard to political matters there is no such docility, although compelled to contribute to his Union's political fund. To-day he is forced to do so, in spite of his power to object under the Trade Union Act 1913; if the Trade Union Act (1913) Amendment Bill 1922 passes, he will not be liable unless he expressly agrees. There is evidence of independence in the results of the General Election in 1918 and of by-elections since, where very large sections of the workers have voted, not for the official Labour candidate, but for the candidate of another political party opposing Labour. This fact undoubtedly explains the strenuous efforts of the Labour Party to formulate a composite political programme which will appear to its Trade Unionist members as an industrial programme, and to non-industrial supporters as one primarily of a social character.

The Worker and the Community

The worker's conception of himself in relation to the community invites a comment. As a substitute for a convincing argument that the interests of the worker are entirely separate from, and opposed to, those of the rest of the community organized on a capitalistic basis, the worker has been assiduously encouraged to develop his "class-consciousness." If by any process of auto-suggestion he can convince himself that what tends to promote the general common weal does not tend to further the interests of Labour, but generally runs counter to them, he may more surely be relied on to adopt an attitude of militant antagonism to continuance of the present organization of industry and society. The efforts of extremists are continually directed to foment this feeling of class-consciousness until it culminates in class-warfare. I have had wide opportunities for gauging the prevalence and depth of the sentiment, and though one found it in active operation among certain groups of men on the Clyde, in Barrow, on the Mersey, and in a few other centres of advanced industrial thought, I never encountered much of it amongst the general body of working-men. They do not accept the proposition that they stand, as beings apart, in a separate category from the rest of the community. Indeed, in the latter days of the war, many Unions, recognizing the interests of their members as consumers rather than as producers, abandoned the policy of increasing wages and strongly urged the regulation of prices instead, so much did the circumstances of consumption affecting their members as citizens exceed in importance matters touching their special interests as workers.

One may carry this a stage further. In spite of the ranting of extremists that the war was an effort of capitalists to advance their own financial ends, and utterly inimical to the interests of the workers, Labour in this country stood shoulder to shoulder with the rest of the community and willingly underwent the greatest sacrifices both in the matter of military service and in regard to the suspension of Trade Union rights and customs. Had the Government at the beginning of the war courageously conscribed every person for national service, many galling disparities would never have arisen, and gross inequalities of sacrifice would have been forestalled, the aggravation of which, towards the end of the war, and not without justification, upset the equanimity of the workers and caused serious industrial upheavals. It should never be forgotten that in the early days of the war universal national service was strongly urged by prominent Labour leaders, but was killed by the cries of "Business as usual," for which members of the Government were alone responsible.

CHAPTER XX
REFORM OF INDUSTRY INSTEAD
OF SOCIALIZATION

The Three Dominant Aspirations of the Workers

The organization of industry cannot continue in its present state of instability; something must be done. The Socialist who would reconstruct industry, the anti-Socialist who would reform it, each assumes it to be necessary to satisfy aspirations of the workers that are not satisfied under conditions as they exist to-day. The three greatest aspirations animating the workers are, in their order of relative importance: first, removal of the ever-present menace of unemployment; secondly, recognition in industry of the worker's human status; thirdly, distribution, as of moral right, of an equitable share of the product. Talk, as I did during the war on over three thousand occasions, to the ordinary working-man, those are the three basic sentiments you find swaying him. All the intricate schemes for reconstruction of industry which the fertile and fervid imaginations of the Labour intellectuals have evolved are largely unintelligible to him, and leave him unmoved and cold. He cares nothing about the delicate and subtle regimentation of industry and society as Guild Socialists would have it; he wholly fails to grasp, indeed, is acutely suspicious of, a Socialist commonwealth constructed and controlled on a vocational or functional basis. The test which he applies to such complex and conjectural conceptions is their efficacy in satisfying those three great fundamental aspirations. But that is too restricted a purview for an aspirant political party, and was astutely declared by the old parliamentary hands of the Labour movement to constitute too narrow a class-basis to support a popular appeal. Hence it was that all the non-industrial doctrinaires—and there are many of them attached to the Labour Party—were set to work to compile a new Social Contract. Scores of pamphlets have now been published descriptive of the policy of the Party on every conceivable topic—political, administrative, judicial, local government, social, and industrial—national, imperial and international. If formulation on paper of ideals of humanitarianism, and quixotic Utopianism, without any consideration of cost or practicability, is statesmanship, the Labour Party's policy is truly admirable. It outlines in glowing splendour a wonderful new mechanism of politics, society and industry, in which every exterior part falls into place with the smoothness and precision of a model engine constructed out of a box of parts—but, like the toy, with no works inside. That this mysterious mechanism may provide in some subtle and not very obvious way, the means of securing the three fundamentals is its only recommendation in the eyes of the great mass of Labour.

If it is right to assume that the ordinary worker's dominant desire is to obtain reasonable satisfaction of these three aspirations, and of the soundness of that assumption I entertain no doubt, for at my three thousand odd conferences and meetings with Labour during the war—at all of which accurate notes were taken of the subjects of discussion—these were the three foremost topics, two questions arise: Are these three aspirations proper ones to be satisfied? If so, how can they best be satisfied with due regard to the interests of the community?

Can and Ought they to be Satisfied?

There is in regard to unemployment but little difficulty in coming to a sound conclusion. Unemployment, and to a less extent under-employment, is on every ground—humanitarian, social, economic—a curse so great that no reasonable effort should be spared to reduce to a minimum the probability of its occurrence, and to mitigate as far as possible its dire effects when once it has supervened. Many will differ as to how far it is right to go in the provision of measures of alleviation, but that is a difference more in degree than in principle. In regard to the investiture of every worker in industry with "human status" there is a more radical cleavage in opinion. While few employers will contest the right of the workmen through their constitutional representatives to voice their demands for settling wages and conditions of employment, and such demands—backed up by the power to apply economic pressure—are effectively voiced by the Trade Unions, most employers will deny the right of the workers "to interfere in the management." It would be quite impossible to have two sets of persons attempting to manage a factory, or to direct the conduct of the business on the commercial side. But between the fixing of wages and conditions of employment, in which it is admitted that Labour should have a real voice, and the actual executive direction of a business in which it is clear that Labour could not exercise a voice, if efficiency is to be preserved and discipline remain unimpaired, there is a wide sphere of matters which are proper to be discussed between employers and representatives of the workers, and which, when discussed and settled, can be left for executive action to the employers. There is ample room for compromise. The confusion surrounding the catchwords of "a voice in conditions," "interference in the management," wants to be cleared away before any more harm is done.

On the question of remuneration there is really, if the matter be closely examined, no difference whatever in principle. Most employers agree with the unions that the worker is entitled to a fair share of the product; they disagree as to what proportion of the product constitutes a fair share—a dispute not as to principle but as to quantum. No employer, so far as my experience goes, would contend that he was entitled in good times to pay his workers nothing more than a bare subsistence wage, and appropriate for himself as profit all the balance of revenue after payment of working expenses and the market rate on capital. What usually happens in bad times is that the workers in employment get, as a first charge on the product, wages much higher than subsistence rates, and the shareholders go without return, which results in great deprivation to many whose meagre incomes consist of such dividends. The more critically one examines the three fundamentals the more one is irresistibly driven to the conclusion that there are no issues between employers and the workers in regard to any of them which cannot form the subject of fair collective bargaining. But that is what is denied by the intellectuals of the Labour Party, entirely on their own a priori reasons. Happily their doctrinaire conclusions meet with scant respect from the general body of workers.

The Vagueness of Labour's Scheme of Reconstruction

There are only two possible courses for the future—either to reconstruct industry on some entirely new basis, or to maintain the present system of organization and introduce reforms which will cover the three fundamentals as a first beginning. That really is the question on which a decision must sooner or later be taken by the nation, and far-reaching national consequences will turn upon it. Labour says: "Destroy the present industrial system, and replace it by something based on public, and not private, ownership of the means of production." Did we know exactly what Labour's scheme of reconstruction is, it could be critically examined in detail, and its practical effect on the prosperity of industry, the welfare of the worker and the good of the community dispassionately considered. But Labour with prudent reticence has not provided us with any official scheme. Different sections of Labour have tabled all kinds of variant and in many cases discordant schemes which agree in one respect only—the elimination of the private employer. All that the Labour Party tender in the way of constructive reorganization is the vague formula of "nationalization and democratic control," Nor will the Party undertake to say what is the method and kind of industrial control—a matter on which depend the whole efficiency and success of industry—which it has in mind. The truth is, the Party has not succeeded in devising any scheme of industrial control on which it can agree, and the Executive Committee, though instructed to report on that question, has either been unable to do so, or have found it expedient to postpone committing itself Yet the Party, after invoking fire from Heaven on the Government as retribution for its policy of opportunism in regard to industry, calls upon the country to witness that Labour has a considered and well-thought-out industrial policy, which it euphemistically calls "democratic control," and announces with ingenuous *naïveté* that it is such a system as will always harmonize with the special circumstances and requirements of each industry! Who is the opportunist? The Government in adhering to continuance of the established organization of industry—on which the greatness of England's trade and commerce has been built up—or the Labour Party, which, without any clear idea of what it would put in its place, would destroy the existing organization in the complacent expectation that by some process of abiogenesis a better system will soar like the Phoenix from the ashes? There would be a short and sharp retort from the members of any of the great Trade Unions, for example the Amalgamated Engineering Union, were the Labour Party to propose to reconstruct that proud organization on the basis of a resounding formula. The Executive Committee of that Union—supposing it, agreed to consider any such gratuitous suggestion from even a Labour source— would insist—at least it always did with me during the war—that general phrases should be reduced into clear, crisp and definite proposals, each one of which could be subjected to a microscopic scrutiny of the most searching kind, sufficient to reveal its true nature, its effects direct and indirect, and its remotest implications. Is not the nation entitled to similar information? In Part I, chapter IX, I outline the injury to industry and the country that would inevitably result, in my judgment, from any socialistic reconstruction of industry. Here I am only concerned to show that when the flowing garments of flowery phraseology are respectfully removed, they are seen to cover nothing but a hollow lay-figure without the least semblance to even an articulated model. This is what we are invited by the Labour Party to set up and worship as the future genius of British industry.

The Recent Change in Labour's Proposals

Labour has started from the wrong end—not to ascertain what are the defects in the present industrial system and the manner in which they can best be remedied—but how to get rid most easily of the private employer under the honest but uncritical and irrational belief that unless he is removed the defects cannot be remedied. This was the notion of Labour in the days when first it embraced State Socialism. Nationalization of industries, under which the Government would replace the private employer, was described in radiant language as "the charter of salvation of the working-classes." Then Labour acquired some experience of the State as a "model employer"—in the Post Office, in the Royal Dockyards, in Woolwich Arsenal, and in other Government factories. With the disappearance of the private employer the workers in such nationalized industries found to their surprise and clamant regret that their conditions were not better, but were worse. The State, they discovered, was not so considerate a master as the private employer—not so disposed to recognize Trade Unions, or introduce Trade Union conditions, or pay standard rates of wages. Was ever a complacently cherished conviction so rudely shattered! Any critical inquirer would have stopped to consider whether after all it was right, with this practical experience, to assume that the only way to improve industrial conditions was to put an end to the private employer. Some prominent Trade Unionists did pause to think, and more than one has told me of his consequent renunciation of Socialism. So the old doctrine died, and some other doctrine was urgently needed—a fitting opportunity for the intellectuals. A new ship had to be constructed on the old keel of the abolition of private ownership, and this time it had to float. And after all, was anything easier? It had become fashionable, during the war, to talk of the rigidity of bureaucracy, and the inelasticity of bureaucratic direction—precisely the same thing might have been said with equal justice about the Trade Unions, for they are bureaucracy *in excelsis*—but no one thought of it. On the other hand, men's ears were dinned with the mobile excellencies of democracy, its extraordinary versatility in adjusting men to their environment, and in modulating the qualities of the latter to its human content, and the air vibrated with theories of political self-determination. Democratic Government was being hailed as the balm for Europe, and what was more natural than that industrial self-determination under the name of "democratic control" should be acclaimed by Labour as the restorative of industry. So the new ship was built and called "Nationalization and Democratic Control." Put into the water in 1918, it still lies a mere hull, unengined, unfinished and unclassed.

But taught by war-time experience, the Labour Party has become more cautious. It no longer contends as it used to do that all industries can be nationalized—an admission, the importance of which should not be overlooked. It would nationalize and democratically control only some of the great national industries, the smaller and less well-organized industries it will leave, for the present, alone. It even goes so far as to admit the economic necessity for the continuance of many middlemen. The industries that it would nationalize are those that were small and badly organized once, but which responded to the enterprise and initiative of the pioneers who made them and so grew great. This, when stripped of dialectics, means that Labour is satisfied that its regime of nationalization and democratic control whatever else it can achieve—and as to that we are left to speculate—cannot supply the enterprise and initiative requisite for the development of budding industries. At what stage in the growth of an industry Labour's machinery of nationalization and democratic control can step in and infuse those two great qualities which are essential for vitality and progress, at a voltage higher than can be generated under private ownership, no information whatsoever is vouchsafed to us.

Those who have studied with a critical eye the official details of Labour's industrial policy in chapter VIII, will have noted that the same veil of indefiniteness enshrouds the practical working out of "nationalization and democratic control." Is it to mean an increased financial burden on the State? No details. How is the requisite capital to be procured when we have performed the national obsequies over the private capitalist? No details, except that it will be derived from a mythical "national surplus" which now, at any rate, does not exist. By what means are the waste and inefficiency which experience has shown to be inherent in bureaucratically administered industries to be obviated? No details. What is the mechanism which is going to compel the home consumer to increase his consumption and the foreign consumer to buy commodities which he will not, and cannot, buy to-day? No information. Where will the secret fund be situated, and how is it to be formed, which is going to finance higher wages and better conditions than under the present scheme of industrial organization? We are not informed—that it cannot be built up from employers' profits is clear from chapter XXVI. For the answers to these practical questions of crucial importance, and to many others, we are left groping in the dark. All we are told is that learned intellectuals of the Labour Party, out of their wealth of industrial research and ample gifts of prescience, when the proper time comes, will open their Pandora's box and reveal the secrets. Is the nation prepared to gamble its existence on that assurance?

Reform of Industry v. Reconstruction

Happily for the country, the ordinary worker is no more intrigued with the intellectuals' proposals for the reconstruction of industry, or society or the State than he is with their schemes for the reconstitution of his Trade Union, all of which he has with contumely turned down. What he is most keenly interested in is whether their proposals are the soundest, safest and quickest way to afford him relief against unemployment, and give him a human status in industry and a fair share in the product. He has not at all accepted the Labour Party's portentous declaration that nothing short of "nationalization and democratic control" can confer those benefits.

Let us then start from the ordinary workers' standpoint. It is fair, it is commonsense, it is characteristically practical. We can say to them with absolute fairness that what Labour is asking the country to do is to take a jump into the unknown, and for the existing industrial system with which we are familiar, and which is always capable of improvement—for that is an uncontrovertible fact proved by our past industrial history—to substitute a new industrial system of which we have no experience, of the practical operation and effects of which nothing whatever is ascertainable, a venture which is subject to risks so grave and possibilities so disastrous as to endanger the whole industrial and commercial prosperity of this country. We can then offer the workers an alternative scheme which, while reforming the fundamental defects that at present exist in our industrial system, will not alter its basic principles. Unless the psychology of the worker undergoes some cataclysmic change, what he will say is: "Take your scheme of reform, if it deals fairly with unemployment, my human status in industry and my share of the product, it will serve as a beginning."

CHAPTER XXI
THE HUMAN RELATIONSHIPS TO
BE RECTIFIED IN INDUSTRY

Before we can construct any scheme of reform of our industrial system we must have a clear idea of what is industry. In the prosaic language of economics it is a purposive production of commodities and services, the immediate object of those engaged in it being to provide, through the result of their work, the material means of satisfying their wants and desires.

Viewed in broad outline, industry will be seen to involve three fundamental processes:

(i) The combination in due proportion of the five things requisite for all production, viz., capital, enterprise, organization, labour—both hand and brain—and natural forces and resources.

(ii) The realisation of the product—industrial work is nowadays useless unless and until the product is marketed. The amount realized depends mainly on the public demand for the product, and invariably the cheaper the selling price, the greater is the demand.

(iii) The division of the realized surplus amongst those associated in production.

Further, it will also be observed that industry necessarily involves six fundamental human relationships, the importance of which has been much neglected in the past.

1. *The Industrial,* i.e. between the classes of persons associated together in industry:

(*a*) Capital and the Administrative Staff.

(*b*) Capital and the Manual Workers.

(*c*) The Administrative Staff and the Manual Workers.

(*d*) Manual Workers between themselves.

2. *The Social*—between industry and the community.

3. *The National*—between industry and the nation. These relationships are of paramount importance. The individual is no longer the unit—in things industrial, it is the group of those associated in production—in things social, it is the community—in things national, the whole people. Each small group is included in, and directly reacts on, a larger group. Labour, in its *Official Policy for Reconstruction after the War*, truly says: "We are members one of another. No man liveth to himself alone. If any, even the humblest, is made to suffer, the whole community and every one of us, whether or not we recognize the fact, is thereby injured." How frequently Labour forgets its own irrefutable proposition! The problem then is so to organize the processes of industry and harmonize the human relationships involved in it, that to the utmost practicable extent productive efficiency will be secured, the human qualities of all those associated in industry recognized, their capacities fully developed and utilized, their aspirations satisfied, and their respective services co-ordinated to promote the benefit and happiness of all of them, the good of the community, and the welfare of the nation.

Capital and the Administrative Staff

Let us first examine the relationship between Capital and the Administrative Staff. In the Administrative Staff, I include every one from the managing director down to the gate-keeper. They are the brains and mechanism of the organization and management, the connecting link between Capital and Labour. The success of an employer's business is dependent on their tact, judgment, and power of governing men, but Capital has not yet risen to that conception. It has not conceded to the Administrative Staff a status commensurate with their enormous private and public responsibilities, nor, except at the very top, adequate financial recognition. The art of managing men so as to get the best out of them and secure their cordial co-operation, is generally considered by Capital to be a customary by-product of technical ability. In truth, it is a special qualification requiring its own special training, exceptional attributes of mind and temperament, and particular fibres of character, of the possession of which technical ability is no criterion whatsoever. If industry is to progress, Capital must elevate its conception of the duties of the Administrative Staff and recognize that administration, even in its lowest branches, is work as skilled as that of an expert craftsman.

Capital and the Manual Workers

We must next scrutinize the basic industrial relationship between Capital and the Manual Workers. Permeating it, we find, as the result of the causes already mentioned, seething discontent and active antagonism—not cordiality—not mutual confidence, but unreasoning distrust. We see on both sides black suspicion twisting the motive behind every action, and the task is to create contentment among the workers, and enlist their hearty co-operation with employers in the process of production.

The Manual Workers *inter se*

The Manual Workers are far from being a happy family. In this country all work in every industry is allocated by tradition or Trade Union agreement to this trade or that trade as its sacrosanct preserve. Woe betide an unskilled man who invades the industrial territory of a tradesman! These rigid lines of demarcation of work are the cause of untold industrial friction and operate most detrimentally to prevent an employer introducing modern methods or installing time- and labour-saving appliances. There is no greater need in industry than for a peace-treaty between the warring Trade Unions under which this system of dividing work into so many water-tight compartments will be modified.

The Administrative Staff and the Manual Workers

The Administrative Staff has not yet attained to a true conception of their great part in industry. I often found that, so far as their relationship to Labour is concerned, they are inclined to regard their general functions as solely to maintain discipline. The preservation of robust discipline is a vital matter. Too often discipline is bolstered up by arbitrary and dictatorial methods, to which means weak men usually have recourse. That, if not productive of immediate friction, certainly sows broadcast the seeds of trouble and unrest. The vital matter, the atmosphere of the shop, is mainly dependent on the conciliatory personalities of the Administrative Staff. What has to be remembered in industry is that despotism is not leadership, and arbitrariness is not good government. "The moral effects of good leadership," as Professor McDougall truly says in *The Group Mind*, "work throughout a mass of men by subtle processes of suggestion and emotional contagion rather than by a process of purely intellectual appreciation." This many employers have yet to learn; they regard courtesy on the part of the Administrative Staff in dealing with Labour as cowardice, and consideration as subversive of good discipline. But consideration is the oil which makes shop wheels go round, and there never was more scope for its application in industry than at the present time, especially in such things as interviewing, selecting and taking on, promoting and dismissing men, and dealing with shop complaints.

Industry and the Consuming Community

Industry as a whole does not appreciate the close relationship between itself and the community, nor its responsibilities to the community. In reality industry has to rely on the community for innumerable services, and for many facilities vital to its existence, and to its prosperity, and for a market for its product. Yet almost invariably strikes and lock-outs are called, regardless of the effect upon the consuming public. In fact, Labour claims the right to use its economic power in furtherance of its own interests, irrespective of the damage to the community. If, under compelling necessity, the community attempts to carry on the services for itself, or provide the commodities of which by organized strikes it is deprived, it is charged with anti-social conduct, and condemned for declaring a class-war against Labour, those who assist being stigmatized as strike-breakers and black-legs. Labour has gone even further in recent years. In a number of cases it has deliberately adopted the policy of depriving the community of essential services through strikes, in order to produce such social hardship as will drive the community to constrain employers to accept Labour's industrial demands. There have also been recent instances of agreements between employers and Trade Unions—as in the building industry—by which wages have been forced up to unreasonably high rates simply because those industries were necessary to the community and, with the knowledge that whatever the resulting cost of the product might be, the community would have to pay. At the same time, the community is largely dependent upon industry, and if the whole of an industry, or each section of it, fulfils its obligations to the community, the community must perform certain duties in return. I speak more fully of these later.

Industry and the Nation

Industry will never progress to vigorous and healthy development unless our conception of the relationship between industry and the nation is radically revised. That conception to-day is mean, stunted, and utterly devoid of any power of inspiration. Industry I have defined, in the language of economics, as the production of commodities and services for the purpose of satisfying the wants and desires of men. On this commonplace process, which sounds so dull in definition, and on none other, the future well-being of our country and the practicability of further social improvements and reforms depend. Production ought, therefore, to be regarded as the principal means of advancing the happiness, social welfare and material prosperity of the nation, and industry, the chief instrument in that beneficent work, as the highest and the noblest form of national service.

CHAPTER XXII
THE RIGHT RELATIONSHIP OF
GOVERNMENT TO INDUSTRY

In approaching the formulation of a national industrial policy, we must first determine the proper relationship of the Government to industry. That involves consideration of what special action the Government can, and should, take in these exceptional times of abnormal trade depression to assist the restoration of industry, and of the position in which the Government should stand to industry in normal times.

1. THE POLICY FOR THE PRESENT DEPRESSION

The present depression in trade and decline in industry are primarily due to the world-war. The causes are not clearly appreciated by the general public; they are international as well as national, and call for action abroad as insistently as for remedies at home.

The causes are: first, a definite lack of demand from foreign markets for commodities of which this country was, before the war, a producer. It was customary, until recently, to hear it said that the countries of the world are crying out for our goods. That is not an accurate statement. A very considerable proportion of the foreign markets, open to this country before the war, has now, for the time being at any rate, definitely disappeared. I have had opportunities of discussing this question with foreign business men who have special knowledge of continental conditions. All were definite as to this want of demand; the explanation they said was simple— the devastation resulting from the war and the absence of settled and stable government. They described the most amazing expedients and contrivances to which resort is made in foreign countries in order to avoid the purchase of what in normal times would be ordinary trade machinery and equipment. Then next comes the inability of continental countries to produce commodities which—to use the compendious phrase in economics—they require to exchange for commodities from other countries, either because their mechanism of production is rusted or ruined as the result of the war, and they have not capital to renew it, or from inability to buy from abroad because of impoverishment resulting from the war, or the adverse balance of exchange against them. When one turns to this country, we see British manufacturers unable to sell to customers in many continental countries because of the uncertain credit of the foreign buyer, and, where credit is sufficiently satisfactory, or constitutes an insurable risk, because of the sharp variations in exchange. A manufacturer in this country may be in a position to do firm business with a foreign buyer at a given rate of exchange which is just sufficient to ensure a small percentage of profit; a violent fluctuation in the exchange at the time payment is effected may entirely eliminate all profit and possibly convert it into a serious loss. Then again, the high cost of production in this country, especially of manufactured commodities where the wages of labour form 60-85 per cent. of the total cost of production, makes it impossible for the British manufacturer to sell sufficiently cheaply abroad, especially in the face of competition of similar goods produced in countries with a depreciated currency which stands at an external value much below its internal value. In addition, some countries to which we have lent money, and which pay us no interest thereon, are erecting heavy tariff barriers against us, and by subsidies and restrictions on coastwise trade and emigration are injuring seriously British shipping and trade.

Establishment of International Peace

International trade implies mutual dependence. If one country goes out of business it injures all other countries, even those that never traded directly with it. Trade must languish in countries where conditions are unsettled. It should be the first aim of the Government in concert with its Allies to establish peace generally throughout the world. That has been authoritatively declared. In accordance with arrangements made by the Council of the League of Nations, an International Financial Conference was convened at Brussels on September 24, 1920. The duty entrusted by the Council to the Conference was to study the international financial crisis and seek for means of remedying it and of mitigating the dangerous consequences arising from it, subject to the provision that no matter included in the then pending negotiations between the Allies and Germany should be discussed. There were eighty-six members at the Conference, representing thirty-nine different countries.

As the chief essential for the recuperation of industry and the revival of trade, the Conference insisted on the establishment of a real, as distinct from a paper, peace:

> "First and foremost the world needs peace. The Conference affirms most emphatically that the first condition for the world's recovery is the restoration of real peace, the

conclusion of wars which are still being waged and the assured maintenance of peace for the future. The continuance of the atmosphere of war and of preparations for war is fatal to the development of that mutual trust which is essential to the resumption of normal trading relations. The world must resolve the rivalries and animosities which have been the inevitable legacy of the struggle by which Europe has been torn."

"The security of internal conditions is scarcely less important, as foreign trade cannot prosper in a country whose internal conditions do not inspire confidence. The Conference trusts that the League of Nations will lose no opportunity to secure the full restoration and continued maintenance of peace."

"The Conference affirms that the improvement of the financial position largely depends on the general restoration as soon as possible of goodwill between the various nations; and in particular it endorses the declaration of the Supreme Council of March 8, 1920, 'that the States which have been created or enlarged as a result of the war should at once re-establish full and friendly co-operation, and arrange for the unrestricted interchange of commodities in order that the essential unity of European economic life may not be impaired by the erection of artificial economic barriers.'"

Reduction of National Expenditure

If trade is to be resuscitated, there must be a ruthless curtailment of national expenditure, an inflexible renunciation of everything resulting in expense which is not absolutely essential to present national existence. On this question the Financial Conference spoke clearly:

"The statements presented to the Conference show that, on an average, some 20 per cent. of the national expenditure is still being devoted to the maintenance of armaments and to preparations for war. The Conference desires to affirm with the utmost emphasis that the world cannot afford this expenditure. Only by a frank policy of mutual co-operation can the nations hope to regain their old prosperity, and to secure that result the whole resources of each country must be devoted to strictly productive purposes. The Conference accordingly recommends most earnestly to the Council of the League of Nations the desirability of conferring at once with the several Governments concerned with a view to securing a general and agreed reduction of the crushing burden which, on their existing scale, armaments still impose on the impoverished peoples of the world, sapping their resources and imperilling their recovery from the ravages of war."

The Washington Conference has made some progress along this line.

The matter was emphasized in more detail in the following resolution unanimously adopted by the Financial Conference:

"It is, therefore, imperative that every Government should, as the first social and financial reform, on which all others depend—

"(a) Restrict its ordinary recurrent expenditure, including the service of the debt, to such an amount as can be covered by its ordinary revenue.

"(b) Rigidly reduce all expenditure on armaments in so far as such reduction is compatible with the preservation of national security.

"(c) Abandon all unproductive extraordinary expenditure.

"(d) Restrict even productive extraordinary expenditure to the lowest possible amount."

The effect on industry of unnecessary national expenditure is immediate, direct, and, at these times, absolutely calamitous. The greater the national expenditure the higher necessarily must be the taxation required to provide for the interest on, and the redemption of the debt. Every penny absorbed in unnecessary taxation is so much money diverted from reproductive industry. If a manufacturer is paying 6s. 8d. in the £ in income-tax and super-tax, the effect is the same as if he worked as a bond-slave to the Government for four months in the year, during which time the Government appropriated the whole of the output of his factory.

Lowering of Taxation

For the restoration of industry an immediate reduction of taxation is imperatively required. The dangerous height to which taxation has mounted operates with devastating results on industry. Many business firms have had to sell securities to pay their taxes; these have been purchased by American investors. The Government points with pride to the improvement of American exchange; at whose expense? Certainly, in part, at that of British industry. While firms have thus to sacrifice capital assets, or even to borrow money to pay current taxation, industry can never be restored, and each month it continues, the period of industrial convalescence is materially prolonged. Case after case has come before my personal observation where employers, content to make a small margin of profit or no profit at all, but only sufficient to cover standing charges and prime costs, have deliberately decided, when faced with certain loss owing to the grinding burden of taxation, rather than embark any new capital in extending their businesses, or in adding to them some new branch of industry which would have provided employment for many men, to put their money on bank deposit or invest it in gilt-edged securities. The effect of such a course on industry and unemployment is disastrous. If initiative and enterprise, which, in this country, form the life-blood of industry, are to escape extinction, then taxation on industry must speedily be reduced. The directions in which business men are pressing for alleviation from the insupportable oppression of taxation are in the reduction of the rate of income-tax, exemption from super-tax of reserves invested in the business, and abolition of the corporation profits tax. The latter falls entirely upon the ordinary shareholders in addition to income-tax; preference shareholders and debenture holders are not mulcted, but receive in full their prescribed rate of dividend or interest less income-tax. The corporation tax thus operates as a severe deterrent on initiative, especially in regard to the starting of new, and extension of existing, enterprises. There is also a growing volume of opinion in favour of funding certain annual national expenditure, e.g. pensions, as an alternative to raising the necessary expenditure by taxing. Better surely the disadvantages of borrowing with the advantages of a revival of trade, than the satisfaction of theoretically sound finance with the misfortune of being overtaken in the race for foreign markets by continental competitors.

Stabilizing the Exchanges

Labour contends that the Government can materially assist industries which cater for our export trade by stabilizing the exchanges. It appears to contemplate reversion to some such system as "pegging" the exchanges, which was customary during the war. The International Financial Conference pronounced on that procedure as follows:

> "Attempts to limit fluctuations in exchange by imposing artificial control on exchange operations are futile and mischievous. In so far as they are effective, they falsify the market, tend to remove natural correctives to such fluctuations, and interfere with free dealings in forward

exchange which are so necessary to enable traders to eliminate from their calculations a margin to cover risk of exchange, which would otherwise contribute to the rise in prices. Moreover, all Government interference with trade, including exchange, tends to impede that improvement of the economic conditions of a country by which alone a healthy and stable exchange can be secured."

On the other hand, "the present chaotic conditions of the exchanges makes international trade," — to quote the Federation of British Industries — "instead of being a matter of reasonable foresight and calculation, a game of chance, in which the rules and stakes are perpetually altering without the will or knowledge of the player."

It does not seem that much can be done in the direction of steadying the exchanges except to put such pressure as is practicable on foreign countries to cease inflation by printing paper money, to balance their budgets, and to stabilize their currencies and re-anchor them to gold, though not necessarily in the same parity as pre-war, at the same time adding to the national wealth, on which sound currency is based, by increasing national production, decreasing consumption, reducing expenditure, and prompting public and private economy.

Revision of Financial Policy

Business men contend that stability and not inflation or deflation should have been aimed at by the Government, and that industry has been gravely injured by the instability resulting from the Government's financial policy of deflating with the object of restoring an effective gold standard. In pursuance of this policy, towards the end of 1919, the bank rate was raised from 5 per cent. to 6 per cent., and Treasury Bill rate from 4½ per cent. to 5½ per cent.; then in April 1920, the bank rate was further raised to 7 per cent.[19] and the Treasury Bill to 6½ per cent. Appended to the Report of the War Wealth Committee, published in May 1920, is a Treasury Memorandum explaining the policy. Inflation and deflation are ambiguous terms; the Government has explained its understanding of them to be the increase or decrease respectively of purchasing power relative to the amount of commodities available for purchase — purchasing power being measured by the amount of bank deposits and currency in circulation. A masterly description of the nature and effect on industry of the Government's policy was given by the Right Hon. R. McKenna at the Ordinary General Meeting of the London Joint City and Midland Bank, Limited, on January 28, 1921. Mr. McKenna drew the distinction, almost invariably overlooked, between "speculative inflation" — a temporary condition remediable by making money dearer and restricting credit—and "monetary inflation"—a more or less permanent condition which cannot so be remedied. In regard to the latter he said: "Dear money and a rigid restriction of credit, so far from proving an effective means of restoring trade to a wholesome condition, could only aggravate our evils." Monetary inflation was due to gigantic war-time borrowing by the Government, not for increasing industrial production, but almost entirely for consumption. As loans remained outstanding after the commodities had been consumed, there was an immense increase of purchasing power relative to the amount of commodities available for purchase. Mr. McKenna pointed out that the first effects of an attempt at monetary deflation would be to cause severe trade depression, manifesting itself in a fall in wholesale prices, due to goods being thrown upon the market by traders who were unable to carry their stocks or who had failed in business; a diminution in production; a reduction in prices; a growth in unemployment; reduced purchasing power of wage-earners, and so a further fall in wholesale and retail prices, and later, in consequence of the trade depression, a decline in national revenue without any diminution of the permanent liabilities of the Government. To pay taxes traders would have to borrow from their banks; to meet national expenses Government would have to resort to bank loans, and credit inflation would again ensue. Mr. McKenna conclusively showed that monetary deflation can only be achieved through repayment of the immense Government loans, which cannot be effected by the imposition of additional taxation, as that would bring immediate ruin upon our commerce and manufacture, but only from funds secured by the most rigid economy in national expenditure, and by increasing the commodities available for purchase through the stimulation of production and of trade.

There are some drastic remedies which leave the patient cured of his disease, but dead from general debility; monetary deflation, as practised by the Government, is one of them. It is no satisfaction to the manufacturer whose works are closed down, or the worker who is unemployed, to be told that the currency is being restored to pre-war parity of exchange. They see in the United Kingdom and the United States—exponents of this process—a larger proportion of the population unemployed than in any other industrial country, and these are the two wealthiest countries in the world, with the greatest foreign trade.

Reconsideration of Reparations Policy

No one suggests that Germany should be relieved from payment of reparations or that the Government should be dissuaded from insisting on payment by any fraudulent bankruptcy on the part of Germany. At the same time there is real urgency for clear thinking and decisive action on the part of the Government in regard to the amount and mode of payment.

The Government's original figure of 20,000 millions turned out to be a ridiculous over-estimate, afterwards reduced by the Ultimatum of London to a maximum yearly payment of 400 millions. To make the payment, the surplus of the value of Germany's exported saleable commodities over the cost of her imported raw materials and food must at least equal that amount. Pressed to provide that surplus she must necessarily undersell our manufacturers in foreign markets, which she will and can do by depreciating the mark in foreign exchange so as to keep its external below its internal value. This results in a premium on German exports, and the undercutting of our commodities in those markets. Mr. McKenna's reasoned speech to his bank on January 27, 1922, is worthy of close attention. "Before Germany could meet her full liability," says Mr. McKenna, "before she could develop her foreign trade to such a degree as to have an exportable surplus of 400 millions a year, the foreign trade of this country, her chief competitor, must dwindle into insignificance." Speaking from the economic point of view, he goes on to point out that Germany can pay annually "to the full extent of the export surplus her trade can give her without forcing the external value of the mark below its internal value ... she can pay in specified commodities, which in our case might include sugar, timber, potash, and other materials which are indispensable to us, but which we either do not produce at all or in insufficient quantities. She can pay also by the surrender of any foreign securities her nationals may possess, so far as they can be traced, and, if the Allies are willing to accept this form of payment, by the direct employment of her labour in reconstructing devastated areas." There can hardly be much question that vacillation in the reparations policy has been productive of serious injury to our foreign trade.

Inter-Allies Debts

The restoration of international trade depends also on a sound and sensible recognition by those of the Allies who are creditor nations of the economic effects of enforcing payment of the indebtedness to them by the Governments of debtor nations, coupled with such action as they, in the interests of civilization and of their own countries, find themselves able to take in the direction of modification. Government war-debts have produced for no debtor country any increase of its national wealth; they can be paid by the debtor country only out of its capital or its income. In regard to the first alternative, no debtor country can possibly, under any scheme of finance, pay its government war-debts out of capital, that is to say, out of home or foreign securities in the hands of its Government or its nationals, or out of cash balances standing to the credit abroad of either or both of them. If those debts are to be paid at all, it must be out of income, that is to say, out of the surplus realized by the export of natural products, manufactured goods, services and "invisible exports," after payment of the expenses involved in producing such surplus, e.g. cost of raw material, labour involved in manufacture, and other costs of production and expenses of rendering the services. Now, the dominant fact to-day is that the debtor nations' available surpluses are either insufficient, or not more than sufficient, to cover their pre-war debts. How then in each case is the surplus to be so enormously increased as to cover the fresh indebtedness resulting from the Great War? In one way only—by enormously increased production, and by a reduction in the national standard of living. Nothing is more certain than the absolute impossibility of any debtor country being able to pay its war-debts under its present standard of production and of living. Supposing, however, it to be practicable, and that it is determined to compel each debtor country to create the requisite surplus, what would be the peril to international trade of such forced payments? Mr. F. C. Goodenough—the Chairman of Barclay's Bank—has explained the position with cogent clarity; his illuminating exposition will be found in *The Times* of April 11, 1922.

First let us consider how much of the needed surplus can be created by increased production. It obviously involves enormously greater output on the part of labour each working hour, the introduction of very greatly improved organization and of time- and labour-saving appliances, which, apart from the new spirit it would demand in industry, would entail a drain upon capital resources for their provision, that, at this present time of scarcity, could not be met, and a general alteration in price levels. Our difficulty to-day is to attain even to our pre-war standard of efficient and effective output. We are living to-day largely upon our capital and not upon income. But, assuming that debtor nations can go some way towards paying their war-time indebtedness by increased production, they plainly cannot go anything like the full length; they must fall back, if pressed, on a reduction of their standard of living which would be primarily effected by a reduction in industrial wages. Then mark the effect upon creditor nations. If wages in a debtor nation are reduced, and costs of production are correspondingly brought down without any equivalent diminution in the efficiency of labour, that debtor nation is in a position, and, if put under pressure to pay its war-debts, is compelled to put its manufactured commodities into foreign markets at prices considerably lower than its creditor nation with a higher standard of living can afford to do. This unfair competition applies not merely to creditor nations, but to all nations trading in the same competitive foreign markets. But, then, follow the matter one stage farther: if the other nations, under the stress of this competition, bring down their costs of production to the same level, the debtor nation loses its preferential position in the foreign markets and ceases to be in a position to pay its war indebtedness.

Even by means of increased production, and a reduced standard of living, a debtor country may be unable to meet its war indebtedness in full. Should it be forced to do so, it must borrow the balance of the money annually due, which can seldom be achieved by external or internal loans, but usually by increase of paper currency which soon brings its own retribution—national bankruptcy. The total amount of Inter-Allied Debts, as between the United States of America, Great Britain, France, Italy, Russia and Belgium, is 4,000 millions sterling, to which, if the Reparation payments of 6,600 millions sterling are added, makes a total of 10,600 millions sterling which does not include the war-debt owing by each country to its own nationals nor by the Dominions to Great Britain. Mr. Goodenough's suggestions were eminently practical, that the amount to be paid by each debtor nation should be fixed as soon as possible, so as to clear away the present disturbing atmosphere of uncertainty, that bonds for as long a period as practicable should be created by each debtor country representing the total amount of its national war-debt, and that these should be gradually offered to the public for investment supported by the national guarantees of the debtor country. Bonds handed by one debtor nation to a creditor nation in respect of a debt could be endorsed by the latter nation to another country in respect of a debt owing by the endorsor to the endorsee, and so find a ready market among investors all over the world. Each country creating a bond would be compelled to provide a fund out of its own taxation for the redemption of its own bonds. The scheme of Mr. Goodenough urgently needs consideration, as the whole question of Inter-Ally indebtedness calls for a decision.

Export Credits

Acting with prudence, and exercising co-operation with business men, the Government can, as experience has shown, beneficially use its credit to assist sound trading between this and foreign countries and to enable works to be carried out which provide employment; and so long as the Government employs the normal machinery of finance and commerce, much can be done in this way to further the restoration of trade and industry. The Export Credits Scheme administered by the Department of Overseas Trade is conferring substantial benefits on industry in stimulating orders from abroad, and developing markets to replace those permanently lost or temporarily closed to us in countries which are, at the time being, potential producers of commodities exchangeable for the commodities we produce. The guarantee of loans so ably administered by the Advisory Committee under the Trade Facilities Act, 1921, is materially encouraging sound commercial business.

Bringing down Costs of Production

But after all is said and done, we are living in a fool's paradise if we think that, even when financial equilibrium and stability have been attained, we shall be able to compete in foreign markets at our present *real* costs of output. Wages constitute the greatest proportion of costs of production in every industry, and wages will have to be reduced—the standard of living of 1920-1 cannot be maintained. A lower standard of profits must likewise be accepted by employers. There must be equality of sacrifice all round. Labour argues that reduction of wages in industry means diminished national purchasing power, and consequently increased trade depression. That is only true when there is an effective demand at existing prices for the output of industry. The object now is to reduce costs so as to get down to a price at which demand may be effective. The foolish expectations nurtured by the working-classes of getting out of the war a higher standard of living than they enjoyed before the war was largely due to the utterly impossible—and sometimes grotesque—pictures painted by members of the Government of "the good times coming." These reductions in cost by reductions of wages and profits can be immediate; any reductions in cost of production through improvement of management, organization and plant or increasing the efficiency of labour's output, while necessary for the permanent well-being of industry, are too slow acting for the present emergency.

CHAPTER XXIII
THE RIGHT RELATIONSHIP OF
GOVERNMENT TO INDUSTRY

2. THE NORMAL POSITION OF GOVERNMENT
IN RELATION TO INDUSTRY

We must now consider the relationship of Government to industry in normal times. Whether or not any particular industries should be nationalized and thereafter conducted as State industries or under some other system than the present, are constitutional questions to be decided by the Government in power in accordance with what they believe to be the will of the people. That the author of this book is strongly opposed to nationalization as a general principle of industrial organization is sufficiently apparent from what has already been written and for the reasons given. Assuming, however, that there is no nationalization of an industry, but that it continues on a reformed basis of private ownership, it is important to discuss under what circumstances the Government ought to intervene in regard to any question affecting the administration and control of that industry, or, indeed, of all industries in general. Our recent experience of Government direction of industries, both during and after the war, assists us in answering that question. If, as during the war, a large supply of munitions has to be organized at a moment's notice, and maintained irrespective of all considerations of economy and industrial efficiency, probably no other course would remain but for the Government of the day to control the industries concerned; but, in normal times, when economy of production is imperative, industrial efficiency essential, and enterprising and far-sighted administration of paramount importance, Government direction has shown itself to be quite hopeless. Employers and Trade Unions are in firm agreement on this point, that Government control of industry spells ineptitude, incompetence, extravagance, and confusion all along the line. We may, therefore, emphasize this as the first cardinal principle regulating the relationship of Government to industry: that the circumstances are few and seldom arise which justify intervention by Government in the economic administration and control of any industry.

Regulation of Factory Conditions

The Government is however bound to assert its right to intervene, in order to prevent the existence of, and, where they have arisen, to remove, industrial conditions which are injurious to the health and welfare of the workers as a whole or any particular section of them. This is action in respect of which every Government would always have behind it the full approval of the social conscience. But for the intervention of the Government in days gone by, the dehumanizing conditions attending child-labour and the employment of women in workshops would never have been removed, and English factories would not be to-day as they are, the first in the world for health, sanitation and good amenities. In the early days of last century, when factory legislation was first proposed, the employers of one large Yorkshire woollen town came in formal deputation to London to protest that, if there were any interference by Act of Parliament with their liberty to employ as they pleased, in their woollen manufactories, young children for such hours as they thought fit, a death-blow would be struck to the trade of England. Those days have gone, and with them that class of employer.

Under the Factory Acts and the skilled and far-sighted supervision of the Home Office Factory Inspectors, an immense amount has been done to promote the health of the workers, the safety of their occupations, and freedom from preventible dangers. None but the most hardened of individualistic employers—and few of them now remain—object to sound and reasonable State regulation in matters such as these. He welcomes it for his own protection.

Conciliation and not Intervention

It is more in regard to industrial disputes concerning wages and conditions of employment that the Government is too prone to intervene. There must always be a Ministry of Labour to keep in close touch with industrial disputes. Such a Ministry, though it should in the first instance leave employers and employed to discuss matters through the conciliation machinery that exists in each particular industry, yet, by discreet and impartial action, can do most valuable work in smoothing over ruptures in negotiations when neither side from motives of dignity or strategy will move. That is a different thing altogether from the Cabinet rushing in. The public will never know the extent to which industrial harmony in this country has been preserved on occasions of stress by the efforts towards conciliation exerted by the Ministry of Labour and its predecessor, the Conciliation Department of the Board of Trade, and sometimes under the greatest difficulties. At times when the Ministry had arranged between employers and Trade Unions a formula for the solution of a wage dispute or the termination of a strike or other industrial controversy, the recalcitrant leaders of some Union, entering into temporary alliance with other turbulent spirits, would speed found in deputation to the Cabinet at 10, Downing Street, and seldom be denied admission. Frequently, other terms would be suggested by the Cabinet for the sake of peace, probably more favourable to the workers than those arranged by the Ministry of Labour. The results were disastrous, the prestige of the Ministry suffered a serious relapse, the repute of the Trade Union leaders who agreed terms with the Ministry was damaged in the eyes of their members almost irretrievably, the rebellious section of the Union was given a resounding advertisement at the expense of industrial constitutional government—no surer way to sow the seeds of disruption and indiscipline in any Union.

Protection of the Community

But it will be asked what is to happen when the employers and Unions concerned in our great national industries decline to come together. In that event, the Government, through the Ministry of Labour, must, as the latter has so frequently done with tact and efficiency, endeavour to bring the two sides to a conference. That can usually be done. The Ministry has power under the Industrial Courts Act, 1919, to appoint a Court of Inquiry, but this power in practice is of little use unless both sides agree. Public opinion, however, can always be relied on strongly to resent employers and unions standing at arm's length; but before it can, or will, operate, a definite open effort must be made to put them into touch with one another. Negotiations once instituted may culminate in an agreement, or end in a rupture, so that a strike or lock-out appears inevitable. Then there is generally but one sound course for the Government to pursue: at once to refer the dispute through the appropriate Government Department to the Industrial Court, and obtain its impartial and experienced decision upon the issue. Whether either or both parties will submit to the arbitrament of the Court is purely voluntary—we have not compulsory industrial arbitration in this country. It has failed in Canada and Australia; it failed here disastrously during the war. If men are to be compelled to accept an award, employers must be compelled, if the Court so decide, to carry on their works at a loss. But the public has no patience with any party to a wages dispute who will not agree to the reference of his claim to an independent tribunal, or who, having agreed to the submission, refuses to accept the award. One of the most important present-day functions of such a tribunal is to analyse the claim and see to what extent the claim is a genuine industrial demand, or part of the revolutionary programme of extremists for squeezing all private profit out of industry so as to force "nationalization and democratic control" or some other favourite socialistic scheme. The one fatal course is for the Cabinet to attempt itself to handle industrial disputes.

Still, after or without an inquiry by the Industrial Court, a strike or lock-out may occur. Then the primary duty of the Government is to stand firm, refuse all concessions, and protect the community; nothing less is adequate for the maintenance of social order. Too often employers and Unions complacently think that the Government should stand aside and let them fight it out over the prostrate public. In saying that they forget the paramount interests of the community. Every principle of democratic government negatives the right of a section of the community so to attempt to enforce its arbitrary will, and where, by refusing an independent arbitration and then calling a strike or lock-out, it does so, it is the plain duty of the Government to provide for the continuance of public services and to maintain a skeleton organization in being for that purpose. This is not acting as strike-breaker between employer and employed. But let not the measures for the protection of the community be taken in stealth. Why should there be any secrecy about the matter? The obligation and intention of the Government always so to act should be openly affirmed. As Labour has officially adopted the anti-social policy of "direct action," the Trade Disputes Act of 1906 should be repealed. Whatever reason of political expediency—there was none in law or in logic—justified the application of the Act to cases of economic strikes between employers and employed, no pretext remains for its retention in cases of strikes against the community, especially where an independent inquiry has been refused. The Government can successfully measure its strength against any such strike, if only it will give the fullest possible publicity to the issues, for public opinion will always split like a steel wedge the solidarity of such anti-social action.

Wages in Unorganized Industries

One particular class of wages questions does demand intervention by the Government. In well-ordered industries, where organizations exist effectively representing the employers and employed engaged in the industry, wages and conditions ought to be left as matters for collective bargaining. There are, however, many industries which are so scattered through the country or so subject to conditions incompatible with good organization as to make collective bargaining impossible. In them reasonable minimum wages and conditions must be secured, and it is the duty of the Government to see that such provision is made, unless it is prepared to acquiesce in "sweated labour trades." Hitherto, the provision has taken the form of a Trade Board for the industry under the Trade Boards Act, and there is no doubt that type of organization must continue in appropriate cases. Much criticism has been levelled against the Trade Boards, on which Lord Cave's Committee[20] has now reported fully. From their inception up to the war, Trade Boards on the whole were successful. The defects that subsequently developed in the system were due to the fact that the far-flung series of Trade Boards, constituted immediately after the war, had none of the experience nor traditions of the old Boards; their chairmen and independent members were very largely persons without practical experience of industrial problems, and necessarily of that category, because of the large number of such appointments to be filled. They did not confine themselves to prescribing minimum wages and conditions—their proper function—so as to avoid sweated conditions, but they attempted to regulate actual wages and conditions, a very different matter. They also applied war-time standards to peace-time circumstances, and that naturally plunged a nascent and struggling industry into great difficulty.

Industrial Research

Industrial research becomes daily more essential for industrial progress. It has been developed to a greater extent in Germany and the United States of America than with us. Much of the industrial prosperity in those two countries is due to the establishment of associations, and, indeed, of highly developed departments by individual firms for industrial research. Much is being done, and still more remains to be done, by individual firms and by trade associations in this country in that direction. There is no doubt that this kind of work can more effectively be conducted in that way than by any Government Department, but, at the same time, a Government Department is required to co-ordinate and stimulate rather than to control such private efforts. In this way, most valuable work is being done by the Department of Scientific and Industrial Research. This will always remain an important sphere for Government industrial activity.

Need of a Real Ministry of Labour

If we are to have anything like effective and efficient labour administration, a Ministry of Labour is essential. Those who call for abolition of the Ministry are truly neophytes in the art of industrial government. Convinced believers, let us assume them to be, in the principle of *laissez-aller*, they actually think that if the Ministry disappeared there would be an end of all intervention by Government between employers and employed. What uninformed criticism! They forget that the Home Office has control of the administration of the Factory Acts—a matter embracing working conditions and welfare of workers which goes right to the root of the Labour problem. They omit to notice that the Mines Department of the

Board of Trade exercises supervision over the conditions of employment and wages of miners; that the Ministry of Agriculture is responsible for the Joint Conciliation Committees which deal with exactly similar questions in agriculture; that the Ministry of Transport does the same in the railway service, and that the Ministry of Health has jurisdiction over health insurance so largely handled by the Approved-Societies-sections of the Trade Unions, and over the administration of the Poor Law relief which so nearly touches the unemployment problem. These various jurisdictions are admittedly to stand—it could not be, and indeed is not contended otherwise. The Ministry of Labour is, however, to disappear, and its responsibilities— unemployment insurance, trade boards, labour exchanges, conciliation of trade disputes, co-ordination of Labour administration in this country in conformity with the International Labour Organization created by the Peace Treaty—are to be extinguished or tacked on as appendages to other departments. The resulting position is too ridiculous to contemplate. Under such circumstances the Government could never be advised on any basis of consistent administration and policy in regard to any labour question; continuous touch would be lost with the representative Trade Union federations; there would be as many opinions as there were departments implicated. Whenever a national strike was imminent in any great industry, the Government would have to organize an improvised committee of the Departments concerned in labour—probably few of them even remotely connected with the particular industry affected—and try to evolve an *ad hoc* policy. We are suffering still from the effects of opportunist action of that kind and want no repetition. And when Government intervention in a national strike becomes inevitable for the protection of the community, he would be a bold man who would prefer negotiations by the Cabinet conducted on no set principle and founded on no experience of industrial conditions, to negotiations by the Ministry of Labour, which does conduct such business on a settled basis of principle, knowing the interconnection of trade with trade and the effect which a concession like the 12½ per cent. bonus to one section of industry produces upon all other sections, and appreciates the danger of settling strikes in the way the South Wales Coal Strike of 1915 was settled.

It has been amply proved by bitter experience that no branch of human activity stands in more urgent need of even administration on uniform and consistent lines than does labour. Granted that employers and employed should settle between themselves so far as possible their own disputes, there comes inevitably a stage when a settlement or failure to settle intimately affects the community. It is then that the offices of a properly constituted Ministry of Labour come into play. If it is desired to leave the public merely as a football between employers and employed then abolish the Ministry. Far from abolishing it, in my view it ought to be consolidated and vested with extended powers. It ought to be made in fact, not merely in name, a real Ministry of Labour. All the powers of the other Government Departments which relate to labour should be transferred to it, so that there would be one central department charged with and responsible for the administration of all labour in this country. A great part of the labour disorganization during the war which has been used as an argument for abolition of the Ministry of Labour, and in derogation of the great national services performed by it, was entirely due to this clash between different departments in regard to labour administration: the Admiralty bidding against the Ministry of Munitions by paying higher wages to the same class of men and settling strikes on more advantageous terms to the workers; the Agricultural Wages Board of the Ministry of Agriculture putting up wages of agricultural labourers to a height that upset the country railway porters who were drawn from them. Innumerable other instances could be given, all directly due to the sub-division of labour administration among a number of different and hostile Government departments. It is not unimportant in this connection to remember that when, in the beginning of 1917, the Ministry of Labour, which was originally a conception of the Trades Union Congress, was formed by Mr. Lloyd George's first Coalition Government, it was intended to transfer to it all the labour powers of the other Government departments. This was fiercely resisted by every department which it was proposed to denude of any powers, and in great measure successfully. As a result of that internecine warfare, the present Ministry of Labour is unhappily but an emasculated edition of the fully endowed central department that Mr. Lloyd George wisely had in mind. The wonder is that it has done as well as it has with such a disappointing limitation of powers. But apart from home labour administration, we shall get into most serious international complications, and very great domestic difficulty, if proper touch is not maintained with, and the interests of the country properly voiced in, the International Labour Organization which exercises now very considerable influence over labour legislation and administration in every country, party to the League of Nations. That cannot possibly be managed if the responsibility is to be scattered over half a dozen partially interested and wholly unco-ordinated Government departments.

If the labour sections of other Government departments were united with the Ministry of Labour, very great economies could be effected: factory and trade board inspectorates could be combined; health and unemployment inspectorates could also be amalgamated; in fact, one central inspectorate could well perform all the four kinds of inspection duties. These are but a few illustrations. The various labour duties performed by the different Government departments are so obviously one and the same that it is inconceivable why the overlapping which exists should be tolerated any longer. It is the one thing in our labour administration that passes the comprehension of foreign critics.

Some of those who suggest the abolition of the Ministry of Labour propose to constitute in its place a National Industrial Council, consisting of an equal number of representatives of Employers' Associations and Trade Unions with a chairman nominated by the Government, as recommended by the Report of the Provisional Joint Committee of Employers and Trade Unions to the Industrial Conference, convened by the Government on February 27, 1919, when the miners' strike was threatening. The duty of the National Industrial Council would be to make recommendations in regard to controversial industrial matters. If the Unions *bona fide* will undertake to use such a Council, or Parliament of Industry as it is sometimes called, for the purpose of promoting good relations between employers and employed, its creation would be of value. That implies the continuance in industry of the private employer. But, on the other hand, if the Unions intend to work for the elimination of the private employer from industry, as they declared their intention to do in the Memorandum annexed by the Right Hon. Arthur Henderson to the Report of the Provisional Joint Committee, then the creation of a Parliament of Industry would be a farce, and merely degenerate into an organized means to the Unions' real end. In any event, the scope of a National Joint Council is limited. No Union will acquiesce in the judgment of other Unions on its domestic affairs—imagine boilermakers accepting the decision of plumbers, electricians and fitters on a question concerning the demarcation of boilermakers' work. As it was, miners, railwaymen and transport workers absented themselves from the Industrial Conference in 1919. Moreover, employers and Trade Unions will always agree, to the serious discomfiture of Government, on reforms of which the expenses are to fall not on industry but on national funds, but the question of such expenditure is surely one to be reserved exclusively for Parliament. The Ministry of Labour has always the General Council to consult, which represents the whole of organized labour, and the National Confederation of Employers' Organizations, reinforced for consultation with any employers' organizations outside that Confederation. If a joint conference with employers and Trade Unions is desired by Government such can always now be easily arranged.

Regulation of Combinations and Monopolies

Combination is inherent in industrial progress; this is fully recognized by Labour. The addendum to the Report of the Committee on Trusts

(*Parliamentary Paper*, 1919, Cd. 9236) signed (amongst others) by such stalwart members of the Labour Party as Messrs. Bevan and Sidney Webb, stated: "We have to recognize that association and combination in production and distribution are steps to the greater efficiency, the increased economy and the better organization of industry; we regard this evolution as inevitable and desirable."

This fact compels the Government to protect the consuming public against exploitation by combinations and monopolies. The principles along which such protective action should proceed are indicated in the Report of this Committee, which has received the official approval of the Federation of British Industries. Shortly put, they throw on the Board of Trade the duty of inquiring into any reasonable complaints, of referring any questions arising out of their inquiry to a special tribunal for investigation and report, and of recommending to the Government action for the remedying of any grievances found to exist by the tribunal. The Federation properly insists upon two safeguards: first, avoidance of any restriction prejudicing the position of British industry in the export trade, and, secondly, caution against any communication to foreign competitors of information regarding British trade associations or combines. There have been suggestions made by some public men that statutory limits should be placed upon dividends of industrial concerns. Such restrictions have in the past been imposed upon the payment of dividends by companies supplying, under powers of statutory monopoly, public necessities like gas and water, but economic history shows conclusively that anything in the nature of a statutory limitation of dividends for concerns not supplying a monopoly but marketing its product in a competitive market is seriously destructive of efficiency and enterprise.

CHAPTER XXIV
THE RIGHT RELATIONSHIP BETWEEN EMPLOYERS AND EMPLOYED

1. CONTENTMENT IN INDUSTRY (*a*)

Reform of the relationship in industry between employers and employed involves three things: securing contentment, achieving co-operation, increasing production; these constitute the dynamic trinity. Only when contentment can be secured is co-operation made possible; without co-operation there never can be efficient production; production alone can create the prosperity which is the sole source of the financial ability of any industry to pay high wages and maintain good conditions of employment. Contentment does not mean stagnation; it means willingness to progress under an accepted system—in other words, evolution.

(*a*) Provision against Unemployment

If we are to secure contentment in industry, unquestionably the first matter to be dealt with is unemployment. A distinction must be drawn between normal unemployment—the result of seasonal or cyclic depressions in trade, which arise from circumstances well-known in industry, either affecting the world at large or peculiar to some country in particular, or special to some national industry—and the abnormal unemployment which has resulted from the Great War. We are now considering normal unemployment. What Government should do to deal with the abnormal unemployment occasioned by the war we have already discussed in Chapter XXII.

Equalization of Demand for Labour

In regard to normal unemployment there are two things only which can be done:—first, to reduce, so far as possible, fluctuations in the demand for labour between one year and another, and one season of the year with another season of the same year, and, secondly, to make the best provision economically practicable for the maintenance during times of trade depression of persons who are unemployed or under-employed. It is most difficult to "equalize the demand for labour." In ordinary commercial business that is a matter largely outside the power of Government, employers, or Trade Unions. It is one of the privileges which is reserved for the consumer. The only directions in which fruitful action can be taken are to provide a system such as exists under the Labour Exchange organization, or that of certain Trade Unions, whereby the workman out of a job can be put in touch with the employer who wants labour of his particular description, and to arrange the execution of public works by Government Departments or local authorities, and the manufacture of stores or equipment for public purposes, the amount of which is more or less standard, so that by postponing some and expediting others some advance is possible towards making more uniform the demand for labour as between good times and bad. But the limits within which this is a practicable policy are much narrower than is generally realized, and immensely more restricted than is suggested by the Labour Party.

Insurance against Unemployment

Although to prevent unemployment is impossible, happily a great deal can be done to mitigate the evils of unemployment when it does occur. Under no system of organizing industry—in spite of the contentions of the Labour Party that under its socialistic reconstruction of industry there would be no unemployment—can any person be guaranteed continuous work. It is possible, however, to spread the income of the industry in good times over bad times, so that when the latter supervene there will be something coming in to the worker for him to live on. This is not a dole as some people call it, but rather in the nature of deferred pay. With that in operation there would be an end to what is called by Labour the "wages system." The worker would no longer be paid wages for such time only as he is employed, but would receive pay for the time he works and also pay during the time he is unable to work because of trade depression. There must be in all industries, both on the side of labour and of the employer, a reserve of productive capacity to meet the peak demands, and all employers with few exceptions recognize that it is their duty to apply some of the profits of good times for the maintenance of this reserve of labour in their industry when unemployed at times other than peak times, and of the general body of labour when unemployed or under-employed at times of trade depression. But the provision against unemployment must be a joint fund to which both the employer and the worker contribute during good times.

Need of a Job-Finding Organization

As ancillary to any scheme for provision against unemployment, there must be some effective organization in existence whose duty it is to endeavour to ascertain where there are any vacancies for workmen in which men who are unemployed can be started. Obviously this is necessary both in the interests of the industry and of the actuarial solvency of the fund provided against unemployment. Unfortunately a substantial number of persons will always exist who prefer not to do work but yet be paid for it.

Insurance by State or Industry

The next question is by whom shall the provision for unemployment be made? Shall it be by the State or by industry, that is to say, all industries acting collectively, or by each industry for itself, or shall it be by individual firms? We shall consider these cases separately.

It is characteristic of the times that when persons have omitted to do what they should have done and then find themselves in difficulties by reason of their omission, they call upon the State to remedy their deficiency. Eliminating the question whether the State out of its own financial resources should make any addition to the fund contributed by employers and employed for provision against unemployment, Government administration of the fund is necessarily less efficient and more expensive than administration by industries or by firms. Some striking figures have been published in *The Times* of January 25, 1922. It was stated at the National Federation of Employees Approved Societies by a gentleman representing the British Xylonite Company that his firm's scheme of unemployment insurance cost only £334 per £10,000 to administer as against the Government's £1,000 per £10,000. It must be remembered, however, that the Government scheme has to cover multifarious trades—organized, semi-organized and those not organized at all. But still, after making all due allowance for that fact, there appears to be no question that a Government scheme does necessarily, from the inability to maintain close supervision, afford opportunities for waste and abuse which would not arise under a system of closer control.

State Insurance

The details of the Government scheme have been described. The Labour Exchanges have, in the face of great difficulties, performed the administration with efficiency, but no one with experience of industrial conditions during the last two years could fail to realize that the administration of unemployment insurance is not proper work to be undertaken by any Government Department. The proper function for the State is to see that all possible provision is made against unemployment but not to undertake the work itself. In 1920 a Committee of Inquiry was appointed by the Minister of Labour to inquire into and report upon the Labour Exchanges. The majority of that Committee reported that "the administration of unemployment insurance by industries on behalf of their own members was the most desirable system in the end, particularly from the point of view of obtaining technical knowledge in the placing of workmen, the creation of a corporate pride in each industry, and a sense of responsibility for unemployment in the industry." The Geddes Committee has recommended that this question should be further explored, and the Minister of Labour is taking steps to do so.

Insurance by Industry or Industries

That industry should provide for its unemployment is obviously reasonable. The taxpayer has no control over industrial conditions, or over the wages which are paid, or the conditions of employment in operation, and in respect of such matters industry is under no responsibility to the taxpayer. Should this provision be made by each industry in particular or by industry as a whole? It would be impossible to form a scheme under which each industry would provide against its own unemployment. There are many industries, ranging from those most highly organized with employers and Trade Unions acting, and accustomed to act, collectively and with some experience of the ratio of their unemployment, down to industries which have no organization whatever nor any collective machinery available for the operation of an insurance fund nor any knowledge of their own unemployment. It is only a highly organized industry that could undertake to provide for its own unemployed, and not all highly organized industries, but merely a selected few—those which are clearly separated off from other industries. To all but the initiated it is surprising how industries are interlocked. If we take, for example, the engineering industry, and industries like iron and steel, nuts and bolts, bicycle parts and innumerable others, there is great interchange of labour, especially unskilled. A large West-end store will be engaged in fifty to sixty different industries. How would its interests in each industry be separated? There is no doubt that it is to the financial advantage of a highly organized clearly demarcated industry to provide for its own unemployment insurance as compared with participation in a State Scheme.

Sir Alfred Watson, the Government Actuary, before the Committee of Inquiry on the Labour Exchanges, pointed out the great financial benefit it would be to the principal industries to provide their own unemployment insurance, and referred to the large margin there would be available for the actual costs of the benefits. In a most interesting pamphlet published on "Unemployment Insurance," Mr. Henry Lesser, the President of the National Federation of Employees Approved Societies, states that in one industrial undertaking employers and employed pay in respect of the National Unemployment Insurance Scheme over £22,000 per year, but that in normal times the persons employed in that particular firm do not receive in the aggregate in unemployment pay more than £800 a year, a case, he says, which may be taken as typical of the whole of the industry in question.

One outstanding advantage which would result from each industry effecting its own unemployment insurance would be the feeling it must undoubtedly engender in the minds of both employers and Trade Unions of their responsibility for the combined working of the industry, and the effect it is bound to have in producing a better spirit between the two parties and amongst the men, who will no longer feel that they are taken on and discharged merely as it suits the interests of the firm. A thorough investigation should be made as to what industries could undertake their own unemployment insurance, and whether it is better that they should do so, or come into a general scheme of insurance by all industries. The ordinary objection of employers and Trade Unions representing "good" industries, i.e. those with a low rate of unemployment, is that they are paying for the "bad" industries with a high rate, but is not that rather the essence of insurance? It may well be that only insurance by all industries acting collectively is possible. If such turns out to be the case, that plan should be adopted ready for carrying into practical operation on the approach of more normal times. Industries which rely mainly on casual labour are a more difficult proposition. Decasualization is essential, and that must be effected by some means of restricting the free influx of labour into the industry, as has been done in the Dock Labour Scheme in Liverpool. The efficiency of the Liverpool method is undoubtedly due to the co-operation between the dock labour employers and the Unions; it has been most strikingly successful. It affords a basis for procedure in very many industries. There must, however, I am afraid, remain a residuum of unemployment insurance to be handled by the State, in the absence of any other authority, on the lines presumably of the present National Unemployment Insurance Scheme, but it would be reduced to small proportions if all the great industries of the country were providing for their own unemployment.

Reform of Present Out-Door Relief System

In connection with unemployment, the present system of Poor Law relief wants overhauling. The provision of relief by the Guardians (in addition to, or substitution for, unemployment insurance benefit) on varying standards in different places throughout the country is extremely wasteful and disturbing to social harmony. If this is taken out of the hands of the Guardians, as has already been recommended by both the majority and minority reports of the Poor-Law Commission, and committed into the hands of some local authority—because local responsibility is essential for the spending of money raised by local rates—it would mark progress of no uncertain kind. Absolute standardization is impossible, because of the varying social circumstances and indeed social outlook in different parts of the country, but, after allowing for this, much greater approximation to uniformity could be secured.

Unemployment Insurance by Firms

Without any doubt the best approach to insurance by industries or by industry as a whole is to start with insurance by firms. An admirable beginning has been made in this direction by the National Federation of Employees Approved Societies—particulars of this scheme can be obtained from the Secretary to the Federation, c/o British Thomson-Houston Co., Ltd., Rugby—it is also described with great clearness by Mr. Lesser in the pamphlet. The experience of the Federation is most instructive. In many works, before the days of National Health Insurance, there were sick clubs which provided for members unemployed through illness, benefits from a fund to which employers and employed alike contributed. Both employers and employed viewed, with considerable regret, the proposed absorption of these clubs into the new Approved Societies established under the Health Insurance Act, and to obviate that fate reconstituted their clubs with the approval of the Insurance Commissioners into "Works Societies," and obtained official sanction for these Societies to administer the State scheme. Later these Works Societies decided to undertake the administration of unemployment benefit at their respective works under Section 17 of the Unemployment Insurance Act, 1920. There were three conditions precedent: first, that the Society must provide for payment out of its own voluntary funds of an additional unemployment benefit equal to one-third of that payable under the Act—that is to say, if the State benefit was 15s. the Society must add to that at least another 5s. out of its private fund and so pay a total benefit of 20s. The second stipulation was that the Society must have a system for ascertaining the rates of wages and the general conditions of employment prevailing in all occupations in which its members were engaged; these particulars were always well-known, and there was not much difficulty about that. The third requirement was that the Society should have an effective system of ascertaining vacancies for employment—this meant some organization distinct from the Labour

Exchanges. Such an organization was finally obtained through the co-operation of the local Chambers of Commerce, who receive from their associated firms particulars of vacancies which the Chambers send on to the different Works Societies. The scheme works exceedingly well. It was first adopted by the South Metropolitan Gas Co., and later by the Gas Light and Coke Co., Messrs. Debenhams, the British Thomson-Houston Co., Ltd., Taylor Bros. & Co., J. T. & J. Taylor, Ltd., and a number of other firms. The Society acts as the State's agent with regard to paying out the State benefits, and in addition pays at the same time a supplementary benefit of one-third of the State benefit, for which an extra contribution is generally levied on the workers at the rate of 2*d.* per week, and most of the employers contribute to the supplementary benefit fund. One cannot fail to be struck in reading Mr. Lesser's pamphlet by the extraordinary success of the Federation's scheme in producing co-operation and good feeling between masters and men. With the experience which firms get through putting into operation a method of unemployment insurance of this kind, the way is opened for the institution of a wider scheme of grouped firms, and ultimately for insurance by industry or industries.

CHAPTER XXV
THE RIGHT RELATIONSHIP BETWEEN EMPLOYERS AND EMPLOYED

1. CONTENTMENT IN INDUSTRY (b)

(b) Human Status of the Worker

The next most pressing reform in our present industrial system is to secure for the individual worker a definite status in industry. To describe what is intended is easier than to define it. At present the individual worker complains that the government of industry is conducted by the employer entirely as the latter thinks fit. He calls it the "domination of capital"; he describes himself as treated with scant or no consideration, and undoubtedly he draws all his industrial inspirations from an atmosphere in which there is little apparent development of his human personality. The worker is right and he is wrong. He forgets that the conduct of industry to-day is not a matter in the uncontrolled hands of any employer. He loses sight of the fact that in all well-organized industries the conditions of employment which prevail have been the matter of extensive adjustment between the employers' organizations and the Trade Unions, negotiated, of course, centrally beyond the horizon of the individual worker.

The Slowness of Ordinary Conciliation Machinery

The real feeling that the worker is trying to express is his sense of personal insignificance in a great factory, accentuated, when grievances arise, by the difficulty, in large works, of securing prompt discussion of them between the workers and the management. All that can be done is for the worker to report the matter to the shop steward of his particular craft in the department, who will no doubt report it to the secretary of his Trade Union district committee. The latter will put it forward for consideration by the committee and take their instructions upon it, and the committee will, in course of time, send down him or the district delegate to the works to see the employer. A discussion will take place, the results of which the district delegate will report back to the district committee. If the matter is amicably settled there is an end of it; if, on the other hand, it still remains in dispute, the district committee may decide to refer it to the executive council of their Union. The executive council will then remit it to the central organization of the employers, to be considered by them at their next meeting. The matter may be then adjusted, or it may be left over for discussion at one of the periodical joint central conferences. While this ponderous machinery is functioning the individual worker is left face to face with the remembrance of his grievance, and it is not surprising that he gradually acquires a sense of inferiority and a feeling of being neglected, through his ignorance that the mills of conciliation grind slowly. The object first and foremost must be to adapt existing, or provide new, machinery in all industries to enable grievances to be speedily discussed in the works in which they arise. It may be found when they are investigated that they involve some issue common to all the works in the district engaged in the same industry. Obviously, then, that is a matter to be discussed between the district employers and the district committees of the Trade Unions, or through the district conciliation machinery, whatever it may be. In course of the district discussions it may be ascertained that the matters of controversy have raised some national question, then, obviously, for the sake of industrial uniformity, these questions should be considered nationally between the organizations representing all the employers in the country engaged in the particular industry and the Trade Unions representing the men, or through the appropriate national conciliation machinery.

These are the general lines along which, as Part II shows, industrial conciliation machinery has developed. In the highly organized industries, there is machinery, district and national, but not as a rule works' committees. The drawback in all industries is the delay.

The Whitley Councils Scheme

The want of such machinery became apparent in many imperfectly organized industries in the early part of the war, and in October 1916, "the Whitley Committee" was appointed by the Prime Minister with the following terms of reference:

(1) To make and consider suggestions for securing a permanent improvement in the relations between employers and workmen.

(2) To recommend means for securing that industrial conditions affecting the relations between employers and workmen should be systematically reviewed by those concerned, with a view to improving conditions in the future.

Of this Committee the present Speaker of the House of Commons, the Right Hon. J. H. Whitley, was Chairman. It comprised representatives of the employers and also of the Trade Unions engaged in some of the great industries. The Committee presented five reports recommending what is now known as the Whitley Councils Scheme.

Joint National and District Industrial Councils

In its first Report (*Parliamentary Paper*, 1917, Cd. 8606) the Committee recommended the establishment for each of the principal industries of a triple form of organization, representative of employers and employed, consisting of National Joint Councils, Joint District Councils and Works' Committees, each of the three forms of organization being linked up with the others, so as to constitute an organization covering the whole of the trade, capable of considering and advising upon matters affecting the welfare of the industry and giving to Labour a definite and enlarged share in the discussion and settlement of industrial matters with which employers and employed are jointly concerned, each Council and Committee exercising such powers and duties as are determined by negotiation between the employers and the Trade Unions in the industry in question.

As part of its second Report (*Parliamentary Paper*, 1918, Cd. 9002) the Committee proposed for trades in which organization is weak or non-existent the adoption of the system of Trade Boards, and for trades in which organization was considerable, but not yet comprehensive, a system of Joint Councils, with Government assistance, to be dispensed with in each case as soon as these industries advanced to the stage when the full organization could successfully be created for them. The Committee also proposed a scheme in its second Report under which the National Joint Council of an industry, once it had agreed upon a minimum standard of working conditions for those employed in the industry, could secure the enforcement of those conditions either throughout a given district or over the whole country.

Works' Committees

Prominently in its third Report (*Parliamentary Paper*, 1918, Cd. 9085) the Whitley Committee emphasized once more the need for the constitution in each factory or workshop, where the circumstances of the industry permitted, of a Works' Committee, representative of the management and the men and women employed, to meet regularly to consider questions peculiar to the individual factory or workshop which affected the life and comfort of the workers.

In the Committee's fourth Report (*Parliamentary Paper*, 1918, Cd. 9099) it recommended the establishment of a standing Arbitration Tribunal to deal with cases where the two sides of a Joint Industrial Council had failed to come to an agreement and wished to refer the dispute for settlement by arbitration.

The far-sighted proposals of the Whitley Committee represent the machinery that is necessary if the government of industry is to be a matter of mutual arrangement between the employers and the employed. Great progress has already been made in establishing Whitley Councils; in some industries they have operated remarkably well, and have succeeded in conferring a very considerable measure of joint self-government on employers and employed. But in other industries where they have been started they have not worked so satisfactorily. On paper no doubt the number of National Joint Industrial Councils which have been established appears large, and the number of Joint District Councils substantial, but their effect in avoiding disputes in some industries is negligible. The reason, in my opinion, is that too much attention has been paid to setting up National Councils and too little to forming Works' Committees. Progress would have been much more marked if employers generally had been prepared to press forward more enthusiastically with the constitution of Works' Committees—they are the crux of the position. It is they which deal directly with the individual worker who is necessarily out of personal touch with the Joint National or District Councils.

The Slow Progress of Works' Committees

There are several explanations of employers' want of sympathy with Works' Committees. In a number of establishments where they were formed the workers used them to deal, not with matters in which the employer and the employed were jointly interested, but with matters of executive responsibility solely appertaining to the employer. This was done sometimes out of keenness, sometimes out of ignorance; in some localities it was a definite attempt on the part of revolutionary elements to use these workshop committees as a means of acquiring the control of the industry. Again, enforcements of discipline were treated as illustrations of the "domination of capital" and tabled by the workers as matters for joint agreement. In some works, it has been surprising to me how far employers have been able to go in discussing matters of discipline, even to the extent of making dismissals for infraction of works' rules a matter for consideration by the workshop committee. That, I am afraid, is a course which cannot be recommended. I have had some experience of the endless agitation which simmered in one yard where that particular plan was followed.

The Success of Works' Committees on the Clyde

In the stormy days on the Clyde in the spring of 1916, I had, as Chairman of the Government Commission for Dilution of Labour, remarkable proofs of the extent to which workshop committees, when loyally supported by employers, operate to create industrial contentment. Up to that time the skilled men in the engineering shops on the Clyde had firmly refused to comply with the "Treasury" Agreements of March 1915, accepted on ballot by their own Trade Union, and declined absolutely to permit any woman to be introduced for the purpose of doing work previously done by a man or even a boy. The Executive Council of the A.S.E. confessed their entire inability to persuade their Clyde members to comply with the Agreement, and left the matter to the Clyde District Committee. We, as a Commission, found the Clyde District Committee willing to assist, but powerless. It then occurred to us that the best way to achieve our purpose of introducing women was to establish in each workshop a workshop committee consisting of an equal number of workers and management. We explained the scheme of dilution to the committee, leaving it to be discussed between the men on the one side and the management on the other, all information being given and objections, so far as possible, being met by us in the course of the discussion. The workers' side of the committee would then report to a mass meeting of the workers and come back in a day's time to a further meeting of the committee, when adjustments, if necessary, would be made by us in the scheme. The result was truly amazing; the men who previously had been adamant against dilution soon realized there was no desire on our part to force some cast-iron proposal down their throats, and that there was a definite opportunity reserved to them as of right for discussing matters, for eliciting information on doubtful aspects, for pointing out and securing a remedy for objectionable features and for introducing safeguards for the protection of their craft. Hostility softened into suspicion, suspicion mellowed into confidence, and confidence in time begat co-operation. Almost insensibly the scope of these committees widened by general consent, and other workshop grievances, apart altogether from dilution, were submitted for discussion and disposed of in the same amicable way. The engineering employers on the Clyde wholeheartedly supported the scheme, and a number of them voluntarily took the initiative in enlarging the sphere of matters to be discussed. It should not be forgotten that this was in one of the most revolutionary districts of the country, where for their own purposes extremists had been long fomenting workshop grievances. When those grievances were remedied in this way there was very little left for the extremists to turn to their own ulterior ends, and the Clyde settled down. After the Commission was dissolved in October 1916, by the

Ministry of Munitions, which did not like to see an outside authority doing successfully what it had previously failed to do, the influence for good of these committees rapidly declined under the hard hand of bureaucratic control.

At first I had entertained fears of Trade Union hostility to workshop committees, because local delegates are apt to think that the discussion of workshop grievances is a matter entirely for them, which, if appropriated by a workshop committee, may impair the necessity for their official existence. This difficulty, however, we surmounted in a very simple way. The committee consisted as a rule of seven or eight members elected by the workers in the shop, and an equal number of the representatives of the management. Notice of any meeting of the committee and of the agenda before the committee would be sent to the district delegate of the Union concerned, who would be invited ex-officio, if he cared, to attend and take part in the proceedings. As a rule the delegate invariably did attend, and his presence was most helpful.

In the course of six months' work the Clyde Commission established nearly 200 workshop committees which met each week, and had the satisfaction of seeing them dispose of workshop grievances and other works disputes in a harmonious, business-like and effective manner. It produced the best possible feeling among the men; they felt—as many of them told me personally—they were no longer under the heel of the foreman, but had an opportunity of putting their complaints fully before the management, being called, of course, as witnesses by the workers' side of the committee. They felt, they said, that their labour was being no longer treated as merely raw material in industry, and that they had at last attained a human status. This, however, we did insist upon, that a worker had to go through the constitutional shop procedure for disposing of his grievance before it could be brought up at a meeting of the committee; in other words, if shop procedure provided for the question being dealt with by the foreman with an appeal from him to the manager, that it should be exhausted before the committee could take the matter up. In the same way the worker had to exhaust his Trade Union procedure, reporting the matter, it may be, to his shop steward, who would follow the progress of the controversy in the accustomed manner.

Executive Management a Matter for Employers

The cause of what I hope is only a temporary stoppage in the progress of Joint Councils and Works' Committees is due to the fact that extreme sections of Labour have taken the view that these Councils and Committees seriously interfere with their projects of bringing industry to an end, so as to enable the workers to acquire control of it, and have, therefore, instigated the workers in certain districts to advance demands going to the very root of the employer's right and responsibility to manage his business, which do not admit of discussion. The employers rightly have objected to this. But for the way in which moderate workmen have unwittingly lent themselves to these tactics, there is no doubt that the scheme for Works' Committees would have made greater headway. To give an actual illustration: One of our mammoth liners, in shipyard after being repaired, required a few hours' overtime on the part of six fitters to enable her to go to her home port to load for departure. The fitters refused to work overtime until the matter was discussed between their shop steward and the management; a discussion took place, the former would not agree, and insisted on convening his workshop committee in a couple of days. The ship was all this time being detained, and eventually had to sail, as she could wait no longer, but as a result of the delay, she missed the tide at her home port. While a limitation on the total amount of overtime to be worked per working week is a matter for legitimate agreement between management and men, when and how the overtime is to be worked is obviously a question for the management. The Whitley machinery is admirable, but however excellent it may be, it can do nothing unless there is the right spirit on both sides—a spirit of compromise and mutual endeavour to arrive at some fair and equitable basis of self-government, leaving it to the employer to manage his works in accordance with the principles that have been agreed. Labour cannot seek to settle the principles by negotiation, and in addition manage the works. No employer claims to dictate what the principles shall be.

CHAPTER XXVI
THE RIGHT RELATIONSHIP BETWEEN EMPLOYERS AND EMPLOYED

1. CONTENTMENT IN INDUSTRY (c)

(c) Remuneration of the Worker

Contentment in industry depends next on a sound and equitable policy for remuneration of the workers. That implies the summary rejection of all attempts to fix wages on abstract formulae which pay no regard to the circumstances of an industry, or conditions affecting the marketing of the product. If we adopt socialistic nomenclature and call the remuneration of the workers "pay," and assume elimination of the private employer, and each industry conducted under "democratic control," even then the gradation of pay between different classes of workers, the rate of pay of each class, the relation between the general standard of pay in one as compared with other industries would depend entirely on the same circumstances as now, and, if the concrete results of past industrial experience are to be disregarded, would be in each case a matter for experimentation, and for practical adjustment and not for pseudo-mathematical solutions.

Uniform National Wages

One of the demands of workers in many industries which, before the war, paid in different districts rates of wages varying according to local economic circumstances, is for uniform national wage rates. This is a result of the war. There was, during the war, no time to consider the wage-circumstances of individual works—the pressing need was munitions at any price—hence Government Departments responsible for production were compelled to treat wages in industries under their control, especially those in which there had been no pre-war defined district practice, on a more or less uniform national basis. Thus, substantially the same standard, as distinct from minimum, rate of wages for the same grade of workers came in time to operate generally throughout the country, in all works in a particular munitions industry. In some of the more highly organized industries the addition of the same war advance preserved district differentials of the same pre-war nominal amount, but the pre-war ratios of the district wages to one another were greatly reduced. So workmen in a particular district, where, for economic reasons, wages had been lower than in other districts, found themselves on much the same wage-level as workmen in the highest pre-war rated district. A difference of 5s. between 35s. and 30s. per week is very different from 5s. between 80s. and 75s. Naturally, the worker will not willingly surrender that position; hence the claim to-day in many industries for standard national rates. It is an impracticable demand under ordinary commercial conditions, save in exceptional cases where you have one employer running all works in an industry, as the Government did munitions during the war, or different employers each possessing balanced undertakings which comprise establishments both above and below average efficiency. The demand for standardization is illustrated in the railwayman's wage settlement; numerous classes of men (excluding drivers and firemen) previously in railway service have been reduced to a small number of grades, and the individual in those grades receives, generally speaking, one of three descending national rates of pay according as his work is in the London area, one of the provincial towns, or in a rural part of the country. Sailors' and stokers' wages are also standardized, the same rates of pay for the same class of man being paid in vessels in the same trade category. It is obvious, however, that neither railways nor shipping nor docks are analogous to industries consisting of an enormous number of widely different concerns. On the other hand, it is quite practicable to have uniform national conditions of employment, overtime, night-work, Sunday-work, etc., and in many industries there is such national uniformity.

Wage-Relationships among the Workers

The war destroyed the delicate pre-war wage-relationship between the different classes of skilled, semi-skilled, and unskilled labour—in some cases the new relationship is a complete inversion of the old. This was partly the result of Government Departments concerned in production—the Admiralty, War Office, Ministry of Munitions—advancing wages of men under their control independently and without reference to one another, in some cases actually enticing men to their employment; partly of strong sectional Trade Union pressure, and partly of the celebrated 12½ per cent, bonus to time-workers, and 7½ per cent. bonus to piece-workers. Since the war, the want of balance has been aggravated by the action of employers and Trade Unions in industries supplying a national necessity, e.g. building, whereby wages were so raised that unskilled men were paid more than skilled men in a trade like engineering. There is no more active cause of industrial discontent. As an illustration of how it operates, at the Dockers' Inquiry, the Transport Workers' Federation protested against any comparison between dockers' wages and those of other workers— they termed it a "capitalistic device" to deprive dockers of their rightful advance. The Transport Workers were members of the Triple Alliance; the railwaymen were also members. A few weeks later the railwaymen were claiming before their Central Wages Board an increase in wage because the dockers had obtained a minimum wage of 16s. per day. It is therefore vital to get back to, and as far as possible preserve, the pre-war wage relationships.

Wages and the Community

Public opinion is beginning to insist, as it ought to do, on recognition of the interests of the consuming community, which in the past have been wholly ignored. If an increase in wages in an industry is, and can be, secured by an increase in price, as when the output is a necessity, the workers in that industry benefit at the expense of the workers in other industries, and of the consumers generally. In other words, the public pays, as in the case of housing. If an all-round increase in wages in all industries is financed by a general increase in prices, then all prices are higher, and the commodity purchasing power of the increased wages is no greater than that of the wages before increase, and again the public suffers from the general rise in prices. Already a beginning has been made in recognizing the interests of the community in placing public representatives upon the Railway National Wages Board.

Are Higher Wages Practicable?

It is essential to realize the practical difficulties in the way of the workers getting the higher wages which all would like to see them receive. There was a Census of Production in 1907 which included all the manufacturing industries and mining, and covered half the wage-earners in the United Kingdom. It ascertained the "net output" for each industry for the year by estimating the selling value of the gross product, and subtracting therefrom expenditure on raw materials, including the product of other industries which were further worked up, and fuel and some other items. The net output thus obtained is obviously for each industry the only fund from which first, wages, salaries, interest on capital, rent, royalties and profits are, or can be, paid, and secondly, taxes, rates, depreciation, advertisement and sales expenses. Professor Bowley, in his *The Division of the Product of Industry*, Oxford: Clarendon Press, 1919, takes the total net output of £712,000,000 for the industries covered by the Census of 1907, and works out how much of it should be allocated against the first set of items. I set out below in tabular form his results:

	£.	Per cent.
Wages	344,000,000	58
Salaries under £160	24,000,000	4
Salaries over £160	36,000,000	6
Interest on Capital at 4 per cent. and rent	48,000,000	8
Royalties	7,000,000	1
PROFITS	133,000,000	23
	£592,000,000	100

Professor Bowley pertinently observes: "How far this 23 per cent., or £133,000,000 together with a relatively small sum (probably well under £10,000,000) for the salaries of managers of companies, is an excessive or unnecessary remuneration for the organization of industry employing 6,000,000 wage-earners and £1,200,000,000 capital, and producing £340,000,000 wages is a question that may properly be debated: *it is this sum that formed the only possible source of increased earnings in this group with industries conducted as before the war and production at its then level*" (the italics are mine). Supposing the absurd: that in 1907 the whole of this £133,000,000 had been taken from employers, and handed over to the wage-earners, the total average earnings of men fully employed in the industries in question, as Professor Bowley shows, would have been only 41s. 6d. per week. Supposing half of the £133,000,000 had been handed over, the total average earnings of men fully employed (including tradesmen) would have been 35s. 2d. per week. But even to have handed over half, would, by reason of the great disparity between the profit-earning power per man employed of different firms in the same industry, have resulted in closing down many of the less profitable concerns. These figures show conclusively that in industry, as a whole, though there may be exceptions in certain particular industries, the ability to pay higher permanent wages depends upon greater and more efficient production.

The Settlement of Wages

Wages and conditions of employment must always be matters of collective bargaining between employers and employed and not for superimposition by Government upon either or both of them. In my view, national settlement of wages and conditions in an industry is essential to wage stability. A national settlement does not, however, involve a uniform national wage. Complete discussion and national settlement entail for each industry the organization of all the employers into one effective federation, and of all the workers, not necessarily into one Union, but into Unions which are embraced in one executive federation. Only where responsible representative and disciplined federations of employers and workers exist in an industry can there be effective national negotiation of wages questions, or in industries in which Whitley Councils exist, between the two sides of the Council. I look forward to the time when the organization in each industry for the settlement of all industrial conditions will be developed into an organization consisting of representatives of (1) employers; (2) administrative and technical and supervisory personnel; (3) Trade Unions, and (4) consumers. Questions affecting the industry as a whole would be settled by all four sections; questions, e.g. of wages, by the representatives of the employers, Trade Unions and consumers. If a wage agreement is negotiated in any industry providing for excessive wages and therefore high costs of production and high prices, is it to be unchallengeable when the industry is a public necessity? There were many such agreements made during and immediately after the war. I see no way of reviewing such agreements when once made; all attempts by Government to do so under the Munitions of War Acts were unsuccessful. The only practicable method of safeguarding the consuming public is to have, as I suggest, efficient representatives of the public present at, and entitled to take an active part in, the joint conferences of federated employers and Unions when wages are being negotiated, as on the Railway National Wages Boards.

Systems of Remuneration

No one can dogmatize and say what system of industrial remuneration should be adopted, whether time, piece-work—collective or individual—premium-bonus, bonus on output, profit-sharing, or co-partnership. That all depends upon the conditions of the industry, its peculiar psychology, especially its past history; it must always be a matter for negotiation. But I am the strongest believer in a fair system of payment by results, as being, under proper safeguards, the best for the worker, the employer and the consumer. A steel worker or boilermaker will swear by it; a carpenter or joiner calls it "the device of the devil." Hence my reference to industrial psychology.

What is a Fair Wage?

Wages are, and can only be, payment for work done and services rendered by the "wages staff." There must always be a maximum limit to wages and a minimum. The employers' maximum is a wage beyond which any advance, with other costs of production remaining constant, would prevent the marketing of the product at a commercial profit commensurate with the nature of the enterprise. The theoretical minimum is a "living wage," i.e. bare cost of subsistence, but the Trade Union minimum wage, which is the practical minimum in industry, is much higher than the subsistence wage. It is a wage which in the particular industry provides for subsistence for the worker and his or her dependants, including therein food, rent, fuel, light, clothing, fares, Trade Union subscriptions, etc., and reasonable enjoyment and recreation. Trade Union minimum rates for different trades varied before the war from one another by "vocational differentials." A skilled man's rate exceeded that of an unskilled man by a recognized excess; the excess is the trade differential in respect of the skill required of the particular tradesman, the length of apprenticeship necessary to acquire it, the nature of the occupation and so forth. The higher rate of the skilled man is naturally reflected, as statistics show, in a higher standard of living. The whole problem in arriving at a fair wage is to determine at what point, if any, between the existing Trade Union minimum and the employers' maximum, the wage ought to be fixed, in justice to the workers, employers and the public.

By way of preliminary I would emphasize that no fair wage can be fixed on any basis of a priori reasoning. It involves constructing a theoretical household budget, adopting an empirical standard of life, with no relation whatsoever to the normal circumstances of any section of the industrial community, ignoring economic conditions, and assuming that industry can or ought to pay a sufficient wage to maintain that standard. That is the fatal method of the doctrinaire. The usual procedure is for the Trade Unions to demand an increased wage, and swear by all the gods that the employers can easily pay it. The employers then assert with equal emphasis their inability to pay any increase. Sometimes a compromise is reached and sometimes not. There should be, and indeed is, a better method of procedure.

First, there ought to be ascertained the wages which the industry is economically able to pay at the then prevailing market prices for its product; we may conveniently call them "ability wages." They cannot be determined by picking out and assuming as typical—a frequent stratagem of Labour—individual firms which are making substantial profits. The industry must be taken on a national, it may be sometimes on a district basis, extreme cases at both ends of the scale ruled out, and a proper estimate struck on methods of accountancy, making due allowance for the trade outlook and for all the expenses and risks present and prospective, which, from the conditions of the industry in question, fall upon the employers. Labour insists on the Trade Union rate of wages being paid by all firms, whether making large profits or none at all. To consider therefore the industry as a whole is equitable. Employers making exceptional profits cannot be taken as norms for wages; so far as their gains are contrary to public policy, they can only be dealt with by a "wise and wary Chancellor of the Exchequer." That an "ability to pay" estimate can be prepared in respect of an industry by competent joint accountants on a basis convincing to Labour has more than once come prominently within my own practical experience. The great point is to prove to the workers that they are getting a fair share of the product of industry under its then existing conditions. It is much more important to satisfy them on that point than to pay them a high wage. If they get a higher wage than the industry can pay, and are not satisfied, they will firmly believe that a still higher wage could and ought to be paid. There is only one way to prove the equity of the wage—to put all the cards on the table, and show the Trade Union representatives at the conference what the exact conditions of the industry are, and what are the maximum wages which the industry as a whole can pay.

Secondly, an exact statement is required of the wages paid in other industries to workers comparable with the workers in the industry in question—these may be termed "comparable wages." They are obtainable from statistics compiled by the Ministry of Labour, but not published in collated form.

There are in practice two objects to achieve. First, to ensure that each grade of worker gets a fair wage which corresponds to the "ability wage," and secondly, to try and keep the wages of workers in one industry in proper wage-relationship with the wages of comparable workers in other industries. If the existing wages are less than the "ability wages," and the latter are either equal to, or less than, the comparable wages, there ought to be an advance of the existing wages up to the ability level, and, in my view, a further advance beyond ability level towards, but not exceeding, the comparable wages-level, if the circumstances of the industry are such, as for example, in respect of foreign competition, that the market price of the product can be increased by the necessary amount. It is so essential for the harmony of industry that the wages of comparable workers should be generally on the same level. There is no difficulty in practice in saying who are comparable workers. Industrial experience and tradition have firmly settled that. In the case, comparatively rare in practice, where the level of ability wages is higher than the level of comparable wages, other considerations arise. Some employers contend that to pay in one industry that can afford it a higher rate of wages than in comparable industries that cannot afford it is to upset the equilibrium of wages in those latter industries, and incite the workers in them to ask for the same wages rates, thus involving a charge upon the whole or a section of the public forming the consumers of the product of those industries with the usual results. Other employers assert that comparable wages are the criterion of fair wages, and as employers have to stand the risk of paying Trade Union wages when profits are not adequate, so, therefore, employers, when profits are exceptional, should be entitled to retain what remains after comparable wages are paid. I do not see why the employer should be entitled to appropriate in such a case the difference between the ability wages and the comparable wages. In my view, if an industry is shown by a joint cost investigation to be able to pay wages which are higher than comparable wages, the amount of the proceeds of the industry beyond the sum necessary to pay wages at comparable rates should be divided equally between employers and workers and consumers—in the case of the latter by a reduction in price. The workers thus secure a share in the prosperity of the industry.

Some wage complexities due to the war urgently need adjustment. Flat additions as war bonuses on piece-work or tonnage-rates are unsettling anomalies; they should be incorporated in new piece—or tonnage—rates. Their existence hinders output. War advances and war bonuses; which, though originally different, are now in practice indistinguishable, should, so far as not withdrawn, be merged into the permanent rate or price—in one-half of industry they have already been merged—difference of treatment only causes unrest. It cannot be too strongly emphasized that high rates of wages do not necessarily mean high earnings—they frequently mean no earnings and no work. Increasing the productive efficiency of labour does increase the ability of industry to pay. Such alone is the one sure road to higher earnings.

Other Essentials to Industrial Contentment

There should be open to the workers in this country an opportunity of rising, that is, of transfer from the wages side to the salaried side of the staff as is afforded by American employers. Why there should be such reluctance among so many English employers to promote men from the wages side I have never appreciated. During the war I had a large number of workmen under me at the Admiralty, who, after the war, were appointed to responsible positions on the administrative side of industry in the establishments of some broad-minded employers, and have abundantly justified their selection.

CHAPTER XXVII
THE RIGHT RELATIONSHIP BETWEEN EMPLOYERS AND EMPLOYED

2. CO-OPERATION IN INDUSTRY

The establishment of co-operation in industry between employers and employed is a matter almost entirely of the mind and spirit; it depends upon the elimination of the mutual suspicion that at present exists; it involves the creation of confidence; it entails the dissipation of certain economic fallacies that obsess the workers and also unprogressive employers.

The Workers' Own Resort to Co-operation

Labour thoroughly well recognizes the productive power of the spirit of co-operation. In certain trades men work in squads, and the members of the squad share in agreed proportions the total price for the squad's collective work. Many shops are paid on the output bonus system or on a "fellowship" basis. Under such conditions the earnings of the squad or shop, within the limits fixed for normal output, depend on the full co-operation of each member of the squad or shop. Co-operation is then recognized as a moral duty. It is almost invariably afforded without stint, if not it is sternly exacted. Many skilled men also paid on output are assisted by semi-skilled or unskilled "helpers" paid a fixed time wage, irrespective of output. Although the increased efforts of the "helpers" result in increased earnings only for the skilled men, in general co-operation is usually forthcoming from the "helpers," and if not it is unconditionally demanded. There is no difficulty in identifying the doctrines to which the workers appeal in justification of their present attitude of non-co-operation with employers—they all come from Marxian Socialism. They are encountered everywhere in workshop, Trade Union branch and district committee, and form the foundations of belief amongst industrial democracy.

The Marxian Argument against Co-operation

Though it is not possible to crystallize the Marxian doctrines with absolute precision of language into a few lines of print, they may be stated in simple words, with tolerable accuracy, as follows:

"Production is the process of applying labour-force to raw material, and the exchange or market value of the commodity which is the product is created by the labour-force expended by the labourer in working. That value, which solely results from the labour so expended, is measured by the time occupied by the labourer upon the production of the newly-created commodity in question. The labourer is paid by his employer a wage which represents the 'exchange value' of his 'labour-force.' But the employer has obtained the 'use-value' of the labour-force, and disposes of the newly-created product in the market at a selling price which, after making allowance for the costs of production before and after the application of labour-force, is higher than the wage paid to the labourer. The excess is 'surplus value.' This surplus value in primitive industry is appropriated wholly by the employer, but in industry more highly developed is apportioned out among the different classes of capitalists in the shape of ground rent, interest, manufacturers' profits, and commercial profit."

In the doctrines of Marx there are three fundamental propositions: the first, that money is the primary form of capital; the second, that the value of a commodity is measured by the amount of labour expended upon it; the third, that the capitalist buys the use-value of a day's labour in exchange for its market value, pocketing the surplus value, which is the difference. As long as we allow these theories to remain victorious, industry to-day is merely a process by which the capitalist constitutes himself the conduit-pipe to the sale-room for the workman's labour, and as the latter passes through his hands filches for himself the "surplus value."

Some Workshop Applications

As I write I have beside me a mass of leaflets, pamphlets and writings, which came into my possession during my recent industrial work, all reeking with this pernicious Marxianism. Some extracts from the *Red Catechism*, handed to me by way of argument in a shipyard, will give an idea of the doctrines:

Who creates all wealth?	The working-class.
Who are the workers?	Men who work for wages and receive only a portion of what they earn, the other part going to keep the idle classes.

Who creates all poverty?	Our capitalistic society.
What is a wage-slave?	A person who works for a wage, and gives all he earns to a capitalist.
What proportion does a wage-slave receive of what he earns?	On the average about a fourth.
What is an exploiter?	One who employs a man and makes him produce three or four times the amount he receives in wages.
How do capitalists become rich?	By employing labour and exploiting it.
The question of merit does not enter into the reward of capital, then?	No. It is only used as a hypocritical subterfuge to hide the robbery of labour.

These are only a few quotations, the list could be amplified enormously.

The Marxian Fallacy of the Origin of Capital

The Marxian proposition that money is the first form of capital is a discordant and disruptive delusion. Marx declared that all capital was derived from the profits obtained by paying labour less than the value it created. On this hypothesis the capitalist assists in no way in the business of production. He is in the position of reaping what he has not sown. He is a bandit who holds up to ransom the whole world of workmen. He lets labourers off with their lives, that is to say, with wages just sufficient for their subsistence and the reproduction of their species, thus securing the maintenance of a supply of labour, on condition that the labourers hand over to him practically the entire value of their labour. As long as such doctrines are taught to the young worker and are accepted by the old, of what good is it to prate about co-operation? It is about as sensible to advocate co-operation between a host and its parasite, between a vampire and its prey, between a highway robber and his victim. Yet that is the vain task on which so many eminent persons are now wasting their eloquence.

The first essential is boldly and openly to challenge this Marxian doctrine of the parasitic character of capital. There will never be, there cannot be, co-operation between capital and Labour until Labour has learned what capital is and the function it plays in production. Labour is ready to learn. I have found it possible to sustain the interest of workmen while explaining that capital consists primarily of things that are not money, of goods upon which people subsist while producing other goods, of factories, machinery, and raw material; that capital is a definite agent in production, capable of application, not merely by the conventional employer, but by every man; that it is something which, when used in production, is consumed, so that he who adventures it must possess such experience and judgment as will enable him to surmount the risk of loss, and obtain a return sufficient to replace the capital that has been consumed, and to recompense the lender for his thrift and remunerate himself for the services he has rendered and the risk to which he has been subjected. These particular aspects of capital, from their very novelty and unexpectedness, catch the immediate attention of Labour, so much so that in some districts the workmen, of their own accord, arranged meetings and invited me specially to discuss with them the character and function of capital in modern industry and the extent to which Labour was dependent upon it.

But realities must be faced. There is no good in evading the fact that while capital is essential and of incalculable benefit to humanity, it can, at the same time, like any other human possession, be used so as to cause inconvenience, injustice, distress, degradation, death. In short, the use of capital may be socially beneficent, or it may be maleficent, anti-social. The invariable example which the workman adduces of its anti-social use is "profiteering" in many of its accustomed forms. It is a great misfortune that there is no precise term in use to describe the particular function of capital as an agent in production. Aristotle distinguished on arbitrary principles which he enunciated, and derived from the conditions of his time, between the natural beneficial use of wealth, which he calls "economics," and the unnatural abuse of wealth, which he calls "chrematistics." His principles are out of date, the terminological distinction which he attempted was sound. This is what happens always in industrial discussion: employers, thinking of the beneficent function played by capital in production, emphasize the dependence of Labour on capital—Labour, thinking of the anti-social uses of capital, and reasoning from the particular to the general, retorts that capital is the cause of all Labour's troubles. If both employers and workers could, by appropriate terms, get down to discussing the same thing, there would be substantial prospect of agreement; to-day there is none.

The Marxian Fallacy of Value

The next notion in the workman's mind subversive of co-operation is his idea, derived from Marx, that "the value of a commodity is the amount of abstract human labour embodied in it." If this be true, as so many workmen now fervently believe, it follows that the employer contributes nothing whatever to the value of the manufactured product, and that the only value-producing agency is labour. In truth neither workman nor employer creates value; both unite to perform services or produce things which other circumstances, e.g. demand, cause to be of value, and they do so because of that value. But the material point is that the Marxian doctrine rules out co-operation. Logically, it implies that the only possible remedy for the present lot of the worker consists in the complete demolition of the present organization of industry. The worker who accepts the Marxian theory of value, with its corollary theory of surplus value, is a weak-kneed individual and a traitor to his brethren, if he be cajoled for a moment into co-operating with his employer, or if he hesitates to fight whole-heartedly for the eradication of the employer, root and branch, from the industrial system.

The difficulty I have experienced in attacking this Marxian heresy is the common one which confronts any opponent of a popular doctrine accepted on faith and not on logic. A reasoned explanation of the fallacy is often not understood, a striking refutation is regarded as an extreme instance to which no reasonable person would ever suggest that the principle applied. When I have put the classic case of a man who discovers a precious stone, picks it up and finds it is worth, say, £50, and have suggested that the labour-force exerted by the finder in reaching down and lifting up the stone and carrying it to a purchaser cannot surely be the sole cause of its value, the answer has at once been made: "That is a case of raw material, and not a manufactured article." I have then taken the case of some manufactured article like "pigs" or "ingots." These when made were of a certain value, but they were put into store as against a rising market and became, subsequently, of greater value. According to Marx, the magnitude of the value of any commodity is determined by the amount of the labour socially necessary for its production and embodied in it under the normal conditions of production, and with the average degree of skill and intensity prevalent at the time. This amount of labour, in the case of the "pigs" and "ingots," was the amount expended when they were first made, but since then, without the expenditure of any more labour, their value has greatly increased. The increase in value cannot obviously be attributed to the addition of "abstract" or any other kind of labour.

It is surprising how many workmen have learned quite glibly the outlines of the Marxian value and surplus value argument, and can express it by rote in flawless Marxian terminology. Even accepting it, as it has been so truly described, as "the greatest intellectual mare's nest of the last century," without any question it is an argument that has to be seriously considered. It must be driven by economic education out of the workers' list of cherished convictions. No good will come of treating it with flippancy, or pouring ridicule upon it. I made it my practice to take up the argument stage by stage, emphasize what appeared to me to be the flaws, and then finish off with a number of practical workshop illustrations of cases where the argument fails egregiously to hold water. To be convincing, and to drive each point well home, takes a considerable amount of time, but it is well worth it. Few persons appreciate the extent to which this Marxian sophistry prevents achievement of the co-operative ideal in industry.

There is just one word of warning necessary. According to Marx, the workman receives from the employer the exchange value of his labour-force or power on handing over to the employer its use-value. Marx maintained, and unfortunately in the past there has been much to add force to his contention, that Labour in return received a wage no more than equal to "bare subsistence" or "bare cost of production of labour-power." In many cases the past level of wages cannot be defended, and it would be foolish to try and vindicate it. But this much can be said, real wages have risen very considerably since Marx's day, and without any overthrow of the industrial system. Such a result is absolutely in contradiction of his prophecy, and at variance with his doctrine. It strongly suggests the wisdom of constructive evolution as opposed to destructive revolution.

The Need of Sympathy in Workshop Life

The power of these economic fallacies is enormously reinforced by the injustice and want of sympathy that too often surrounds the industrial relationship between employers and employed. That atmosphere is due to old-fashioned employers holding fast to crude individualistic notions of industry, to the idea that a workman is the animated machine—ἔμψυχον ὄργανον—of the Greek philosophers—an "economic unit" without soul, sensibility, ideals or aspirations, who still labour under the discredited obsession that justice and sympathy are incompatible with discipline and the firm handling of labour. Of course, justice and sympathy can have no place in a creed where labour is merely one of a number of troublesome items of the cost of production. Neither is shown, neither is expected. That type of employer has never recognized that capital, brains and manual labour fill separate and distinct rôles in industry. He looks upon himself as the all-dominant personality and Labour as his feudal and dependent hireling.

Now domination, or any attempt at, or suspicion of it, is quite incompatible with co-operation; in fact, the least semblance of it in industry will speedily kill any latent spirit of co-operation. Nor does it matter in the slightest on what ground the domination is based or asserted. It may be on intellectual superiority, technical experience, organizing capacity, social standing, I care not what; it is the poison of all industrial harmony. As soon as it appears there is straightway an end of all co-operation in any democratic organization, and sectarianism and strife mark the reaction that immediately ensues. Mutual agreement is the essential basis of co-operation, both from the objective and subjective points of view. To secure agreement there must be the spirit to agree, and the existence of that spirit depends almost entirely on the knowledge and belief that matters of industrial controversy will be considered and adjusted on principles of justice and equity. My experience of industry has left me convinced beyond all doubt on one point—there is, deep down in the heart of the British workman, a sense of justice and fair-play. Often it takes time and trouble to vitalize it, to assist it in freeing itself from the tentacles of ignorance, Marxian sophistry and revolutionary formulae which entangle it, as weeds do a swimmer struggling to gain the surface, but in the end, if it gets a chance, it will assuredly triumph.

The Need of Strict Justice

The unenlightened employer has not yet given it a chance. He does not believe in its existence, nor in its efficacy as a moderating influence. There are no conceivable circumstances, he will tell you, which Labour will not unjustly use for its own aggrandisement, if an opportunity coincides with power. That in the past has, unfortunately, been the tradition on the part of reactionary employers no less than on the part of Labour. In regard to either justification or excuse, no distinction whatsoever can be drawn between the two. Propositions and proposals founded on equity and reason can, with confidence, be submitted to the workman's sense of justice. In many instances during the war, I have appealed to this sense of justice with signal success in shop matters of peculiarly acute trade controversy. Even in regard to victimization disputes, always formidable questions, productive often of almost intractable controversy, that is to say, cases of dismissal, fine or reducing, on grounds alleged by the men of the prominence of the "victim" in furthering the interests of his Trade Union, or because of alleged breaches of unwritten shop law, invented, it would be said, by some vindictive foreman. When masters and men have failed to adjust the difference—the former taking their stand on "their right to maintain discipline," the latter on their duty "to protect their Trade Union interests"—I have invariably found it possible to settle the dispute by getting down to principles of fair-play. If the workman who has been "dealt with" was a shop steward, and was really using his employer's time for doing his Trade Union branch work when he might and ought to have been doing his shop work, the men have accepted the position that, after notice, the employer is entitled to take exception to that procedure. On the other hand, if he has only been utilizing for Union business the many periods of time which occur in the best organized shops when he is "waiting for work" or "standing by," and has done it in such a way as not to interfere with his shop work, then the men claim that he has only done what he was entitled to do, and that an employer who objects to him doing Union business under such circumstances is really out against the Union. Most fair-minded people would probably draw the same inference.

The Money Value of Sympathy in Industry

There are to-day many employers, managers, under-managers, and foremen who still act on the dogma that there is nothing to be got out of the sympathetic handling of labour. "It's so much cutting air," more than one has said to me. If an employer of this type honestly believed there was money in it, he is far too keen a business man not to try it. But to many employers Labour is still only a machine which, as long as it runs in any sort of way, is to be left severely alone; when it jerks or sticks it is to be lubricated with smooth words, professions of the employer's anxiety for its welfare, "soft sawder," for which the men, naturally, have the utmost contempt.

The Sympathetic Handling of Labour a Special Art

A very large number of employers have not realized yet that the sympathetic management of labour is a special art, calling for peculiar qualities of temperament and tact. Until that is accepted as sound economics there can never be co-operation. Technical experience is the usual qualification required of a foreman, seldom, if ever, is the least regard paid to his ability to handle men sympathetically so as to get the best out of them. Yet that, much more than technical capacity, contributes to workshop efficiency. There are many persons wholly unfitted by nature to have the charge of men, more especially to perform the responsible duty of taking on and discharging them. Their presence in a shop is a chronic source of irritation, and keeps the men's backs perpetually up. Co-operation, under such conditions, cannot exist. An outsider entering the shop can feel the strained relationship almost intuitively. A sort of nervous tension seems to pervade the place. No cheery words are exchanged between men and manager, as the latter passes through the shop. A notice is often found in the office: "Workmen must wipe their feet before entering." As a workman said to me: "No such direction is given to anyone who comes to place an order," How much better to say to every one, "Please wipe your feet." If a workman wants to see some one in authority he is kept hanging about, losing his piece-work earnings, or is brusquely told that the manager is engaged, while all the time he sees customers admitted with welcome to the office. One manager frankly told me that but for his clerk, who artfully got rid of the workman always wanting to see him, he would never have had any time to do his business. That indicates the attitude of mind that good employers are fighting against. It is not considered by unprogressive employers any part of the recognized duty of a manager to apply sympathy, understanding, and tact to the treatment of Labour. There is no doubt it requires very great time and patience and prolonged study and investigation of numerous circumstances which are on the surface trivial. A manager is often loath to devote to work of that kind time and energy which he thinks, and which many employers certainly think, can more profitably be spent in technical and commercial activity.

An Illustration of its Successful Application

But assuming that management will accept the teaching of the best employers that the sympathetic handling of labour is an employer's duty, and, apart from that, is good business, the problem then will be how to make and sustain such an appeal to the worker that he will be induced to co-operate with the management. A similar problem confronted myself during part of the war period when, as Director of Shipyard Labour, I had charge of the labour in some 2,500 firms, employing something like one million men. Output had to be secured and maintained at all costs, so when any trouble occurred my Department had to intervene if the management and men failed to come to a speedy settlement. When forming the Department I gathered together a small band of enthusiastic and far-sighted employers and Trade Unionists, and in conjunction we made a determined and intensive effort to get right down *au fond* and strike the chords in industrial human nature, on whose vibration co-operation is dependent. Some simple principles were formulated, which, later, as experience grew, were modified in detail. These were made the basis of the appeal, not merely in mass meetings, Trade Union lodges, and elsewhere among the men, but also, with the assistance—and it was loyally given—of the employers, carried into daily workshop practice. At the time when these principles were first put into operation, there were close on 200 strikes a week in the 2,500 firms. After a twelve-months' regime the strikes which had fallen regularly, month by month, came down to under ten a week. Some employers denied that the principles had anything to do with the diminution of strikes. One of the most prominent described them as "so much pap." But the Trade Unions took a different view, and I hold many personal letters from some of the principal Unions attributing the whole of the improvement to the sympathetic regime that had been put into operation—it was really nothing more than carrying sympathy and strict justice into all the details of workshop life. Far be it from me to suggest that any State department, without executive responsibility, can run labour as well as a private employer who has that responsibility; the point is that enormous improvement in the co-operative spirit between employers and employed can be effected by the adoption of a well-developed *methodized* system of handling labour based on sympathetic principles.

Co-operation is a vital essential for the reconstruction of industry. It is the true antidote to revolution. It will only be forthcoming in industry when sound economic conviction operates in an atmosphere and environment of justice and sympathy. As long as economic fallacy is allowed to permeate the minds of employers and employed, leading them to reject or belittle the material advantages of co-operation by representing it as inimical to their respective interests, and as long as the want of sympathy and justice continues to feed that fallacy, co-operation will never emerge as an integrating force in industry. The remedy is, therefore, obvious.

CHAPTER XXVIII
THE RIGHT RELATIONSHIP BETWEEN EMPLOYERS AND EMPLOYED

3. PRODUCTION IN INDUSTRY

The Importance of Production

It is unnecessary to stress the national, the social, the industrial need for production. That does not mean more output with no improvement in the ratio of efficiency. It means more output accompanied with increased efficiency and therefore lower cost of production. It is on cheapness of output that the demands of the home and the foreign consumer for commodities largely depend. Restriction of output means for the community high costs of commodities, less purchasing power, a lower standard of living; it means that there will not be available either the wealth to finance social reforms, or the capital required for industry, and therefore worse conditions and less work for the workers; it means reduced export trade and adverse exchanges. Apart from production, there is no fund from which labour can be paid, the only fund is that consisting of the commodities and services and values which are produced. As the fund is made greater by the joint efforts of employers and workmen, so can the wage paid to the worker be increased. One worker is needed to realize the goods, values or services produced by another worker. If both increase their output as much as is reasonably practicable, each has the maximum available for exchange, and both can secure for themselves the greatest possible standard of living. On the other hand, if one particular worker limits his production, say, by one-half of its reasonable maximum, he not only injures himself and his dependents, because he throws away the opportunity of disposing of one-half of his labour, but he also injures the other workman who, directly or indirectly, exchanges with him, and who would like to exchange the whole of the goods and values and services which he produces, but who is prevented from disposing of more than one-half by reason of his opposite number's selfish and stupid action. The present national standard of living can by no human ingenuity be maintained under to-day's conditions of output.

What Production Depends on

Lord Weir has truly pointed out[21] that there are only four methods of improving the volume and efficiency of our national production:

(1) An increase in intensity of effort per operative hour;

(2) An increase in the number of operative hours per individual per day;

(3) An increase in the number of operative individuals;

(4) A perfecting of methods, processes and organizations, by which waste of operative hours is eliminated.

Accepting this as an accurate statement, which it is, of how alone output can be increased, I wish to point out the immediate obstacles to an achievement of these four objects. They are these:

In regard to (1)—the workman's low conception of work, his tendency, in many trades, to lose time, his inveterate belief in restriction of output.

In regard to (2)—the conception of organized Labour that the present 47- or 48-hour ordinary working week is a social reform with which no tampering will be permitted, and that if in times of trade prosperity more hours are necessary, they ought to be worked as overtime.

In regard to (3)—the insistence of the Trade Unions, in this country, on their rigid lines of demarcation of work—in other words, on certain work being always reserved for certain Unions, without reference to the prevailing industrial or commercial conditions.

In regard to (4)—the opposition of the workers to the introduction of time- and labour-saving appliances, or of payment by results—and Lord Weir adds: the killing of the spirit of enterprise among employers, as the result of the taxation policy of the Government; the lack of reciprocity and co-operation on the part of the Trade Unions, amounting to active obstruction; and bad statesmanship on the part of the employers' organizations.

To state these four methods in their order of relative practicability, they run (1), (4), (3) and (2). All the obstacles enumerated above to securing greater production by methods (1), (4) and (3), are the fruit of unsound economic theories that have for many years past been sedulously instilled into Labour, and are now accepted by it as part of its everyday rule of life and conduct.

The Workers' Notion of the Secret Fund

Foremost, in normal times, comes the erroneous belief that all the aspirations of Labour for increased remuneration, shorter hours, improved conditions of employment, can be satisfied to the full out of the existing profits of employers and current production. This has been argued incessantly before myself. It is honestly believed that all that is necessary to liquidate the demands of Labour is to devote to that purpose part only of the existing profits of industry, in their entirety said to be appropriated by avaricious employers. The sole impediment is considered to be the greed of employers, coupled with the fact that as industry is now organized they hold the money-bags. But this error can be exposed if the demands of Labour are reduced to a definite charge per annum on the industry in question, and each particular establishment involved. It can usually be shown on the actual accounts in typical establishments, at any rate in the engineering and shipbuilding industries, that the demands of Labour could not be met out of existing profits. In fact, in many cases, if the whole of employers' profits were handed over to Labour, and Capital left without any return whatsoever, the demands of Labour could not be satisfied to anything like the full extent.

This delusion is one of the most pernicious in industry, because of its widespread acceptance and its fatal results. It has been fostered by the war conditions, as has already been explained. Employers made profits which exceeded in many cases those retainable under the Munitions of War or Finance Acts, and so it frequently did not matter to them what rate of wages they paid in order to expedite work. Moreover, war advances, far above the rate of wages, were distributed under order of the Government Courts of Arbitration to cover the increased cost of living arising out of the abnormal conditions resulting from the war. These war advances were generally paid by Government, in addition to the contract price for munitions. Thus the workman saw very high nominal rates of wages paid, and the employers at the same time making much greater profits than they could by law appropriate. Nothing was, therefore, more natural than to suppose that all demands could on the current basis of output be satisfied out of existing profits.

"Passing it on"

Accepting, as will some sections of Labour, that their demands cannot be met out of employers' profits on present output, the alternative is, they say, that the manufacturer must raise his selling price by an amount sufficient to cover the extra cost. In this it is assumed, of course, that the rate of production remains the same. It is a fixed idea that every manufacturer and the owners in every industry can raise prices without any difficulty whatsoever. In discussing this delusion, as I have frequently done, it becomes quite obvious that workmen do not appreciate the effect which an increase in the cost of production has in reducing the ambit of the market for the sale of the commodity in question, or in lessening the demand for it in a specific market, with consequential curtailment of employment, and undermining of standard rates of wages. The regulation retort is that any trade not able to pay proper wages ought not to live. That, of course, depends on what is "proper," When the wages are starvation wages, every one will agree the industry ought not to live. When the wages, though sufficient to cover (1) subsistence, are not sufficient for (2) reasonable amenities of life, nor to allow adequately for (3) trade-skill, there may be difference of opinion, according to the circumstances of the particular industry, whether it should be maintained or not. When, however, full and adequate remuneration is paid to cover (1), (2) and (3), it is suicidal policy for Labour to insist on such advances in wages as must kill the industry.

In advancing the contention that if the employer cannot, out of his existing profits, pay the advance on wages claimed, it should be added to the sales price, workmen invariably repudiate as wholly immaterial the resultant effect on trades other than their own, and especially on the consuming community. If those claiming the advance are engaged in what is inelegantly called a "key industry," that is to say, where their output is raw or semi-raw material for other industries, it is obvious that any rise in its cost may inflict serious damage on both employers and employed in the dependent industries. But the workman's retort is "let them pass it on." I have had that put to me on hundreds of occasions. The effect on the community is dismissed as quite irrelevant.

During the war, the fashion of general advances in wages to cover increased cost of living came into vogue. The consequent reaction on prices set up the "vicious circle" known to all economists where a general advance in wages raises prices, thus forcing up the cost of living, and so creating a fresh demand for a further increase in wages. Over and over again by simple illustrations I have tried to make this "vicious circle" clear to workmen. I have always been much impeded by one circumstance. In the early days of the war, in certain districts, as soon as a general advance in wages was awarded by the wages tribunals, or conceded by Government, the various lodging-house keepers put up their rents for rooms, or their charge for board. This was stigmatized by Labour as "profiteering." Arguing by analogy, the workpeople contended that when a general rise in prices followed a general advance in wages, it was entirely due to profiteering. It was never admitted by the workmen that any part of the rise in prices was the natural, inevitable, logical result of the general advances in wages, through the increase of purchasing power operating on the same supply of commodities. War experiences have equally confused workmen's minds with regard to the effect of high wages on the volume of employment. Whatever glimmering suspicion the workmen had before the war that an advance in wages in many industries tended directly, through increased cost of production, to bring about unemployment, has now practically been dissipated by the war. Time after time, I have been told that none of the general advances in wages during the war has ever caused unemployment. The explanation, of course, is that during the war workmen were not to any great extent producing commodities for an ordinary commercial market, but munitions of war for the Government, and all they could turn out the Government could take, so insatiable was its demand.

The Workers' Belief in Restricted Output

We come to another dangerous and widespread fallacy, the assumed advantage of restricting output. This declares itself in many varied forms. One of the commonest is a definite limitation on the tonnage, or feet lineal or square of the day's work. When the day's work is completed the workman, if paid on time, will frequently remain at work, but doing nothing until the "hooter goes." In other cases if paid on a piece-work basis, the workman will sometimes leave the shop after his day's work or "stint" is finished. I have investigated cases where workmen coming on at 7 a.m. finished their day's work and went home by 10.30 or 11 a.m. Other methods of reaching the same end are less open. The operative, instead of finishing his work early and then allowing his machine "to cut air" for the rest of the day, will with nice calculation slow down all day long so as to spin out the allotted day's work more or less uniformly over the working day. Industrial experience during the war has proved the existence, to an almost inconceivable extent, of this latter method of limiting production. Perhaps I can best illustrate it from some cases within my personal knowledge. In one instance some boys straight from a board school were put on to do a simple operation from which men had been withdrawn for more arduous duty. Working at the men's piece-prices, they averaged £4. 15s. per normal working week against the men's £2 10s. That meant the boys turned out—nor were they any the worse for it physically—almost twice the men's output. Women I put on to replace men at some simple machining operations made, after a short period of training, £6-£10 per week, against the men's £4-£5. The women were paid the men's piece-prices for the operation. In another case men who were working on piece-work, after learning of the announcement of the Minister of Munitions that under no circumstances would piece-prices be "cut," speeded up their output by 120 per cent. These are only a few selected illustrations out of a large number.[22] They are concrete exemplifications of the appalling extent to which the false doctrine of limiting output is rampant in industry—operative as an active orthodox Trade Union principle.

By limiting output the workman genuinely believes that he is performing a moral duty to himself and to his trade. He argues first, that he is reducing unemployment by making the work go round; secondly, that he is keeping up the value of his handicraft by putting a premium on its application. Workmen have described to me the difference between possible and actual production as being "their reserve fund." Over and over again this policy has been justified to me by reference to the action of commercial trade combinations which pool orders and limit the output of the works of certain of their members in order to ensure business for other members less fortunately situated, and also by reference to groups of manufacturers who systematically keep up prices by "keeping the bottom in the market" through restricting the quantity of their output that is offered for sale. The workmen will tell you in words to which no economist can object that value is due to utility and to limitation of supply. What he overlooks is that all that is thereby established in practice is a minimum rate of wages, and that maximum earnings depend on maximum output. There are many classical instances, well within memory, where unemployment in certain trades was in fact almost entirely abolished by restricting the output of those employed, notably by discontinuing the then existing systems of payment by results—"blood money" as it was called. These recollections live. But, as a matter of fact, these instances prove nothing. They occurred just about the commencement of a depression in trade, and, in fact, the extra cost of production subsequently caused by the limitation of output, accelerated the unemployment in those very trades. Still working men, like most men, argue from particular cases of personal experience to universals.

The only way to attack the heresy is from the concrete illustration drawn from the United States of America. There restriction of output is not merely unknown, it is definitely repudiated by the Trade Unions. Unfortunately, many labour intellectuals who have no knowledge of American conditions pervert the facts and hold up to execration the industrial organization in the United States of America. "Scientific management," they have told the British workman, "is merely cunningly devised slavery in which the shackles of serfdom are so precisely adjusted that the workman is a mere cog, helplessly and inhumanly enmeshed in a grinding anti-social mechanism." The average workman, however, pays little attention to rhetoric and rodomontade, from whomsoever it may emanate, and I have succeeded in satisfying bodies of workmen as to the value of production by taking an American establishment and giving the output, hours and remuneration per man per annum, or any other convenient period of time, along with the output, hours and remuneration per man for the same period in a comparable establishment in England. The output will be expressed in pounds sterling of wholesale market prices. This really does sink in. Then the moral can be driven home. The vital truth can be shown that in a well-run establishment, as output increases, the cost of the fixed charges per unit of production decreases. Consequently every percentage increase in output—assuming no "softening" of the selling price—results in a larger percentage increase in the amount available for division between workmen and employer. If that division is effected on equitable lines, there is an obvious advantage to the worker. That is why the workman in the United States of America can take home much higher real earnings than his brother in this country. It is not difficult to satisfy the hard-headed practical English worker that these higher American earnings are neither manna dropped from heaven nor doles from more compassionate employers.

If there is scepticism as to the value to Trade Unions of production, there is complete apathy as to the necessity of production for the nation's sake. What is wanted is to secure conviction of the need by simple homely illustrations. The extent to which in any community increased production conduces to plenty, and plenty to employment, good wages, a higher standard of living, and low prices is beyond the present ken of Labour. In other words, the proposition that the prosperity of a country depends upon the production in the country obtains no credence whatsoever; it is generally treated by working men as a sheer irrelevance.

On the other side of the account some reactionary employers, and under-managers and foremen, cling to the hoary fallacy that however high the output may be, workmen are never worth high earnings. Such persons seem to think that the payment of high wages, even when accompanied by high output, is a reflection on the management of the shop. They constantly argue that high wages degenerate the workmen, and lead to lost time. In order to reduce earnings, when they are considered to be inordinately high, the piece-prices are "cut," and time-allowances are "docked." This is a peculiarly English folly. No American employer would dream of it. The results in England are disastrous. With the fear of having his trade-prices reduced, the workman will not "go all out," but will limit output and maintain his earnings at such a figure as he thinks will not stimulate the employer to reduce prices or time-allowances. In commencing a piece-job the operative will deliberately go slow so as to get a high price fixed, and thereby allow for any future cutting. The employer ought to know that the more jobs that pass through or over a workman's machine or bench in the shift or working day the greater is the number of jobs over which standing and fixed charges and the invariable portion of the working costs are apportioned, and, therefore, the smaller is the debit on each operation and the lower is the cost of production. If the employer can get high production, it is to his direct interest to allow high earnings for it. This is well accepted by American employers, and represents normal shop practice in the United States of America.

Introduction of Time- and Labour-Saving Appliances

Anyone acquainted with industry in the United States of America and in England cannot fail to notice one further striking contrast. In the United States of America time- and labour-saving appliances, machines and methods are being continually put into service by employers, and loyally operated by labour. It is recognized as being in the joint interests of them both. It clearly is. Anything that results in a net reduction of output-cost, after allowing for extra interest and depreciation, benefits not merely employers, but also employed. In England, however, workpeople seriously regard time- and labour-saving devices as inimical to their interests, and subversive of trade-rights. It is contended that the introduction of such devices leads to the displacement of labour and to unemployment. In this connection labour has learned nothing from experience. Improved machinery has enormously bettered the worker's lot. In the United States of America the resultant reduction in output-cost is admittedly the reason for the much higher real wages of American workmen as compared with their English and Scottish confrères. Nor has it led to unemployment in the United States of America. There is no reason why it should do so even temporarily. The introduction of time- and labour-saving appliances is always a gradual process in any factory. Ordinary foresight and organization by an employer ought to enable any men displaced still to be retained in employment. But many English employers have impeded the introduction of labour-saving devices by haggling over the readjustment of piece-rates in respect of the installation of machines giving improved output. The American employer, on the other hand, tries, after allowing for the costs of the new machine, to maintain, as far as possible, the old piece-rates, with the result that the workmen's daily earnings are increased by its use. The English employer is inclined to think that he is justified in reducing piece-rates so long as the workmen's daily earnings are maintained. It is unnecessary to point out which policy is most likely to attract the wage-earner to the use of improved machinery.

Payment by Results

Nothing in industry is surrounded by so much confusion and ignorance, both among employers and employed, as the question of payment by results. The value of this method of payment in promoting production is indisputable. I have many actual cases in mind where the introduction of piece-work in place of time-work resulted in an increase of output up to 110 per cent., thereby materially reducing the cost of production. Yet while in some trades, for example the cotton trade, the operatives refuse to work on any basis other than piece-work, in other trades, for example carpentering and many sections of engineering, piece-work is considered a "pestilential system" [sic] tending to unemployment, degradation of the worker, and untold evils. It is in regard to payment by results on the premium bonus system that the greatest misconception prevails amongst both masters and men. That is a system under which a time is fixed for each job. If the job is done in less than the fixed time, the time saved is divided in a definite proportion between employer and worker—generally half and half in England—and the latter paid for his portion at his ordinary time-rate. The system has provoked in this country, unlike the United States of America, the greatest animosity on the part of the Trade Unions. Their point is that on a piece-work basis, where the man is paid a definite price for each article or operation, the more he does the more he is paid. For all time he saves in finishing an article, he receives the full benefit, the employer's benefit being the lower cost of production resulting from increased output. What right then, it is argued, has the employer, like a parasite, to make anything out of the time which the worker saves on the premium-bonus system. The argument is plausible, but misleading. It entirely overlooks the fact that under a piece-work system, where the workman is paid for all the time saved, prices are necessarily fixed on a much less liberal basis than time allowances on a premium-bonus basis. In the latter case, just because the employer gets a share of the time saved, he can adjust the rate generously, or as rate-fixers put it, "fix the price loosely." If production is to be furthered in this country, the whole system of payment proportioned to output must be lopped free of its perversion by certain employers, and emancipated from the prejudice of Trade Unions. When displayed intelligibly in its true economic characteristics, the system will speak for itself. The actual rates to be fixed under any particular system are, of course, a fair matter for collective bargaining.

Subdivision and Simplification of Process

An idea is commonly encountered among the rank and file that to keep up the labour costs of every operation or job is the best way to maintain the general value of the labour of the operatives concerned. An illustration may be taken from the engineering industry. In engineering, as is well known, England was the pioneer. The practice in the early days was for a skilled turner or millwright, or other craftsman, to undertake a job, perform all the necessary machine and bench operations, and carry it through to completion. Later, as work increased in volume, and still later in diversity, there gradually evolved a differentiation between the turner and the fitter, and in more recent times, between turners and fitters and other kinds of engineering craftsmen. But the essence of the business was that every person concerned in the work should be a tradesman, or skilled man. In recent times, the employers succeeded in establishing "their right"— which is now being questioned—to promote unskilled men, perhaps shop labourers, to work certain classes of machines, capstan and turret lathes, etc. These men were graded as machinists, and when the trade became organized generally received about three-fourths of the skilled turner's rate. They were designated "semi-skilled" men. The point to be observed is that any operation among the many thousands that constitute skilled work is deemed to be a "skilled operation," performable only by a skilled man, and if in special circumstances it is undertaken by any other person, supposing such an improbable case, it carries the full skilled rate of pay. Very similar, but somewhat less rigid, conventions exist in regard to semi-skilled work. The inflexible way in which the engineering Unions enforce these trade practices has certainly reserved exclusively for skilled men a large sphere of work, but it keeps up production costs, and retards development of the industry. Whenever a new and improved machine has been introduced, a machine, say, of a type where the skill was mainly in the machine, and no longer to anything like the same degree required of the worker, there has been a constant struggle between the Unions and the employers as to whether the machine should or should not be operated by a skilled man. Sometimes the employers have won, sometimes the Unions—it is a pure question of relative strength. But the obvious waste of skill in employing one skilled man on one of these machines when he could manage two or more, and the payment of the skilled rate, all added to the prevailing limitation of production, have discouraged English employers from installing up-to-date appliances and so cheapening production.

This is not all the story. In the United States of America the invariable practice is to subdivide every job into its simple constituent operations, allocate each simple machine operation to a machine expressly designed, or "set up" or "rigged" for that special operation, and capable of being tended by an unskilled person after a small modicum of training. So also in regard to non-machine operations, that is to say, assembling or fitting. Each operation is allocated to a special person, in the first instance probably quite unskilled, who becomes proficient and efficient at this one line of work. There is little or no haggling about the remuneration of these unskilled operatives. The volume of production and the consequent ability to pay high wages obviate that. It is never contended by the Machinists' Union that all of these subdivided operations must be done by skilled men, and by them only. Yet in England it is practically a rule that no man in a Union engineering workshop may lift a file and do the smallest amount of "rough" filing unless he is a skilled fitter.

It is a platitude to insist that the natural and efficient evolution of industry involves subdivision. It is, in fact, the governing condition of efficiency and low production cost. It is equally evident, from American experience, that there is nothing in subdivision really hurtful to the skilled men, their trade, or their standard of remuneration. Subdivision in the United States of America has led to an enormous output. All the vast number of machines in service must be set up, repaired, and periodically overhauled. Only the skilled men can do that. The machine "tenders" or "minders" must be supervised. That, again, is work for skilled men. All the tools for the machines must be ground, repaired, and in most cases "set up"—more work for which skilled men alone are suitable. In short, in the United States of America, the skilled men enjoy better conditions, a higher status, and receive greater real wages than the skilled men in this country. The latter must be helped to realize, and quickly, that their present policy of preserving for skilled men exclusively each simple constituent operation now included in skilled men's work is detrimental to their interests, is stifling industry, and strangling the trade of the nation.

No "Niggling" at Prices

At the same time, a stern caution must be administered to certain employers. With labour charges forming so large a proportion of the costs of production, some employers are constantly on the alert to pull down wages by fair means or foul. A slight alteration is made in the method of manufacture, or some device that would not deceive a first year's apprentice is fitted to a machine, and it is then claimed that the work has become such as entitles the employer to put unskilled or semi-skilled men on to it, or alternatively, to reduce the skilled man's price. Sharp practice of that sort sours the shop. It intensifies enormously the difficulty, at present great enough, of the good employer, struggling to reorganize his business fairly and properly on efficient and honest subdivision lines. Present trade customs, as long as they effectively exist, must be honoured. No employer should be entitled to vary the accepted trade grading of the work or its accompanying rate of wages or prices unless there is a genuine and substantial change in process or machinery which in reality supplants the skill of the worker and manifestly increases production.

So far as improvement of production is concerned, the difficulty first, last, and all the time is the bitter enslavement of the mind of the worker, and, if I may borrow the phrase, the "collective mind" of the Trade Unions, by economic fallacy, and this must be attacked and vanquished before any real progress can be made. The remedy is education.

CHAPTER XXIX
THE RIGHT RELATIONSHIP BETWEEN
INDUSTRY AND THE COMMUNITY

If too little consideration for the community has been exercised by industry—and that is unquestionably proved in the foregoing chapters—the community has scarcely realized its duties to the workers in industry.

The Formation of Sound Public Opinion

Industrial disputes in the long run must be decided by the force of public opinion. In the past there has been far too great an inclination on the part of the public to dissociate themselves from industrial controversy as though it concerned them not. Apart from the direct economic effect of any great strike upon the consuming public, the community is under a definite moral obligation to try and reach a right conclusion on the issue and to use the weight of its opinion to secure a fair and equitable settlement. In the course of any strike of importance immediate tribute is paid by both sides to the power of the public. This is evidenced by the various statements of their respective cases which emanate from each side. Labour is specially sensitive to the control of public opinion, and is the first to realize the hopelessness of protracting any strike against which public opinion is hardening. Therefore, both in regard to ascertainment of facts and an intelligent determination of the merits of each industrial controversy, the public is laid under great obligations. It is one of labour's chief complaints that the average shareholder makes no effort whatever at general meetings of his company to ascertain the facts in regard to strikes or lock-outs, or to regulate his investments with some regard to his company's treatment of its workers. This complaint is justified.

The Responsibility of the Consumer

Every consumer has definite responsibilities. In the middle of last century he was almost omnipotent, and industry's chief object was to meet, indeed to anticipate, his desires. His power to-day is not so unrestricted by reason of the competition between consumers in different nations for limited world supplies, and because of the better organization of employers and employed. But still the consumer has immense power, and in the interests of industry, society, and, indeed, of the nation, he ought to realize his duties. The day has long gone past when it was thought that all expenditure by a consumer, whether in necessaries or luxuries, conduced alike to the benefit of trade and the increase of the national wealth. It is now recognized that at all times the supply of labour and raw material and capital—"the wealth heap," as Mr. Hartley Withers graphically describes it in his *Poverty and Waste*—is limited. If, therefore, any consumer demands that more luxuries be produced than necessaries, there must be fewer necessaries for those who want them, and those at higher prices because we are expending on luxuries capital and labour and raw materials otherwise available for the production of necessaries. Even if at any time the supply of necessaries exceeds the demand, that does not justify the production of luxuries. If luxuries are demanded, capital and labour and raw materials must be more or less permanently hypothecated for their production. If, on the other hand, luxuries are dispensed with, then capital and labour will be diverted to the production of necessaries, with consequent reduction of prices and improvement in real wages of workers as the supply of necessaries increases. As capital more or less automatically tends to flow to whatever class of production affords the greatest remuneration, it is really only the consumer who can control in what particular class of production it is invested. A question will always remain: What is unreasonable luxury? That is, of course, a question which each person must answer for himself, but anything, as I view the matter, is a reprehensible luxury when its production results in the consumption of wealth or attraction of labour which is needed for more urgent national purposes. If any consumer is in doubt, he can save instead of spend. He can invest his savings in industry, or, if not, leave them on deposit with his bank, which can do it for him. By this means new permanent industries will be started, production of necessaries increased, wages and purchasing power improved, and a definite service rendered to the community by the establishment of undertakings which, if sound and properly managed, will supply employment, and increase and circulate wealth in a way the production of a luxury could not attempt to rival. The consumer has a duty nowadays to think.

There is a much smaller supply of wealth than most persons realize, which accentuates the duty of every person to use his income in the manner most beneficial to the community. In his book *The Division of the Product of Industry*, Professor Bowley shows (p. 47) that if we take the tax-paying income for 1911 of residents in the United Kingdom derived from home sources, viz. £742,000,000, and from it subtract (i) earned incomes—giving no earner more than £160 per annum—(ii) farmers' incomes, and (iii) endowed charities, the balance left is only £550,000,000. Subtracting from this latter figure the pre-war amounts required for national saving and national expenses there remained only 200 to 250 millions "which on the extremist reckoning can have been spent out of home-produced income by the rich or moderately well-off on anything in the nature of luxury." This sum would have been little more than sufficient to bring the average wages of adult men and women up to a minimum of 35s. 3d. weekly for a man and 20s. for a woman, which Mr. Rowntree in *The Human Needs of Labour* estimates as reasonable—with prices as at July, 1914. Professor Bowley puts it in yet another way. Before the war, there were about 10,000,000 households each containing on an average about 4½ persons, of which nearly 2 in each household were wage-earners. If the total home income had been divided equally round, the average net income per family, after all rates and taxes were paid and an adequate sum invested in home industries, would have been nominally £153 from home income, which, if the balance of income brought home from abroad and not re-invested abroad were also divided equally round, would be increased to £162 per annum. The equal distribution of income would, of course, have enormously increased prices. Professor Bowley observes: "When it is realized that the whole income of the nation was only sufficient for reasonable needs if equally divided, luxurious expenditure is seen to be more unjustifiable even than has been commonly supposed."

The Brussels International Financial Conference said: "Above all, to fill up the gap between the supply of, and the demand for, commodities, it is the duty of every patriotic citizen to practise the strictest possible economy, and so to contribute his maximum effort to the common weal. Such private action is the indispensable basis for the fixed measures required to restore public finances."

The Duty of the Citizen

The principles of Labour policy which I have outlined are generally in the direction of freedom and in its best sense individualism, looking rather to the development in industry of co-operation than to struggle and the use of power to settle differences and express the balance of economic forces. But industrial freedom and individualism impose correlative responsibilities on all citizens, especially in regard to the maintenance of efficient social services. At first sight, any mention of social services may appear a contradiction of the argument developed so far. Social services to many minds are inevitably associated with relief in the narrow sense of the word, conceived as a concession to the clamour of Socialist theorists. In reality they are the growing expression of an increased social sensitiveness. No State can be healthy which is based on a foundation of hardship and suffering. Certain abuses must be removed, and certain conditions remedied. In any advanced economic society the State must take action, has taken action, and will in future extend its action. The social conscience, to anyone who reads history, is a real and growing force. But to be sound and effective it must of necessity be based upon voluntary individual co-operation.

As things are to-day, we must recognize that State activity in social services is in many branches ahead of the understanding of the ordinary man. It has, through the nature of our political machinery, developed in a specialized manner, which throws a heavy burden upon legislators and administrators whether voluntary or official. There is a consequent confusion, lack of co-ordination, and overlapping of effort which leads to waste, not merely of money, but of what is, in the long run, more important— human enthusiasm, effort and efficiency. In dealing with this problem, the individual is of vital importance. The average citizen must know more, take more interest, and render more service, if order and economy are to take the place of confusion and waste. The necessity for this individual interest is reinforced by the present financial situation.

We are, as a nation, recovering, in fact, becoming slowly convalescent, from the effects of war-time and post-war inflation of money and credit. We have realized that sound finance and the balancing of the Budget are the necessary foundations of prosperity. Other European nations are still enjoying the temporary delusive prosperity that can always be obtained by inflation and dishonest finance. To carry the economic argument one stage further, we must realize that the State can only carry non-producers to the extent to which industry can obtain a surplus, after providing for wages, interest, replacements, etc. The State cannot, by any arrangement of taxation, loans or administrative activity, provide an artificial standard of life, which is not earned by human individual activity. There is, therefore, urgent need for education in finance, in both its public and private aspects. Some of us are learning the lesson by the bitter experience of high rates and taxes, others by the hardships of unemployment. But out of this experience much good is coming. We are learning the true and permanent bases of national prosperity. The dangers of Great Britain to-day are not to be found in Red Revolution. Democracy will fail, if it fails at all, from a lack of understanding of economics and finance. Politicians without scruple or foresight may hold out bribes of immediate material advantages, trusting to some juggling of figures to enable them to redeem their promises. During the war, the National Savings Committee, by a steady education in economics—converting financial theories of currency, goods and services into the terms of men and munitions—educated the general public into the social consequences of spending and thrift. The control of national finances so established under the patriotic stimulus and urgency of war is no less necessary in peace.

The history of social legislation in the twentieth century is the expression not merely of democratic pressure, but of the increased social sensitiveness to the national conscience, awakened by individuals of outstanding merit protesting that certain evils should no longer exist. As the industrial revolution worked itself out, it was possible to ascertain, by patient investigation, its weaknesses and evils, and to provide certain remedies. Based on a steadily growing prosperity, its record is worth reciting; a wide extension of education providing in increasing degree an opportunity to the able men and women in all ranks of society to develop their individuality; a general standard of education which proved its value in increasing temperance, diminished crime, and growing sense of public spirit, culminating in attention to the physical condition of school-children, that in normal times would have given every child a happy healthy childhood. In public health, the elimination of the most dangerous infectious diseases, a steady improvement of sanitary conditions, and an education in preventive medicine, that can be proved by statistics to have been directly remunerative. On the positive side, an extension of infant welfare work, which, relying on the natural affection of mothers, and calling upon them to develop their own individuality, has for a small expenditure reduced the infant death rate by half. Health Insurance on a contributory basis has lessened the sham of sickness in the wage-earner's family, and as the results of the quinquennial valuations of Approved Societies are more widely known and understood, will overcome any remaining adverse criticism. Old age pensions have removed the fear of an old age spent in dependence on grudging relatives, or on the Poor Law, with its deterrent associations. The treatment of unemployment has gained in efficiency and thoroughness by the steady gaining of experience—the Labour Bureaux, Unemployment Insurance, the use of State credits to finance international trade and guarantee extensions of industry at home are laying foundations of a new order—the irregular activities of voluntary organizations and local authorities in emigration have developed into an Imperial Scheme for Overseas Settlement. Under the existing conditions of financial stringency, we have to consider how this burden can, in the future, be borne. How much of the national income can, in the years immediately to come, be devoted to services admittedly admirable in their objects? One fact becomes clear: at all costs we must hold on to the main essentials in the public services and keep the machinery in working order so that it will be ready for expansion when financial conditions make it possible. The fall in prices, resulting in a reduced cost of living, lower war bonuses, lower cost of materials, is bringing, and will bring, even further relief to the taxpayer and ratepayer. The adjustment, however, lags behind the change in individual circumstances, and is the cause of much criticism of those in authority. If, however, this policy of holding on to essentials is to be carried out, there will have to be an increased measure of economy—economy, not merely of money, but, in its original Aristotelian sense, of management of a household. This can only be done by attention to details, by a higher standard of public spirit, by which the services in health, education, etc., are looked upon by those who benefit as something for which they pay, and for which, in the long run, they are responsible. If the desire for education were widespread, there would be an immediate economy in school attendance officers, rota committees, and all the machinery devised to block the holes in the educational net. If the individual standard of care for health were raised as it can be raised by such movements as health weeks, baby weeks, etc., there would be a consequent reduction in the expenditure on Public Health. But the largest measure of economy of the household management type would come through a co-ordination of the activities of national departments, local authorities and voluntary organizations. Attention has recently been called to the advance of expenditure due to the system of grants-in-aid to local authorities, by which local authorities are led to spend money on the false assumption that the ratepayer will gain something to be paid for by the taxpayer. The discrepancy between the rating system and the tax-paying system is the root cause of many difficulties, but a wider understanding of finance would obviate the grosser evils.

Under our English system of government, all recent legislation has been of specialized character dealing with specified classes, or a particular evil. As each need was recognized, a special administration was set up to deal with it, and we now have innumerable inquiry officers, inspectors, officials of various grades administering Acts of Parliament and regulations in varying ways. The whole relationship of national departments and local authorities requires revision and reorganization. Owing to the burden of rates on the ratepayer driving the local authorities to rely more and more upon subsidies from the National Exchequer, and to their refusing to undertake new burdens, social services have been identified with departmental activity, red tape and bureaucracy. Local government has suffered from a gradual atrophy.

Now, under pressure of financial stringency, is the time to overhaul our social machinery. It needs the services of the best brains that the country can produce. The problem has two aspects. First comes financial policy.

Owing to the complexity of administration, no local check can exist on the total expenditure in any area. Inquiry is urgently needed, on the lines of the national return known as the Drage return, setting out for each local government area the sums paid by the local authority, Health and Education, etc., the Poor Law, and the National Ministries of Pensions, Labour, etc. At present the facts are not known, and, indeed, are not available. Secondly, in administration, we need a co-ordination of investigation and inquiry, and some measure of co-ordination in the payment of relief; at the very least, a register of assistance by which overlapping in payments and machinery could be avoided. The extent to which either of these movements could be successful depends almost entirely upon local interest. Any scheme set up by Government would but add to the general confusion. Economy in this sense is a strict inquiry and attention to detail, and is a service which can only be rendered by those of business experience and ability. Finally would come a reorganization of the Poor Law, not in any spirit of hostility to those who have done such admirable work in spite of abuse and misrepresentation, but a reorganization on to new areas coinciding with the other areas of local government, and more nearly adjusted to the present industrial conditions.

As a social policy, the insistence on economy will seem dull, but the comment of the old lady about husbands that the good ones are dull applies equally to social policy. The future development of social services must depend upon the economic and financial future. No one under present conditions can advocate fresh channels of expenditure, or the widening of existing channels. This is not a confession of failure, or an admission of social stagnation. We can no longer measure social reform by the gradually increasing sums of money spent in particular specialized services. We must, for a future as long as we can foresee, measure social progress in the terms of the social service that the individual is prepared to render. As a preparation we need two elements: (1) wider economic education; (2) wider knowledge of social conditions, and the provision for dealing with social evils. For the first the development of the Savings Movement is a guide. Started in 1916, with the twofold function of economic education and the provision of facilities for the small investor, it has grown into a financial instrument of unlimited possibilities.

In the six months ending March 31, 1922, £93,000,000 have been invested in Savings Certificates, a sum which is more remarkable when one considers the conditions in industry during this time. By a wise foresight, arrangements have been made by which local authorities can borrow from the Public Works Loans Commissioners 50 per cent. of the money raised in the area of any local authority. In brief, this means that £46,500,000 per annum of new capital is being saved, and made available for works of public improvement if required, while another £46,500,000 will be available for the repayment of ways and means advances which will thus set free bank credits for the financing of private trade. It is a steady regular funding of the floating debt by money which is actually saved. As a measure of comparative magnitude of millions it is well to point out that the total cost of Old Age Pensions for the past financial year was £21,750,000, and the total cost of Poor Law in the year ending March 31, 1920, was £28,500,000. This measure of success has concealed to some extent the other function of the Committee, viz. economic education. In the last analysis the problem of unemployment becomes one of finance. So far as it can be alleviated by measures of insurance or relief or emigration, taxation and rates will provide the means, but beyond all compulsion, the individual has a measure of responsibility. Wise spending, the avoidance of waste and extravagance, will do more to restore the foundations of industry and credit than any action by Government. Just as during the war it was possible to divert goods and services from private ends to the main national need of providing men and munitions necessary for victory, so to-day a conscious control of individual expenditure, including a measure of personal thrift and saving, will mean lower rates of interest, a larger amount of credit, and a general improvement of trade and employment.

As regards the second element, viz. the wider knowledge of social conditions, foundations are being laid by voluntary effort. In all the big industrial areas a growing measure of interest is being taken in social conditions. The pre-war voluntary associations are realizing their inevitable connection with the Government Departments and local authorities. Councils, representative of local authorities and voluntary associations, have been formed, based, not on the Victorian ideal of the Lady Bountiful, but on the juster, saner ideal of a common citizenship owing service to the community. Practical steps are being taken to reduce the chaos and overlapping in effort and money: in one place a survey of local conditions; in another a handbook of information on the local provision; in yet another a system of mutual registration of assistance and relief, and finally, an investigation into the total sums spent out of public funds in social services. Underlying it all is the personal service rendered by social workers, as welfare workers, Guilds of Help, prohibition officers, infant welfare workers, etc. Out of experience has come the understanding that two types of co-operation are needed: first, the co-operation of experts in co-ordinating questions of policy; secondly, the co-operation of individual citizens in solving the problems of the individual in trouble. From a wide experience of industrial unrest there is a firm conviction that the hard cases, the unintentional injustices, the administrative difficulties, summed up by the phrase "red tape," are a more fruitful source of trouble than the larger grievances.

This advocacy of personal service in many fields and in differing degrees is not the vapouring of a social visionary, but is an expression of the genius of our race. Every reform, every method of social advance, has owed its existence to the enthusiasm of volunteers trying a new idea, finding it work successfully, and then convincing others that it should apply throughout the country. It is not muddling through, but the onward march of individual freedom, which includes a freedom to combine and a freedom to persuade and convince others that a new way is the right way. The Teutonic method of social improvement by compulsion, not for its own sake, but for military purposes, influenced English thought for a generation. The result is seen in a development of the State far beyond the capacity or desires of our people. The remedy is to be found, not in a further treatment of homœopathic doses of the same medicine, but by relying upon the natural, healthy development of the national spirit through and in the individual.

The uncovenanted service that is needed from each member of the community "is inspired service that is not measured in cash, about which there are no overtime disputes, and in which time and a half or double time is welcomed rather than objected to. And is not that the kind of service for which the world is pining? Unless we can do away with the nicely balanced give and take we shall not make progress in alleviating the sufferings of humanity." And there is an even broader vision. As against the extreme Socialists who preach class-warfare, and try to sever class from class, there is only one true antidote—some strong, compelling, active principle that tends to bring together all classes, not for selfish ends, but springing from an ever-present sense of the brotherhood of men.

FOOTNOTES

[1] This is only the number directly affiliated; there are in all 2,350 divisional and Local Labour Parties and Trades Councils.

[2] Reprinted, with additions, as *The Revolutionary Movement in Great Britain*. Grant Richards, Ltd., 1921.

[3] A good exposition of this school of Socialism is to be found in Professor J. A. Estey's *Revolutionary Syndicalism*.

[4] Rt. Hon. J. R. Clynes; Messrs. J. A. Hobson, J. J. Mallon and Misses Susan Lawrence and Mona Wilson.

[5] The shop stewards, normally, are persons elected by the men of each craft in each department of an engineering shop to act individually, or through a "convener" of all the shop stewards of the particular craft as the connecting link between the men of that craft in the works and the district delegate or district committee of the craft Trade Union.

[6] Messrs. Adamson and Gosling.

[7] Small Holdings and Allotments Acts, 1908 to 1919; The Acquisition of Land (Assessment of Compensation) Act, 1919; Small Landholders (Scotland) Acts, 1886 to 1919; Land Settlement (Scotland) Acts, 1919 and 1921; etc.

[8] See *Land Nationalization*, by Harold Cox, 2nd Ed., 1906. Methuen & Co.

[9] A similar Bill was introduced in the Session of 1922.

[10] Joint Committee of Trades Union Congress, Labour Party, Co-operative Unionists—Final Report, 1921—(Co-operative Society, Ltd.).

See also:—

1st	Report Civil Service Association.	*Times*,	April 17,	1922.
2nd	" " " " "		July 18,	"

[11] Sir Wm. Mackenzie, K.B.E., K.C., is President.

[12] "The Geddes Committee."

[13] In fact many railway men work more than 8 hours per day, receiving, for the excess hours, overtime pay.

[14] The National Union of Railwaymen and the Associated Society of Locomotive Engineers and Firemen.

[15] The principle had been agreed in January 1920.

[16] Now the General Council of the Trades Union Congress.

[17] The propriety of this disqualification has been referred by the Minister of Labour to a Committee for consideration and report. (See *Labour Gazette*, July 1922, p. 287.)

[18] The total value of the *effective* allocations is £2,630,000, inasmuch as approximately £160,618 will not ultimately be payable.

[19]

1921.	April 28.	6½	per cent.
	June 23.	6	"
	July 21.	5½	"
	Nov. 3.	5	"
1922.	Feb. 16.	4½	"
	April 13.	4	"
	June 15.	3½	"
	July 13.	3	"

[20] Committee of Inquiry into the Working and Effect of the Trade Boards Acts—*Parliamentary Paper*, 1922, Cd. 1645.

[21] Address to Glasgow Chamber of Commerce, Oct. 18, 1920.

[22] See other illustrations reported by me to the Government, p. 302, *Industrial Problems and Disputes,* by Lord Askwith.

INDEX

For convenience of reference this index is divided into Parts as follows:

PART I. ACTS OF PARLIAMENT, STATUTORY ORDERS, ETC.

Health Insurance Acts

Industrial Courts Act. 1919

Labour Bureaux (London) Act, 1902

Exchanges Act, 1909

Local Authorities (Financial Provisions) Act, 1921

Metropolitan Common Poor Fund (Outdoor Relief) Regulations, 1922

Mines Acts

Mining Industry Act, 1920

Ministry of Transport Act, 1919

Munitions of War Act, 1915

National Health Insurance Acts (see Health Insurance Acts)

Insurance Act, 1911

(Part II Amendment) Act, 1914

(Part II) (Munition Workers) Act, 1916

Outdoor Relief (Friendly Societies) Act, 1904

Overseas (Credits and Insurance) Amendment Act, 1921

Trade (Credits and Insurance) Act, 1920

"Peels Act," 1825

Prevention of Employment Bill, 1919

Price of Coal Limitation Act, 1915

Railways Act, 1921

Reform Act, 1832

Representation of the People Act, 1832 (Reform Act)

Regulation of the Forces Act, 1871

Relief Regulation Order, 1911

Right to Work Bills

Roads Acts, 1920

Shops Acts

Trade Boards Acts

Trade Disputes Act, 1906

Facilities Act, 1921

Unemployed Workmen's Act, 1905

PART II. PERSONS

Marx, Karl

Miliukov, Dr.

Morris, William

Owen, Robert

Palme Dutt, R.

Plender, Sir William

Postgate, R. W.

Pratt, Edwin A.

Rew, Sir Henry

Roberts, Rt. Hon. G. H.

Rowntree, B. Seebohm

Runciman, Rt. Hon. Walter

St. Aldwyn, Lord

St. Davids, Lord

Schuster, Col.

Shackleton, Sir David

Shadwell, Dr.

Stamp, Sir Josiah

Stuart-Bunning, Mr.

Thomas, Albert

Thomas, Emile

Thomas, Rt. Hon. J. H.

Vandervelde, Emile

Wallace, Dr. Alfred R.

Watson, Sir Alfred

Webb, Mr. and Mrs. Sidney

Weir, Lord

Whitley, Rt. Hon. J. H.

Williams, Robert

Withers, Hartley

Wolfe, Humbert

PART III. PLACES

PART IV. PUBLICATIONS

"Bolshevism, an International Danger" (Miliukov)

"Call,"

"Case for Capitalism" (Withers)

"Case for Land Nationalization" (Hyder)

"Co-operative Magazine,"

"Daily Herald,"

"Division of the Product of Industry" (Bowley)

"Economic Liberty" (Cox)

"Edinburgh Review,"

"Evening Standard,"

"German v. British Railways" (Pratt)

"Group Mind" (McDougall)

"Guild Socialism Restated" (Cole)

"Historical Sketch of State Railway Ownership" (Acworth)

"Histoire des Ateliers Nationaux" (Thomas)

"History of British Socialism" (Beer)

"History of Trade Unionism" (Webb)

"Human Needs of Labour" (Rowntree)

"Industrial Democracy" (Webb)

"Justice,"

"Labour and the New Social Order,"

"Labour International Handbook,"

"Labour Leader,"

"Labour Party and the Countryside,"

"Labour Supply and Regulation" (Wolfe)

"Land Nationalization" (Cox)

"Life and Labour in London" (Booth)

"Nineteenth Century,"

"Official Policy for reconstruction after the War,"

"Organization du travail" (Blanc)

"Poverty and Waste" (Withers)

"Prices and Wages in the United Kingdom" (Bowley)

"Progress and Poverty" (George)

"Quarterly Review,"

"Red Catechism,"

"Revolutionary Movement in Great Britain" (Shadwell)

"Revolutionary Syndicalism" (Estey)

"Right to Work" (Marriott)

"Socialist,"

"Socialist Standard,"

"State and Revolution" (Lenin)

"Sunday Times,"

"Two internationals" (Palme Dutt)

"Times,"

"Trade Unionism and Political Action,"

"Unemployment: A Labour Policy,"

"Workers' International" (Postgate)

PART V. ORGANIZATIONS

Amalgamated (Society of Engineers) Engineering Union

American Socialist Party, Connection with Socialist Labour Party

Bolsheviks

British Socialist Party

Building Trade Unions

Communist Party of Great Britain

Electrical Trades Union

Electoral Labour Committee

Fabian Research Department

Fabian Society

Federation of British Industries

General Federation of Trade Unions

General Workers' Union

"Hands Off Russia" Committee

Harmony Community of Equality

PART VI. SUBJECTS